MICROSOFT POWER APPS

An Operational Handbook for all Levels to Mastering the Microsoft Power App Tools and Creating Business Applications

Michael J. Harrison

TABLE OF CONTENTS

PART ONE: POWER APPS FUNDAMENTALS

If you are a beginner, you need to tune into the fundamentals of Power Apps. In this book, we are going to be taking you through all of the fundamentals.

CHAPTER ONE

INTRODUCING POWER APPS

What are Power Apps?

Now if you are looking for a fast way to build a business or personal application, you can use the Power Apps. It is a combination of different applications, services, and connectors that provides a fast-paced setting to build an application.

Working with the power application you can instantly build applications connected to stored data within the Microsoft data verse or in other online or on-premises data sources.

It is very easy to assume that when you use this kind of application, you are not going to be getting the best services or quality. However, when you make use of the power application to create an application, you are working with a program that has excellent capabilities that transform your business operation offline into a digital platform.

The History of Power Apps

Power Apps is relatively young in history and was only out to the public in April 2016. Then, In less than a year by the end of 2016, over 124,000 users from 46,000 organizations from as many as 143 countries have been able to create several websites and mobile applications using Power Apps.

By august of 2016, Microsoft then integrated Power Apps into **share point online** list. This way, a user can create a customized app, by just selecting the command bar on the custom list at the top of SharePoint Online. Then you are going to find the application in the **Custom** view which makes the user able to have access to the Power App just by connecting to the internet and in their SharePoint Mobile application.

This way, it is easier for people to create applications without wasting time as there are a lot of inbuilt templates to hasten the process of making an application.

What are the key benefits of the Power Apps?

There are a few key benefits to using the Power Apps.

1. Now one of the big selling points for Power Apps is that it dramatically cuts down the time of creating an application. If you are a business or company that is very cautious of time, then Power App is the way to go.
2. You are not required to learn any code as all of the templates is already available for you. Now if you want to add your code to it… Well, that is fine. As there is still an opportunity for people who want to work with codes.
3. Power Apps is integrated with Microsoft and some other third-party services. For example, Microsoft Dynamics 365, Salesforce, Adobe, and
4. Since the Power App is part of the access Power Automate, then most of its activities can be automated. And that includes things like notifications, approvals, documents, or record routing. Power Apps can work with the power automate engine so that the developers and users to create some automation based on the behavior of end users
5. Before Power Apps, creating applications used to be an expensive ordeal. But with Power Apps now, things have just gotten cheaper. Since when you are working with a Power App, you do not need to learn code, the cost to develop an

application is way cheaper than some of the alternatives out there.

6. Since this is the modern age and a lot of people are beginning to wonder when AIs are going to take over. The truth is that they already are. You just don't know it yet. So Power Apps as the capability of incorporating AI's into the apps and also add intelligence to the business apps with an AI Builder feature. This way, you cut out data scientists and other advanced AI developers to build another model.

What data sources can we use?

The Power Apps data source provides you with all of the necessary data that you need to effectively work. You can store these banks of data in the cloud so that you can access them from where ever you want to access them.

A Power App data source for example is Microsoft Excel. You can store tables in OneDrive or in cloud storage that is connected to your Power Application. There are certain connectors that you need to be able to communicate with the data source. However, importantly, that also helps you to connect with some other useful services.

SAMPLE APPS

Now you can create an application with Power Apps using **Sample apps**. So here we are going to be taking you through how to create one with the different sample applications. Here is what to do.

- To open a sample app. The first thing to do is to sign into the Power Apps.
- Then click **Create** on the left pane.
- Then when you go to **Start from a template,** select a sample app from the list of sample apps there like the cost estimator, etc.
- Then you need to update the app name and then choose to **Create** an app.
- If you want to then connect the app to the data storage, then you can select **Make my App.**

- Then when you choose to **Connect to storage** from the choices that are available choose **Done.**
- Use F5 to see a preview of what you have done.
  To then save the app
  1. Go to settings to review the default settings.
  2. Then choose **File.**
  3. And select **Save as.**
  4. Then enter the app name.
  5. Choose to **Save.**

CANVAS APPS

To create a **canvas** app with specific **templates** for specific scenarios. For example, to track budgets and to schedule a vacation.

The first thing to do is to have a cloud storage account so that you can create an application from templates and store the sample data for the template.

If there is no license for the Power Apps, you can also create one for free.

Here is how to create an app:

- To open a sample app. The first thing to do is to sign into the Power Apps.
- Then click **Create** on the left pane.
- Then when you go to **Start from a template,** select a sample app from the list of sample apps there like the cost estimator, etc.
- Then you need to update the app name and then choose to **Create** an app.
- If you want to then connect the app to the data storage, then you can select **My App.**
- Then when you choose to **Connect to storage** from the choices that are available choose **Done.**

To then run the app, here is what to do:

- Use F5 to see a preview of what you have done.

- You can also see the default behavior for the app by then creating, updating, and deleting sample data, and checking if the data in the cloud storage account show the changes that you made.
- To go back to the default workspace, simply select ESC.
- The next thing that you want to do is use Ctrl+S to name the app and then click on **Save** so that the app saves.
- Then you can share the app with others within your organization.

MODEL-DRIVEN APPS

The model-driven app template involves a system that focuses on the components like the forms, views, charts, and dashboard with the app designer tool. Furthermore, the kind of relationship that connects the tables makes it possible to permit the navigation between them and make sure that the data is not unnecessarily repeated.

With the app designer, you can build a simple or complex app without code or very little code if any.

PORTAL APPS

You can create a powerful experience allowing users to sign in from external-facing websites with different identities. You can create and view data with the Microsoft database or you can browse your content anonymously.

You can essentially use the Power App platform to create a code for the canvas apps. Furthermore, as a professional, you can also use the power apps to create and even import code parts into the canvas apps with the Microsoft Power platform CLI. However, there are APIs that you will not find in the canvas apps. However, you can determine if it is available when you search the APIs.

Review Question

- What is Power App?
- What are the different kinds of apps that can be made with Power App?
- How can a user run a Power App?

Summary

In this section, we went through a brief introduction to what Power App is and what it is used for.

CHAPTER TWO

SUBSCRIBING TO POWER APPS

In this chapter, we are going to be taking you through the steps of practically working with the power application.

How to get Power Apps

- To work with Power Apps, go to PowerApps.com.
- When you hop on the site, select **Start free trial** then an entirely new window pops up for you.

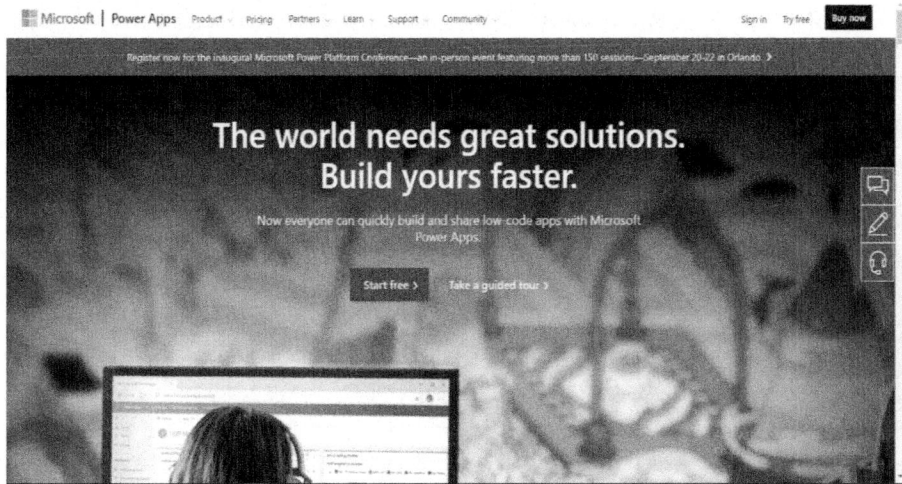

- On a side note. Before you can work with the Power Apps, you either need a work or school Microsoft account.
- Now if you do not want to go straight to power apps, you can go to Office.com. And login with your work or student account. Then you can select it to start building the app.

Which plan do I need to access a data source?

Power App has two basic plans: A pay as you go plan and a subscription plan.

The pay-as-you-go plan is just $10 per active user monthly. It is the best plan when a business wants the flexibility that comes with the ability to pay only when the user works with the app monthly.

Then there is the subscription plan that is categorized into two: which are the per app plans and the per usage plan.

The per-app plan costs $5 monthly and allows the business to work with one app or portal per usage.

You can use the per-app plan to run an app or a portal per user plan and stack licenses to gain access to an additional as the needs change. You get an AI builder in this plan. But you are also going to need Microsoft 365 admin center that has either global administration or billing administration roles.

You can use the second plan at only $20 to run all of the portals per user.

SUBSCRIBING TO POWER APPS

Obtaining a suitable Email Address

Now you cannot use the normal personal email address to sign up with the Power Apps. You are going to need a work email or a business email. You cannot use the normal email address that ends with, for example, Hotmail, Gmail, outlook, etc.

Your work or school email address has to be backed with the Azure Active Directory so that you can first sign up for a trial license.

What are the Licensing Options?

Now you can find out the license that you have by Signing into the Power Apps with the work or school credentials. Then when you enter the page choose the gear icon on the upper right corner and choose the **plan(s)**

Licensing Portal and AI Builder Apps

The AI builder license comes as an add-on to your Power Apps, the power automates, or the 365 licenses. This means that you can go ahead and start the AI builder trial. Once you start the Power Apps, you get the option of the **Power automate**, the dynamic 365, and the provision to create a Microsoft power platform.

Now you are not going to get the AI builder add-on in the Microsoft 365 business premium license.

Accessing Power Apps via Microsoft/Office

To access the Power Apps from the office,

- First sign into your Microsoft 365 app page.
- Then look for the app on the home page in the category of **Business Apps** and you can just search for the app in the search box.

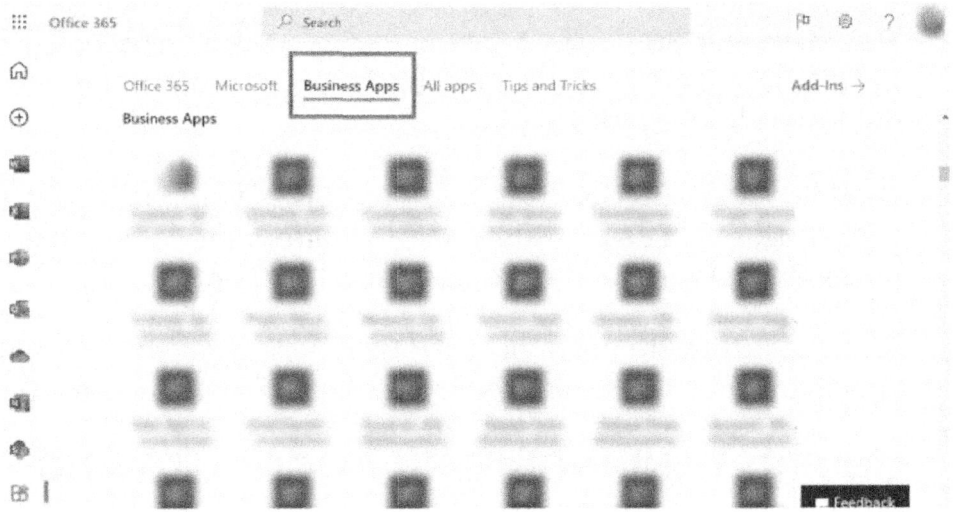

WHAT IS OFFICE 365?

Office 365 is a cloud-based Microsoft productivity platform that has software like, Word, Excel, SharePoint, Exchange, Teams, and others.

Since it is cloud-based, you can have access to all of these tools from anywhere and at any time easily.

MICROSOFT 365: CONSUMER VS BUSINESS

Microsoft provides two plans for people. One is a business plan and the other is a home plan.

Microsoft 365 for home gives you a premium value of Microsoft Word, Excel, PowerPoint, Outlook, Teams, OneDrive, and Editor. Plus, 1TB of one drive space. All of this for just under $10.

While the Microsoft 365 business plan is divided into three categories. It is the business basic, app for business, business standard, and the business premium.

The Microsoft 365 business basic plan, gives you the basic Excel tool for just $6.

The Microsoft 365 apps for business give you, plus basic apps like word, excel, and PowerPoint; apps for a business like Access, and Publisher, Just for $8.25.

The Microsoft 365 Business Standard gives you basic apps including exchange, Access, Publisher, SharePoint, Outlook, Teams, PowerPoint, Word, and Excel just for $12.50 per month.

And the premium plan at only $22, will give you iTunes, Azure, Outlook, OneDrive, SharePoint, Exchange, Publisher, etc.

UNDERSTANDING WORK ACCOUNTS AND PERSONAL ACCOUNTS

Work accounts and personal accounts are two different things. Yes, it is very easy to confuse the two. But the thing is that if you log in with a personal account, you are going to be getting different services from what you will be getting when you log in with a work or school account.

The work or school account is connected to your company or your school and when you change jobs or change schools, these changes too. Microsoft for school is integrated with Office 365 business mailbox, Azure cloud services, SharePoint, and others. A business office 365 email address is a Microsoft work account.

And for students, you are going to get discounted services for all of the plans of office 365.

Now the personal account on the other hand is for your usage and does not change no matter who you are working for at certain times. For example, an outlook.com, or a Hotmail.com account is a personal account.

Which Microsoft/Office 365 Plans include the Power Apps?

There are four different to get the Power Apps and they are Office 365, dynamics 365 enterprise application, per user per app (2 app packages and the per-user unlimited app.

- With Office 365, there are no additional charges. And the qualifying license is the business premium, the business essentials, the F1 plan, and the E1-E5 enterprise plan.
- To get the custom apps you need the canvas apps and the standard connectors.

Does the plan I want to Buy Include Power Apps

If you are using an Office 365 business premium plan, then you can work with the Power App.

Accessing Power Apps via Dynamics 365

There are no additional charges with dynamic 365. The licenses that you need are customer service, field service, talent, business centers, retail, and others. The custom apps are canvas or model with premium and custom connected added to it.

WHAT IS DYNAMICS 365?

If you want to impress your customers, then you can use Dynamics 365. With Dynamics 365, you are going to be getting an armory of intelligent business applications allowing you to deliver your services faster and break those barriers.

There are connected business applications to optimize the business operation and encourage innovations and communicate better with customers.

Dynamics 365 has platforms for sales, services, marketing, customer data, commerce, financial protection, and supply chains.

How much does it cost?

Depending on the services that you need from Dynamics 365. It can cost from $20 to as high as $2000.

LOGGING ON TO POWER APPS

Enter powerapps.com and then enter your work or school account. If you are a first-time user, you can use the service for free in the first month, and subsequently, you are going to have to start paying for the services.

CREATING AN APP

Overview of other Administrative Areas

From the Power App administrative center, you can get features that can help the admin to perform their tasks effectively. You can create and manage the work environment databases and the data policies from the admin center.

Review Questions

- What are the different licensing options for Power App?
- How do you log into Power Apps?
- What is Dynamics 365?

Summary

Summarily, Power Apps provide you with cool new features. But there are a few things that you are going to need for you to have an account in the first place and create an app.

CHAPTER THREE

CREATING YOUR FIRST APP

Now that you know what Excel is, there is still the need for you to know a few things before you create your first app. In this chapter, we are going to be taking you through all of those details.

PREPARING AN EXCEL DATA SOURCE

To prepare your data as an Excel data source, you have to go through the following steps

1. The first thing to do is to format the data as a table in Excel
2. Then you need to store the excel file in cloud storage. Preferably Dropbox, Google Drive, OneDrive, and One Drive for Business. You can also gain access to more cloud locations with the updated Excel version of connectors
3. You can add Excel as a data source for the Power App. There are two ways to do this and they use slightly different versions of connectors.
4. The first version is from Excel: this way you can automatically add excel and create 3 screen application by first creating a canvas app with data that you get from an Excel file.
   Once you are done, you are going to find an application. And once you are done with that, you are going to then see the data source has been added using the one drive connector.
5. The other method is to add a new data source.
   This way, create a blank canvas app then decide to then add a new excel data source.
   If you use the Excel Online connector, then you can work with excel files inside the document libraries supported with a graph. The old Excel connectors have a lot of limitations and one of them is that just one user cloud can work with the excel file at once. Furthermore, you cannot access files from SharePoint.

With the newer Excel Online connector, you get faster, robust, and flexible services that support multiple users and allow you to work with as many standard document libraries. Before you add Excel as a data source, you need to look for Excel Online connectors from the connector lists.

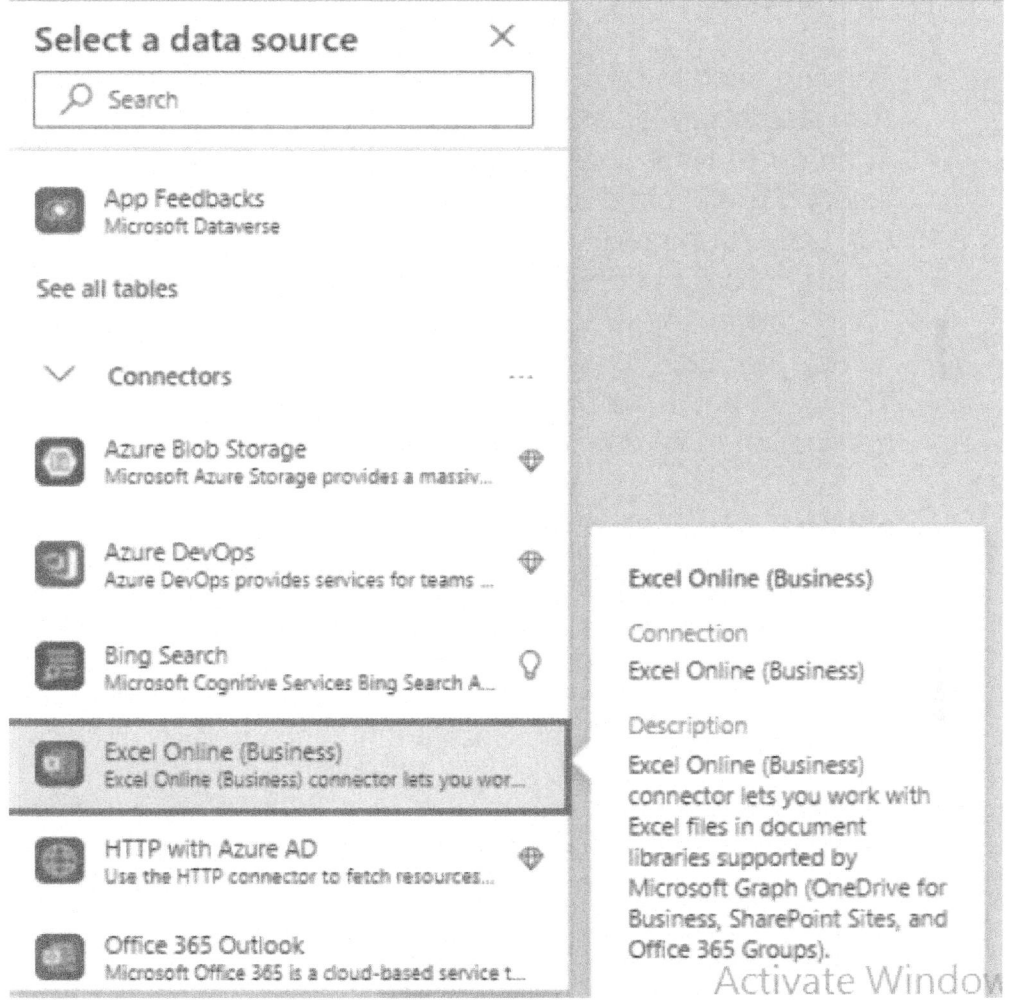

- The Online Business connectors make it easy for you to choose from more locations in other to find the Excel file.
- After choosing the Excel file and the table inside, that adds a new excel data source to the application, then you can go further to verify usage of the newer version of the connector with an Excel icon instead one drive icon from outdated connectors.

CREATING AN APP

Creating an auto-generated app

There is one feature in the Power App that everyone needs to learn to use and that is the feature of creating an app automatically from data inside the Power Apps.

- The first thing to do is to go to the Windows store, install the Power App studio and log in with a work or a school account.
- Then go to **New** and choose any of the popular **Connections** or select **More** in other to choose from 20 connection options that are currently supported.
- After choosing a connection, look for the list and select **Connect.**
- Then Power App is going to read the data and structure to create an app for you.
- Then you have the option to run, customize, save and share the application that you have created.

Creating an app from share point

After creating an app from the SharePoint list, the app is going to show as a **View** from the list. You can as well run the app with iOS, Android devices, and web browsers.

So to create an app with the SharePoint Online:

- Go to SharePoint Online and open a list then choose **Integrate > Power Apps > Create an app.**

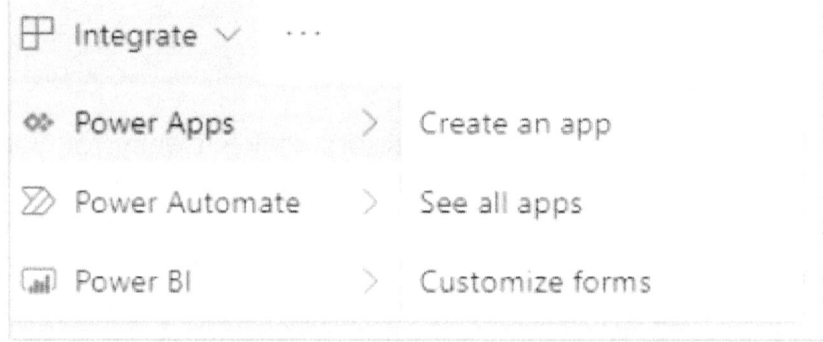

- A panel appears next. Type the name of the app and choose **Create**

Name your app to get started. Power Apps will open so you can customize your app.

Name

MyNewApp

Create   Cancel

- If you are using a web browser, a new tab pops up showing the app that you have created based on the list. You can then customize the app from the Power App studio.

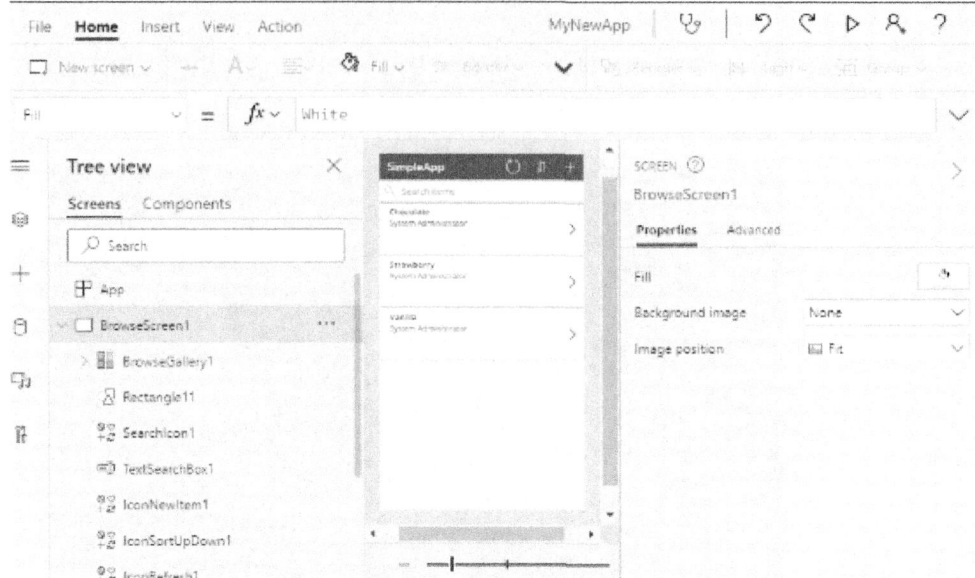

- Then you can refresh the browser tab that has the list by first choosing it and then selecting **F5**. Then you can follow the following steps so that you can run or manage the application.
- If you want to run the app, click **Open.**
- If you want others within the organization to have access to the app, choose to **Make this view public.** And to let others be able to edit the app, select **Share it** and choose **Can edit** permissions
- If you want to disconnect the view from the share point, choose **Remove this view.** And to remove the app, select **Delete.**

Examining the screens at runtime

In Power Apps, there are multiple screens with label controls, Button controls, and other controls with data and support navigation.

UNDERSTANDING THE AUTO-GENERATED APP

Adding, deleting, and rearranging screens

Here is how to add a screen:

- Go to the Home tab and choose **New screen** then choose the screen you will like to add.

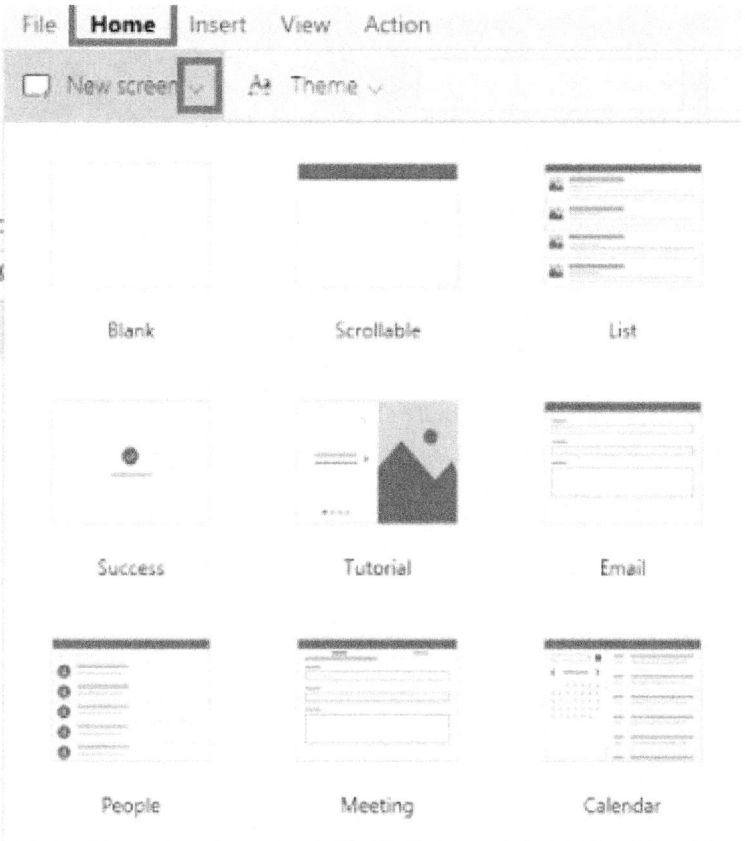

- Then go to the right-hand pane and enter the name of the screen and enter the **Source.**

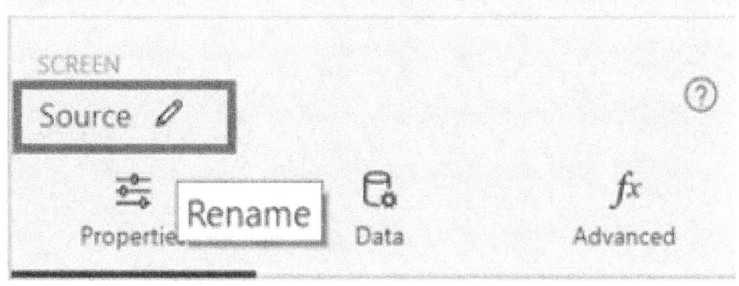

- Then add another screen and name it **Target.**

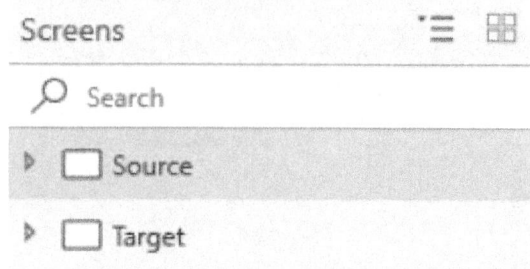

Then to rearrange the screen here is what to do:

- Go to the left navigation bar, then hover above the screen that you will like to move, then choose the ellipsis button that pops up and choose, **Move up** or **Move down.**

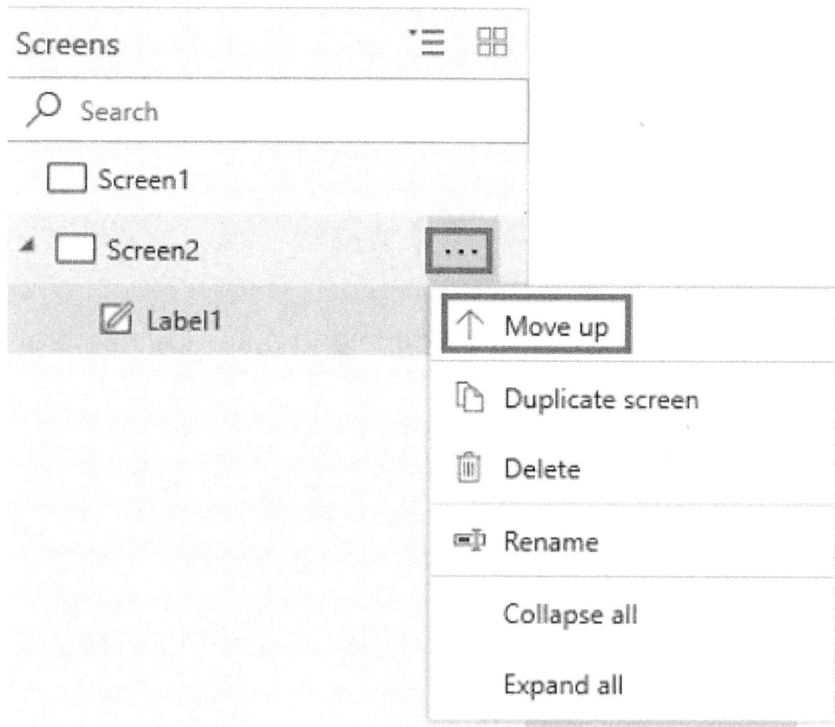

UNDERSTANDING HOW SCREENS ARE CONNECTED

Understanding forms and cards

A card form is used in views for apps that are model-driven. These card forms are created in other to present data in a compact way suitable for a mobile device. Take, for example, the default card form for the My Active Accounts view that defines the information shown for each account row.

Here is how to create a card form:

1. The first thing to do is to sign in to the power apps.
2. Then expand the data, and choose **Tables** then choose the preferred table and select the **Forms** area.
3. Then go to the toolbar and choose to **Add the form.** Then choose **Card form.** Also, you can open a preexisting form and type in a card form so that you can edit it.

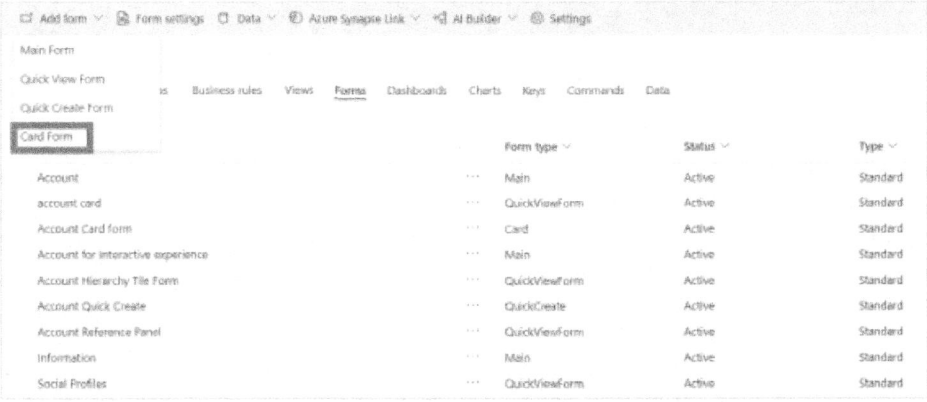

4. Then you can add the number of columns that you want. We prefer that you have a limitation to the number of columns so that the entire form will show well on a small screen.
5. Choose **Save** and choose to **Publish.**

Then you need to add a card form to view

- The first thing is to sign into power apps as usual.

- Then expand the data and choose the table you prefer, then choose the **Views** area.
- Choose your preferred view, then go to the **View designer toolbar** and choose **Switch to classic.**
- Choose the custom controls from **the common tasks pane.**
- Then select **Add control.** Then from the control list, choose **Read-only grid** then select **Add.**
- Then when you are on the **Read-only grid** properties page, set the card flow properties and choose **OK.**
- Then choose **OK,** if you want to remove the **Custom controls** properties page.

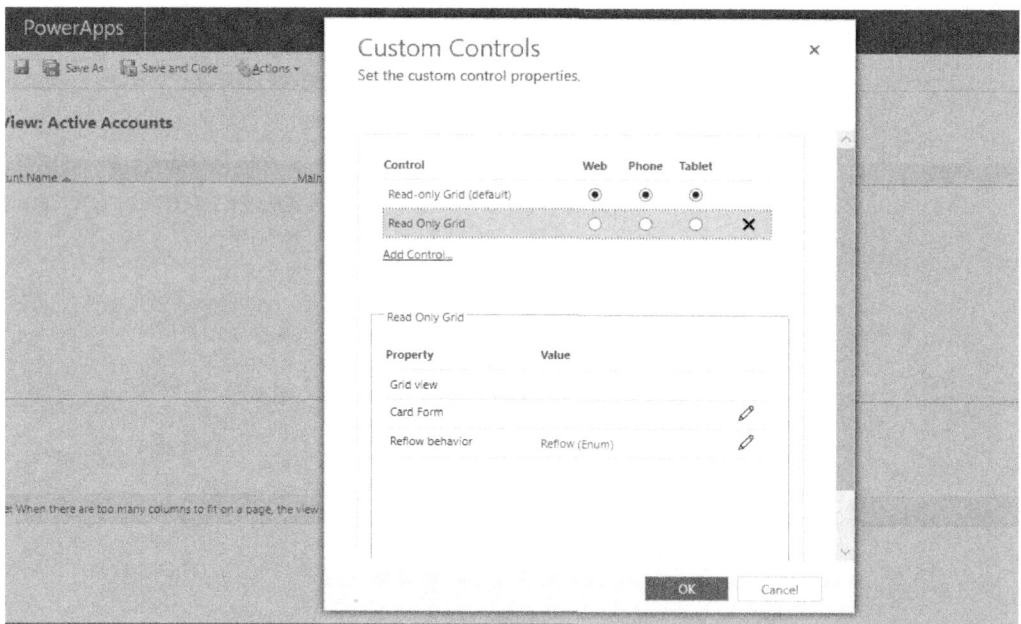

- Then enter the **Classic View** designer toolbar and choose to **Save and Close**

SETTING APP PROPERTIES

There are a few properties in Power Apps. They include:

Default -- which refers to the value of control before any configuration was done by the user.

Delay output -- this is set as true so that it delays action when inputting text.

Display mode -- in the display mode, you can edit, view, or disable. You can configure **Edit** when you want the user to make inputs or **View** to just show the data or **Disabled** when you want it to be disabled.

Items -- referring to the source of data appearing in a gallery, a list, or a chart.

On change -- refers to the action that needs to be active if the user wants to change the control value.

On select -- refers to the action that manifests when the user selects a control.

Reset -- refers to if the control goes back to the default.

Text -- refers to the text that appears in control or the user types inside a control.

The tooltip -- refers to the text that pops up when a user hovers over one of the control.

Value -- this refers to the value of input control.

Visible—refers to when the control pops up or does not.

Saving and opening Apps

To save any changes to the app you make on the power apps studio, choose to save from the file menu that you see on the left, and then follow these steps:

1. If you have never saved an app before, go to the **File** menu and select **Save** and you are going to go automatically to **Save as.** Pick a location. Preferably **The cloud** and name it. Then choose to **Save.**

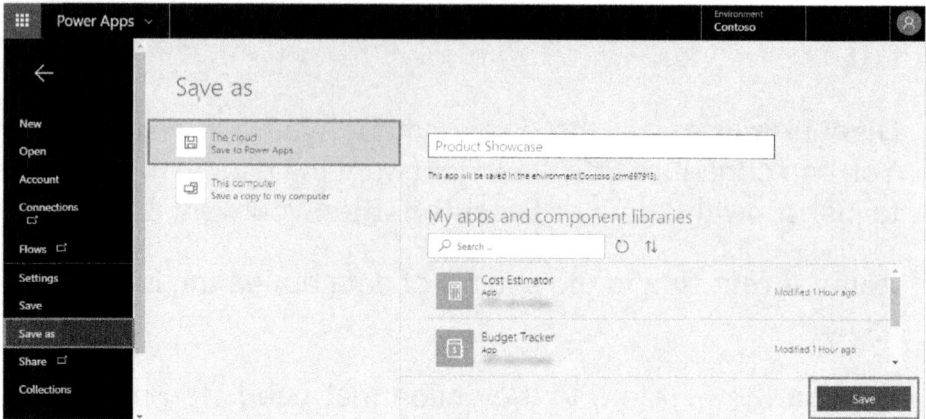

2. If the app has been previously saved, then you can add a version-specific note or add a comment.

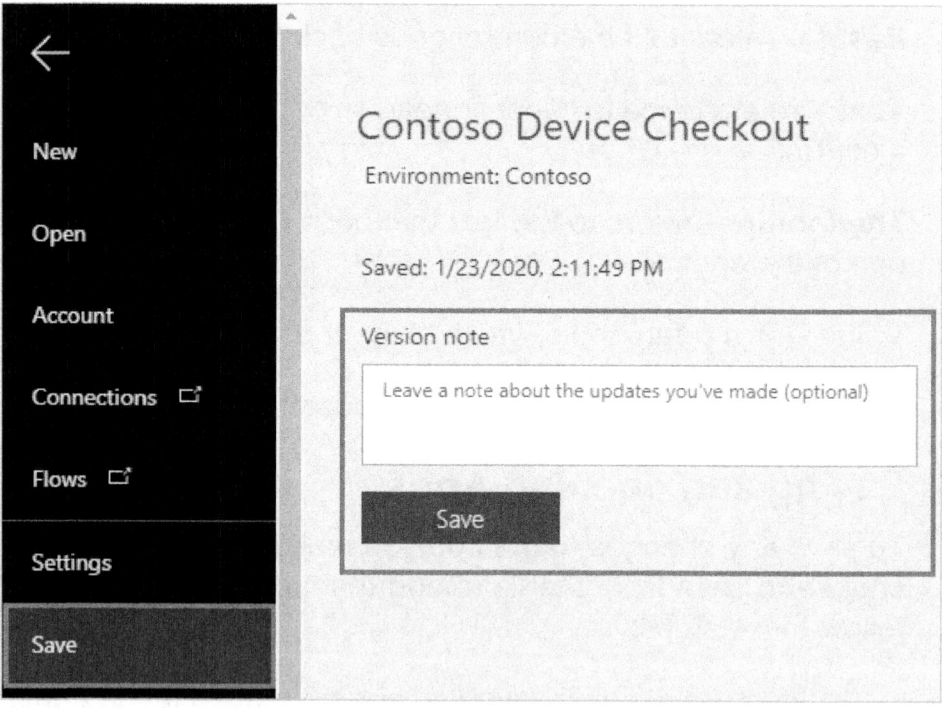

3. You also have the option to save the app every 2 minutes. Once you save the app, a version of the app is going to be saved periodically without you pressing the save action.

Review Questions

- How can one prepare an Excel data source for Power App?
- What is the Power App designer?
- What is an auto-generated app?

Summary

Powerapp.com is important in all of these. We can now create apps with the Power apps and know some of the properties of the power app when you are working with it.

CHAPTER FOUR

SHARING APPS

In this section, we are going to be taking you through the steps of sharing apps with end users after creating them.

SHARING APPS WITH END-USER.

Now there are a lot of options you have once you build a canvas application that addresses the needs of a business. You can specify who owns the app and who has access to them for modification and even to share them.

But before you begin to share the application, there are a few things that you must do first. You have to first save the app to the cloud online and then publish it. Then the other thing that you need to do is name the app. And it is that simple.

Here are the steps to then share the app:

- First login to the Power Apps.
- Then go to the left pane and choose the application.

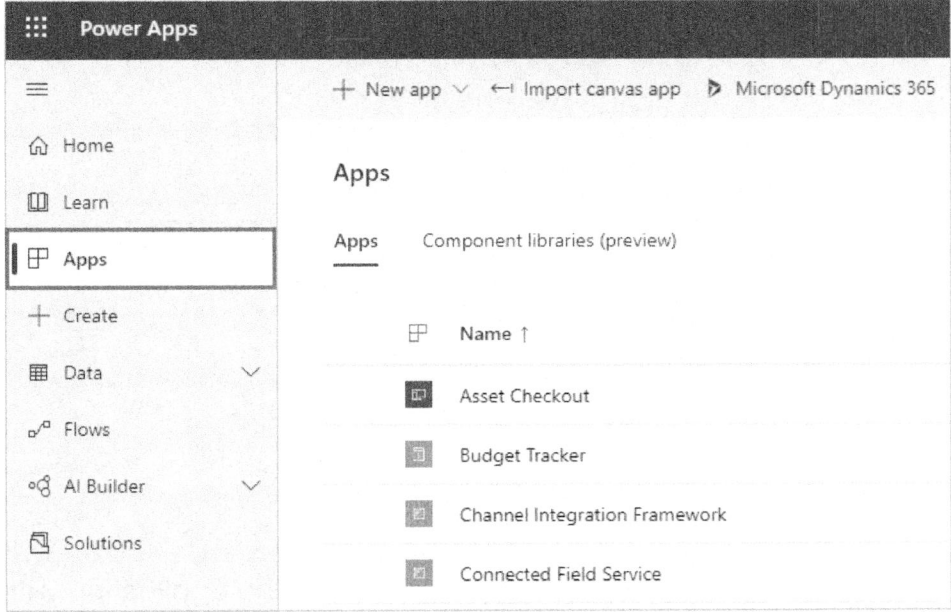

- The next thing to do is choose the application that you want to share by selecting the icon of the app.
- Then go to the command bar and choose **Share.**
- Then you can specify the name or the alias of the user or the security groups in Azure Ad with whoever you want to share the app with.
- If you want to give everybody in your organization, permission to run the app, select **Everyone** from the sharing panel. As a user, you also have the opportunity to find the app by filtering the app list to organize apps.

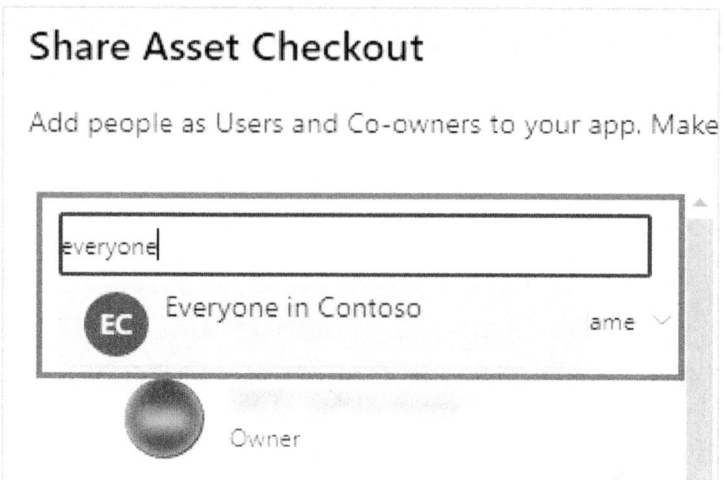

- You also have the opportunity to share the application with a list of aliases, friendly names, or combinations of the aliases as far as the aliases are separated by semicolon. Now, if a lot of people share the same names, but different aliases, the first person found will be added to the list. A tooltip only appears when one of the names or one of the aliases already has permission or cannot be resolved.
- If you prefer the users to edit and share the application, choose the **Co-owner** check box.

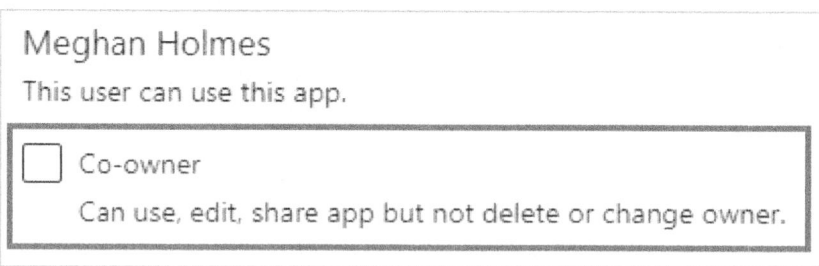

- From the sharing user interface, there is no option to give co-ownership permissions to a security group when the app was created within a solution. Nevertheless, you can give the co-ownership permission to a security group for apps inside a solution with the set-power app role assignment cmdlet.

- If the app is connected to data that users are going to need access permission specify the appropriate security role: take for example, that the app might connect to a table that is in the Dataverse database. Once you share that app, then the sharing pane is going to notify you to manage the security for the table.
- And if the app user connects to the other data sources like an excel file that was hosted by OneDrive for business make sure that you also share the data source with those users that you share the application with.
- And if you are going to help people to find the application, mark **send an email invitation to new users'** checkbox.
- Then under the share panel, select **Share.** The users can then run the app with the power apps mobile on a mobile device or from an app source on the Microsoft 365 platform. As a co-owner, you can then edit and share the app inside the Power Apps

  The user can select the link in the invitation to run the app if you used an email invitation. However, when a co-owner receives an invitation, they also are going to receive another link that runs the app so that it can be edited on the Power Apps studio.

  After giving the permission, if you want to change the user or the security group here is what to do:
- If you want the co-owner to run the app but you do not want them to share it or edit it, unmark the **co-owner.**
- If you do not want to share the app with a user or a group, choose the icon "X"

SPECIFYING OWNERS AND USERS

Creating users

If you host Dynamics 365 in a GCC high cloud region, you have to then create an application used for all of the environments in Dynamics 365 that you will like to back up.

Then to create the user:

- The first thing to do is to login into the Microsoft Power Platform Admin center via the system administrator.

- Then go to the navigation pane and find **Environments** then choose one of the environments in the list.
- Then go to the **Settings** tab and find **users + permissions,** then find **application users.** This brings out the application users' page
- The next thing to do is choose **+new app user** to bring out the **Create a new app user** dialog box.
- Then choose one of the business units and select **+add an app** so that you can have it.

Setting up Security Groups

When you want to create a security group so that you can then add members to the security group, here is what to do:

1. First, log in to the Microsoft 365 admin center.
2. Then choose the **Teams and groups** icon, then select **Active teams and groups.**
3. Pick **+add a group.**
4. After this, you can switch the security group type by adding a name and description for the group and choose to **Add > Close.**
5. Then pick a group that you made and choose **Edit.**
6. Select **+add members.** Then pick the users that you will like to add to the security group and choose to **Save> Close** multiple times to find your way back to the **group's** list.
7. Now that you know how to add a user, removing a user is just as easy. What you are going to do is choose the security group that comes after members and choose **Edit.** Then pick **Remove members** then choose x for the members that you will like to remove.

Setting up External Users

Now when you want to set up external users, there is an easy way to do it and it does not take much.

- The first thing to do is to add the external user into the Azure active directory as a guest: enter the global admin center for the app menu if you have administrator access.

- Then enter the user section and choose **Guest users:** you then have the option to add guest users here.

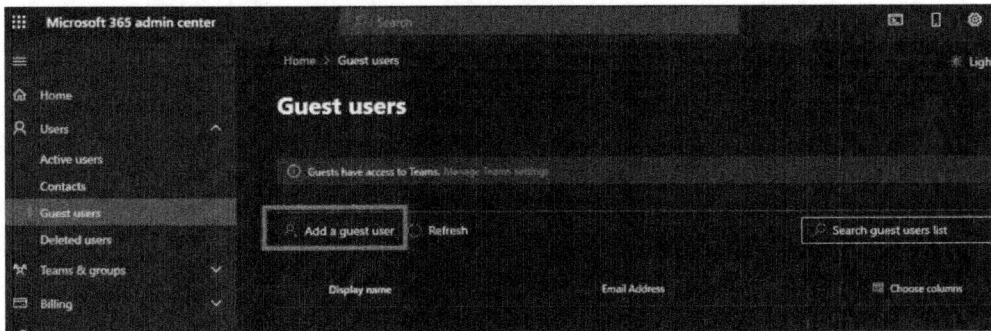

- Then in the new user setup screen, you can then indicate if you want to create a new user account for the organization or if you will like to send an invite to a guest user with the email that they have. Then you can assign a name, email address, first name, and last name.

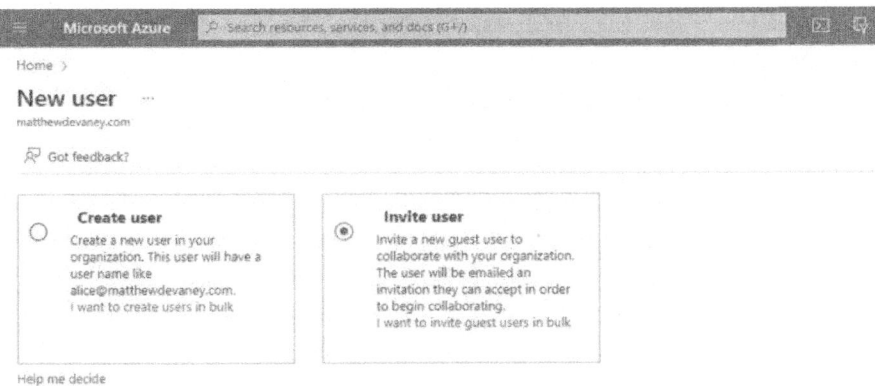

- If you are inviting an external user, then the invite is going to be sent by email to the person.
- However, the external user will need a license for Power App before they can use an application in the organization. However, when you try to give the guest user a license on the global admin center, you cannot assign the license. The assign license tab cannot be seen as a guest user.

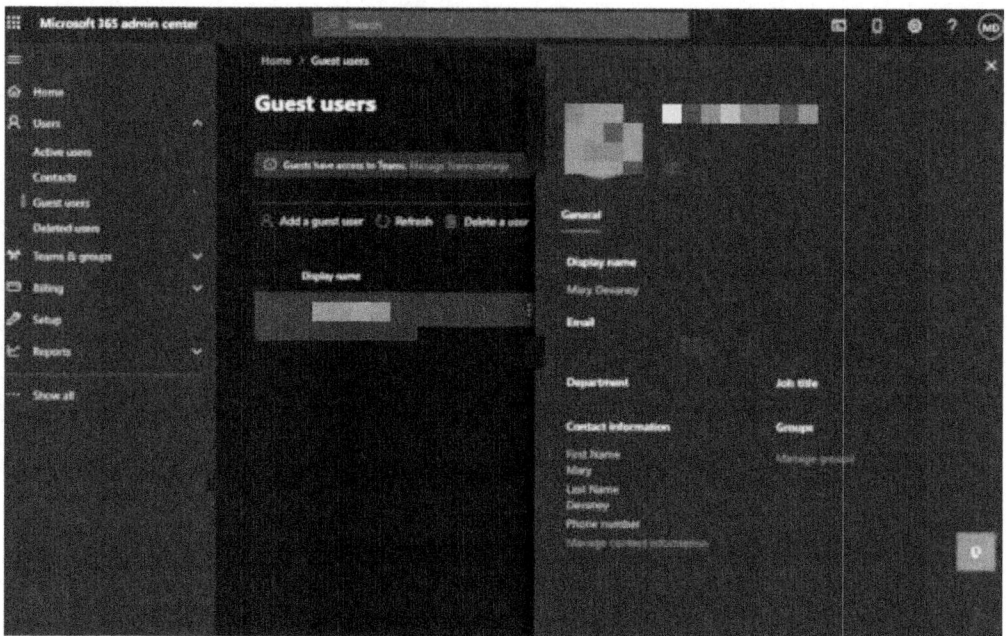

- So you have to create a group for the external users inside the Azure Active Directory the assign a license to each group member. Then enter **portal.azure.com** then open the Azure Active Directory.
- Choose **Groups** from the left pane.

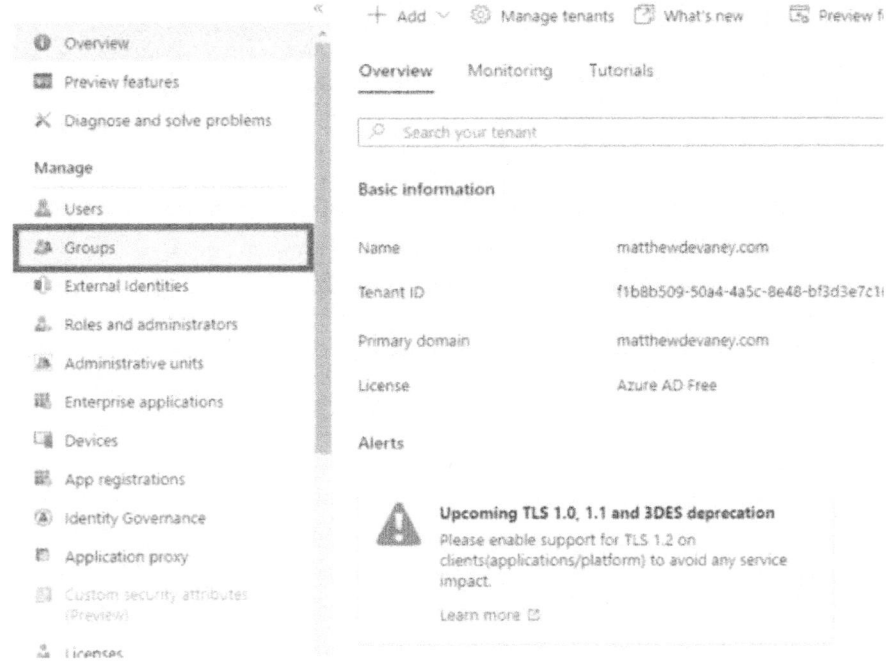

- Then place the new group.

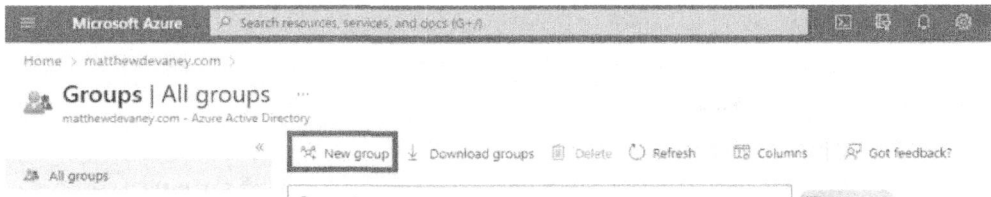

- Enter the group and type security then give the group a name and describe it. Here, you have to make yourself the group owner.

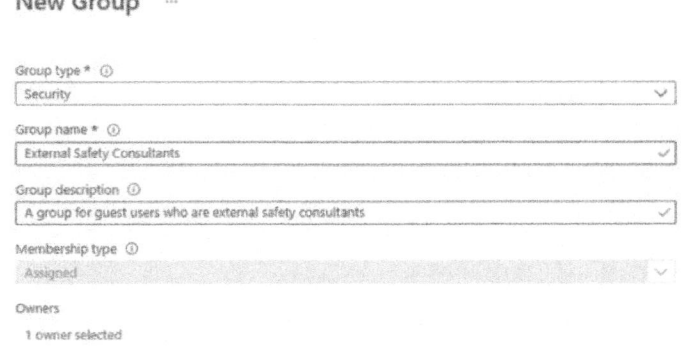

- Then you can choose the **Member**, then add an external user to the group and close the menu then choose **Create**. The new group then appears in the group list.
- After creating the new group, you can then assign an external user the license for the power apps.
- Go to the **External Safety Consultants** group.

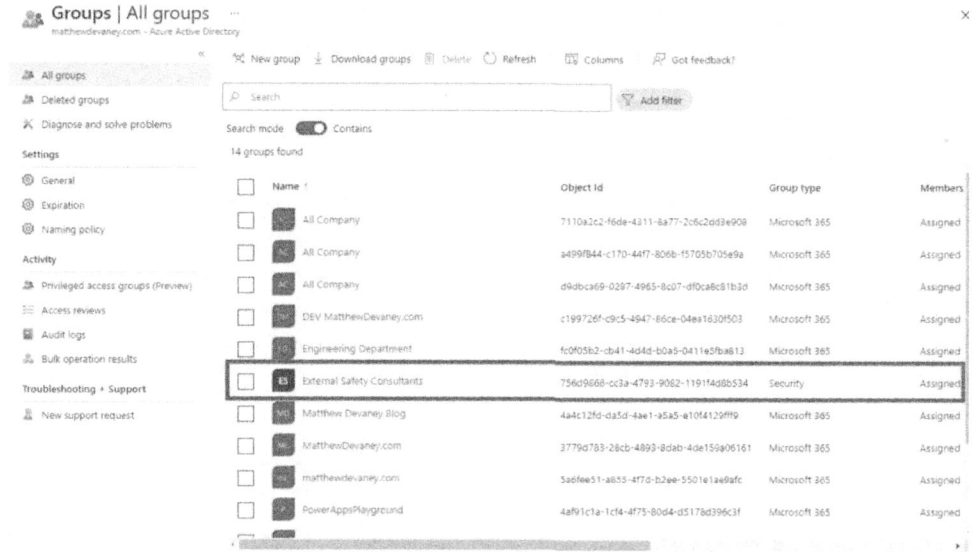

- Then enter the license menu and choose **Assignments.**

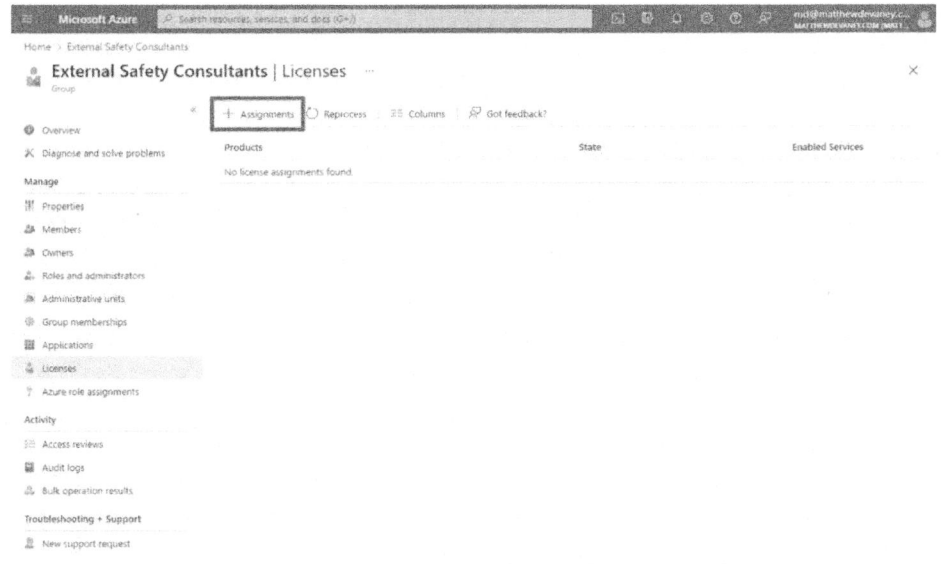

- Then when you go to the Update licenses assignment screen, choose the licenses required by the external user to be able to run the app. The requirement for licensing may varies depending on whether it is a premium connector, an independent canvas app, or a customized SharePoint list form.

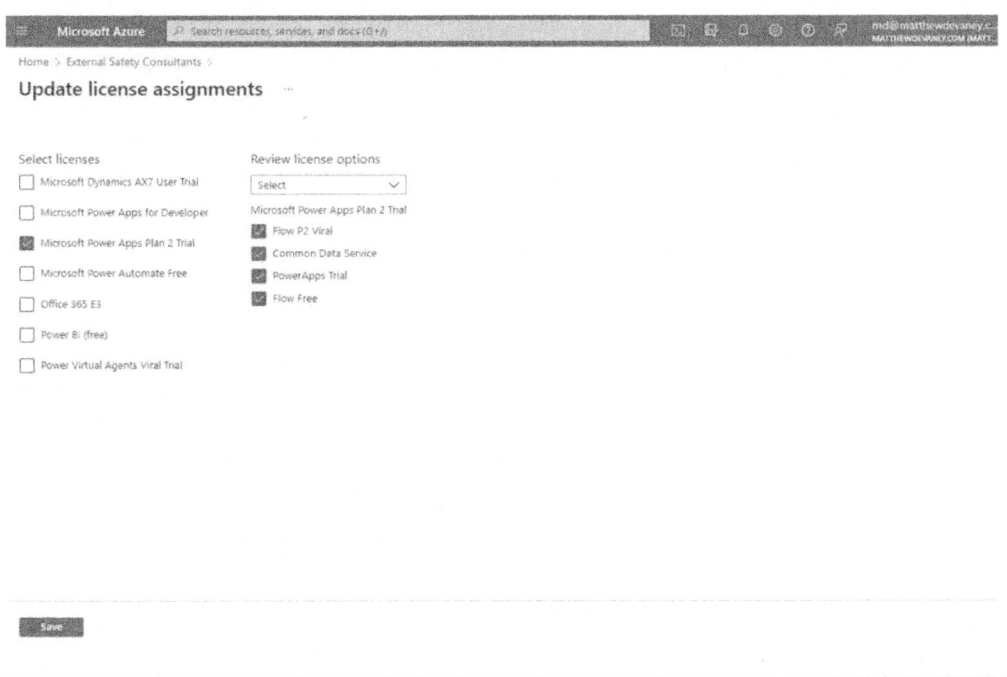

- Once you are done, choose, and save.

Sharing App Data Sources

When you share the app with other users some connectors like SQL, SQL Server with SQL, or windows authentication are shared automatically with the app. However, some other forms of connections need the users themselves to create a connection and then assign security roles to each user.

Now, you can decide to share the app with or without the connection in just these few steps:

- Go to **Data** and select **Connection**.
- Then enter the connection that is needed.
- If you see the **Share** button on top of the navigation or if you see the share button only when you choose **More commands,** that means that the selected connections can be shared with the other users.

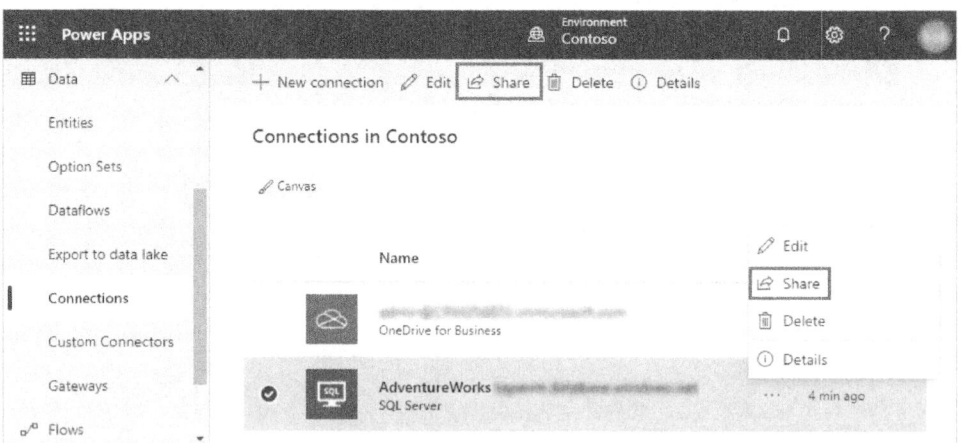

Installing the Mobile Player

The Power apps mobile can run the following apps: Model-driven apps, canvas apps, Dynamics 365 Marketing, and Dynamics 365 customer service.

Then there are the steps to install the mobile player.

- You have to first sign in with the Azure Active Directory. You can sign in with the Microsoft Authenticator on your mobile device when you enter the username after being prompted. Then you must approve the notification that was sent to your device.
- Then look for the application. If you created an app or one was shared with you, you can use the power app mobile to run it.

UNDERSTANDING THE ENVIRONMENTS

Just like everything around us that we can see and touch and store, or manage stuff Is an environment, so also is the Power App environment the place where you can store, manage and share the business data for the organization, Chatbots, and flows. It is also the place where you can separate applications with different roles, security requirements, and target audiences.

Now the application you are creating and the organization that you work for determine how the environment works.

1. All of your apps or Chat-bots can be built in one environment
2. You can create a different environment that will both group the tests and the production versions of the applications and the Chatbots
3. You can create a different environment that corresponds with some specific teams or departments within the company, with each of them having the relevant data and the application for each of the audience.
4. You can even create a unique environment for different global branches of your organization

Creating new environments

The environment is created with the Azure Active Directory tenant and everything in it is only accessible by users that have the tenants. Furthermore, the environment is bound to the geographic location where it was created and when you create an app inside an environment, the app and all of the items that were created within the environment are routed to the data centers within the geographical location.

Here are the steps to create an environment:

1. Sign in to the Power platform admin center first
2. Then go to the navigation pane and choose **Environments** and choose **New.**

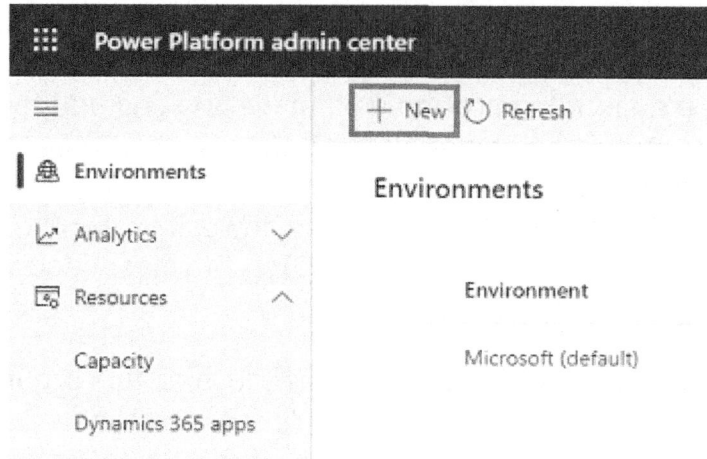

3. Enter the name of the environment, the type of environment, the region, and the description of the environment then select **Next.**

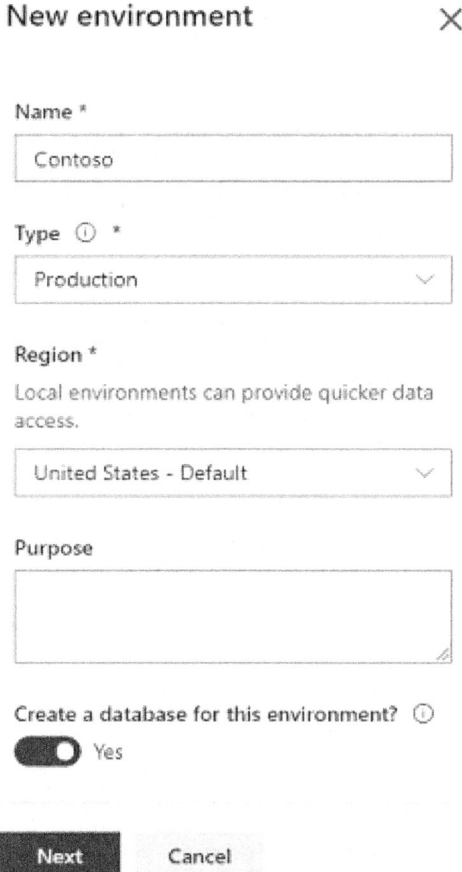

New environment   ✕

Name *

Contoso

Type ⓘ *

Production   ⌄

Region *

Local environments can provide quicker data
access.

United States - Default   ⌄

Purpose

Create a database for this environment? ⓘ

◖ Yes

Next   Cancel

4. Then enter the following and choose to **Save.**

← Add database   ✕

Language *

Default language for user interfaces in this
environment

English   ⌄

URL *

Contoso

crm.dynamics.com

Currency *

Reports will use this currency

USD ($)   ⌄

Enable Dynamics 365 apps

In addition to Power Apps. Learn more

◖◗ Yes

Automatically deploy these apps

Sales Enterprise   ⌄

Security group

Restrict environment access to people in this
security group. Otherwise, everyone can
access. Learn more

+ Select

[**Save**]   [Cancel]

If you wanted to, you can also create an environment without
databases.

- First sign into the admin center
- Then enter the navigation pane and choose **Environments** then choose **New.**

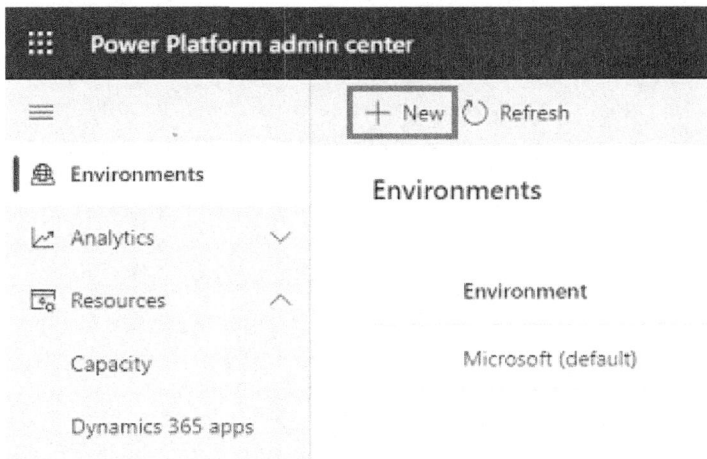

- Name the environment, the type, the region, and the description, and choose to **Save**

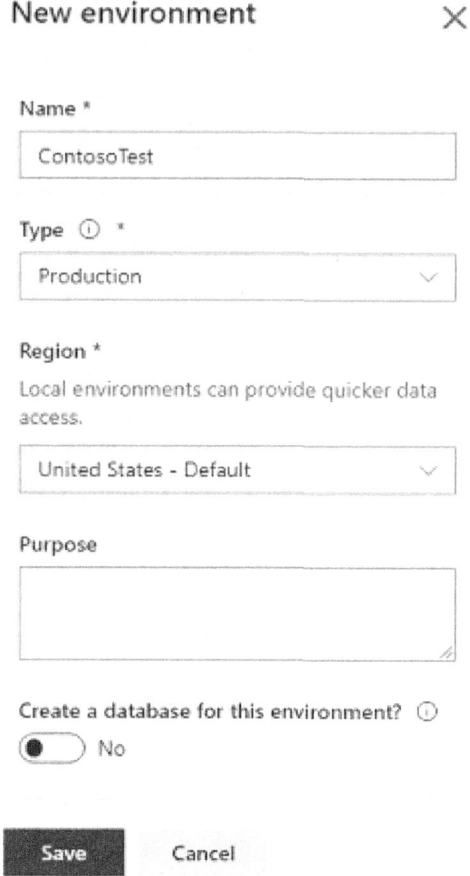

Choosing an Environment Type

There are six different environment types in the power platform and we are going to be taking you through all of them one by one very briefly.

- **The production type**: it is used for permanent work within an organization and the user has full control. Only people with a power app license or an administrator can create these types.
- **The default type**: here each of the tenants has a default environment created automatically. And the users have limited control. But the licensed users have the role of environment maker.
- **The sandbox**: these are the polar opposite of the production environments that offer things like copy and reset. They are used

both for development and testing and are different from production. The user has full control when used for testing. But only user access is needed

- **The trial**: this is used for short-term testing and they are cleaned up after a certain period. The security control here is full.
- **Of the Developer Environments:** if you have a development plan, then you can use this. This way you can add other makers.
- **To the Microsoft Dataverse for teams**: the Dataverse for teams is created automatically for the chosen team after creating an app in teams with the power app. You have limited control and the admins have a limited set for the team environment.

Setting Environment Permissions

There are two inherent roles to providing permission in an environment. And they are the environment Admin and the environment maker.

The admin role can add or remove users or groups from the admin or the environment maker, they provide a Dataverse database for the environment, and they view and try to manage the resources created inside an environment. And they prevent data loss by setting the policies.

The environment maker, on the other hand, creates resources within an environment.

To set the permission:

1. Sign in to the power admin.
2. Then enter the **Environment** and choose one of the environments.
3. Go to the **Access** tile and choose to **See all** for the environment admin or the environment maker.

MOVING APPS BETWEEN ENVIRONMENTS AND TENANTS

You have the option to move apps between environment and tenants simply by following the steps we are going to give you in the section below.

Exporting an app

- First, enter the **Power App** you will like to export and choose the **Export package** on the top panel.

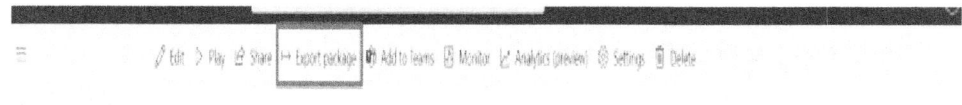

- Then on the page for the **Export package**, type the name and description for the power app and select **Export.**
- When you export the app, it is going to notify you to also save the application in the local system. Then you can save the app the way that it is.

Then we are going to tell you how to import in the section below:

Importing an app

- Then in the tenant site that you are sending then select **Apps** from the left navigation and choose **Import** canvas app.

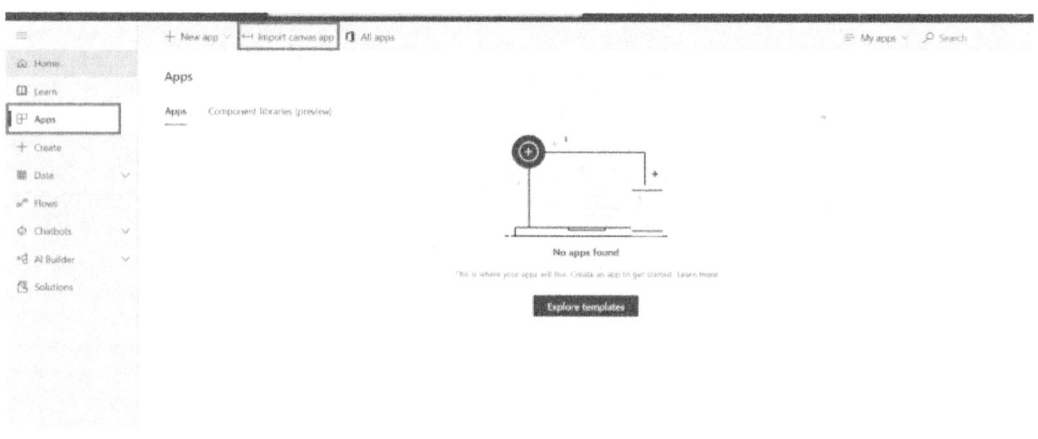

- Then when you enter the page for **Import package,** select **Upload.**
- Then you can choose the specific zip file from the local system that you want to import and choose **Open.**
- While on the package details page, select update. Then select **Setup.**
- Select **Import** from the review page.

- Once the import is successful, then the page is healthy.
- Then you can select **Open App.**

Updating a Data source versioning Apps

Then to update the data source, here is what to do:

When the app is open, go to the **Data pane** and choose **View > Data source,** then choose the connector and select **Remove** in the screenshot.

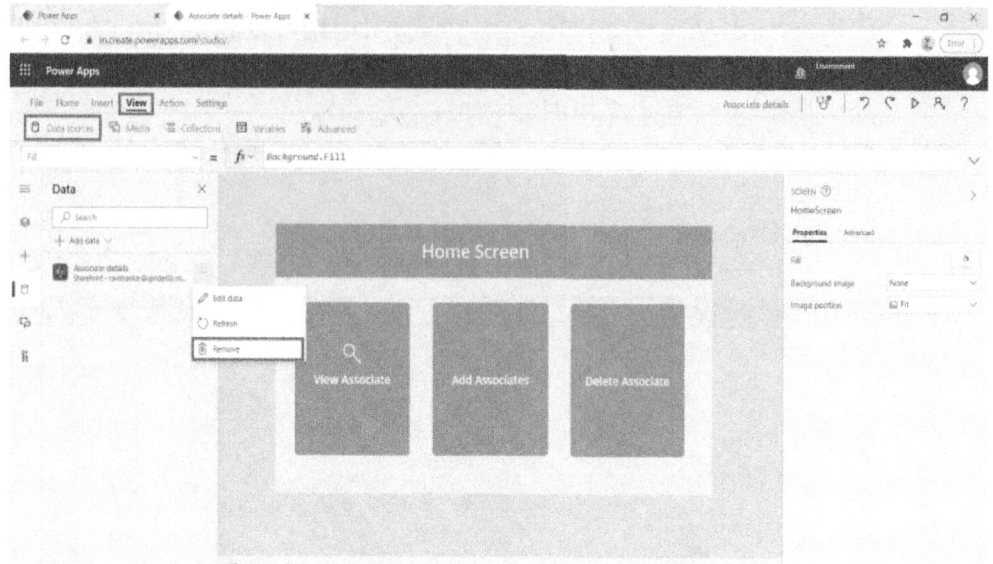

Then choose **Add data** and select **Connectors** then choose **SharePoint.**

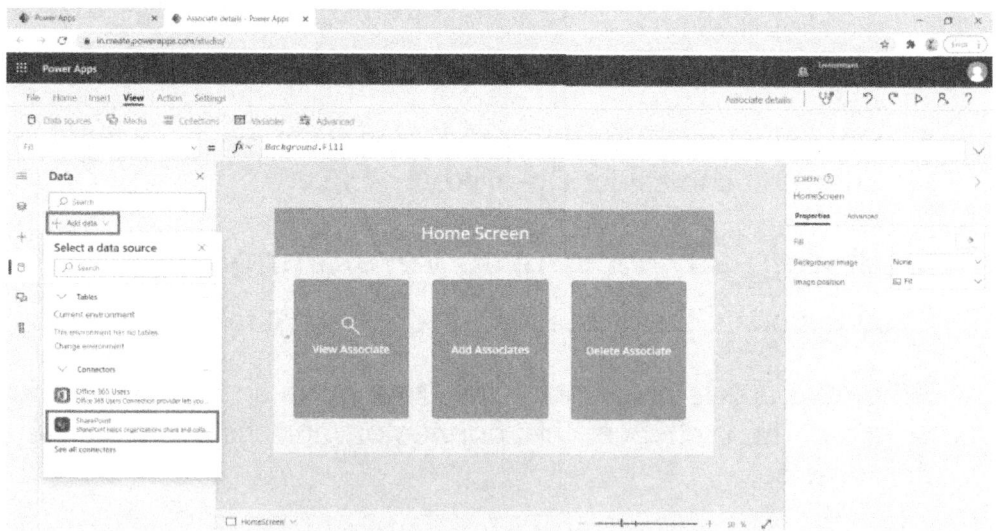

When you are in the **Connect to SharePoint** site, choose the URL that you will like to use and select **Connect.**

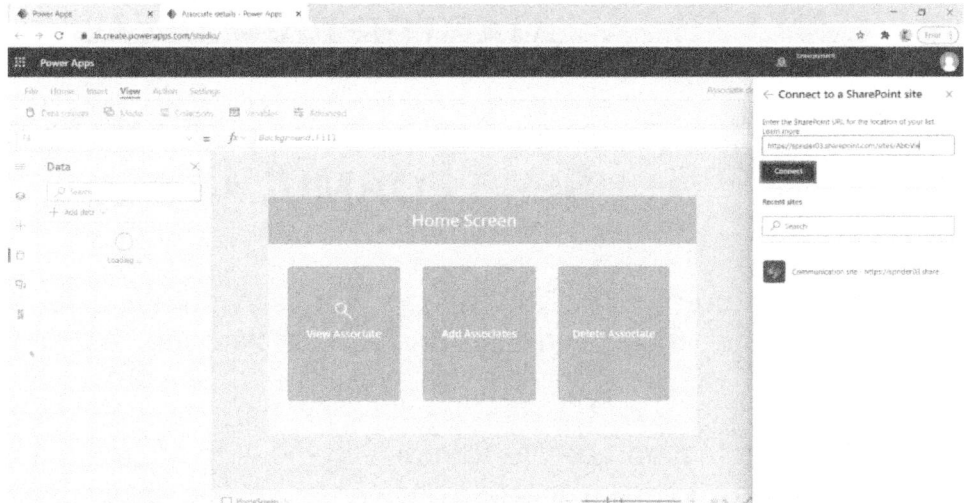

In choosing a list, check the lost you prefer and select **Connect.**

And now, you have successfully moved power apps across tenants.

Review Question

- How do you share an app with others?
- How do you set up the Power App for External users?
- How do you set up the Environment permission?

Summary

Voila, it is that easy. You can now run apps, share them, and set security roles for users in your organization. Now it is on to the next section of using formulas.

CHAPTER FIVE

USERS FORMULAS

If you have created a Canvas app, you can create a formula that calculates the values and also performs tasks, and responds to the user's input.

Just the way that you create formulas in Excel to populate a cell or to create tables and make charts, in Power Apps. The difference however is that you need to configure the controls and not cells; you configure them for applications and not for spreadsheets.

So you can use a formula to add a command of how an app responds when a user selects a button, or inputs something.

MAKING FORMULAS

When you enter specific data into an Excel cell, the cell always carries that data the way you typed them. In Power Apps also, you can add data and don't expect it to change when you set the text property of the label to the specific sequence of the character covered with double quotation ("")

Here is how to make a formula to show simple values:

1. The first thing to do is select a blank canvas app.

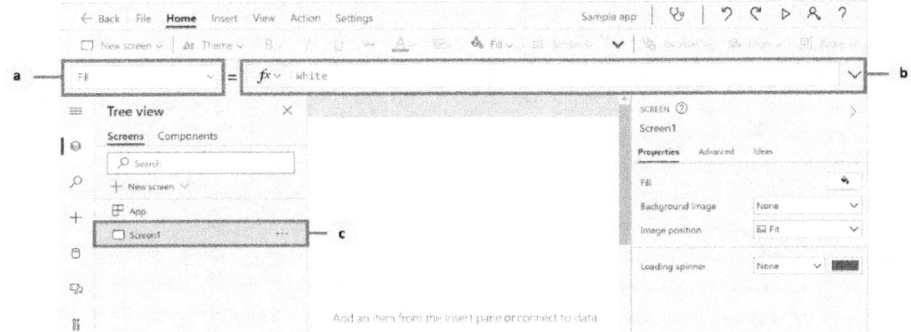

2. Then add a label control to the screen.

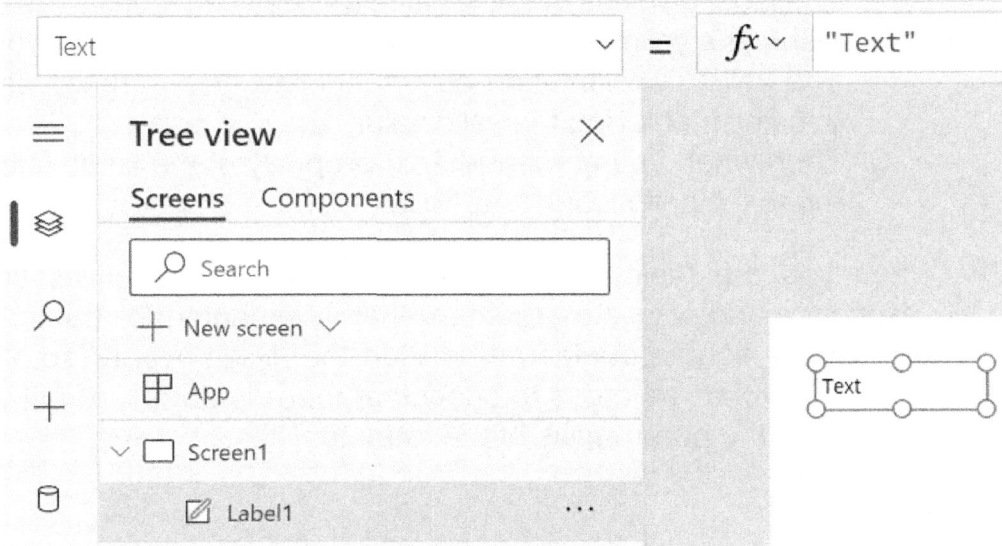

3. After you add the label, the property list displays the properties of the text, which is the actual control. Automatically the value of this property becomes TEXT.
4. Configure the value for the **Text** property into "Hello world" by then entering for example "Hello World" and surround the string with a double quote inside the formula bar

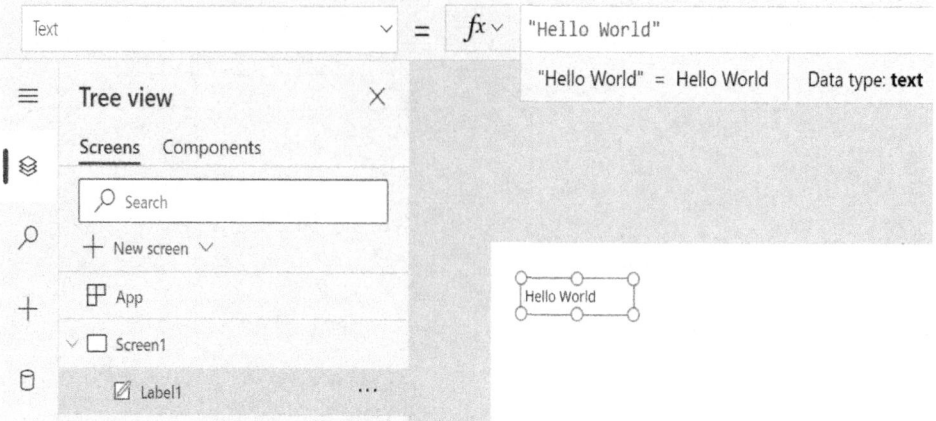

5. The label displays the new value the way you type it. The screen displays a yellow-colored exclamation point icon when you type. The yellow exclamation points indicate errors, however, once you finish entering the valid value, they go away.
6. Then when you are in the Text property of the label, substitute the text " hello world " for SUM(1,2,3)

When you are typing into the formula bar, it also gives you the description and also the argument that is expected for this function. just like the double quotation mark on the: Hello World" so also the screen shows a red cross to show that there is an error until you go and type in the parenthesis of the formula.

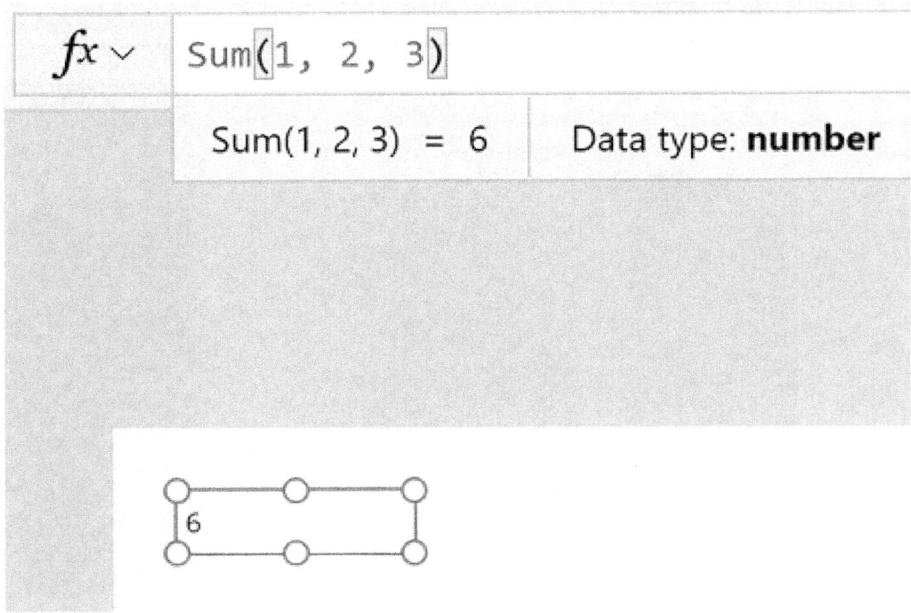

Adding comments

So to add a comment, we are going to be using a Power BI report to see the stock volume for three companies both by their dates and the managers of their accounts. So we are going to be making a line chart and a slicer for the companies on Power BI.

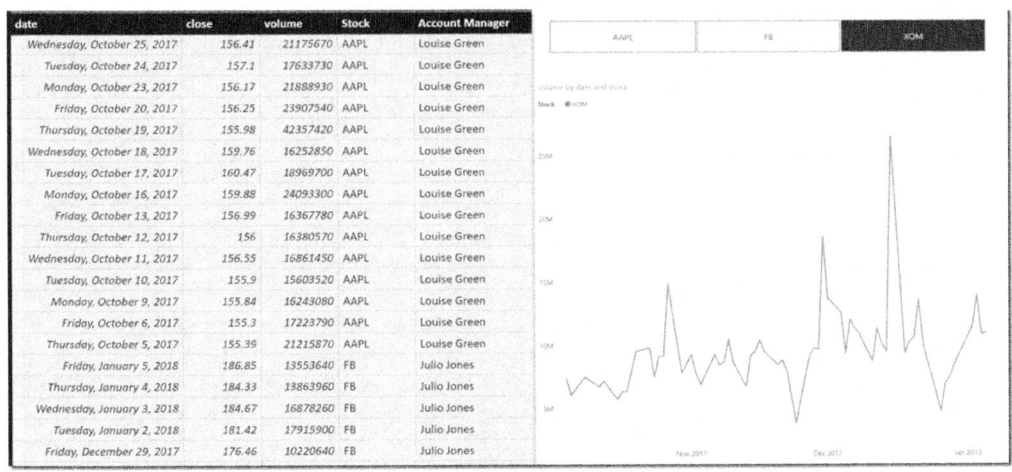

- Then place that report to the Power BI service, then you can edit the report. Then go to the store and add the power apps custom visuals.

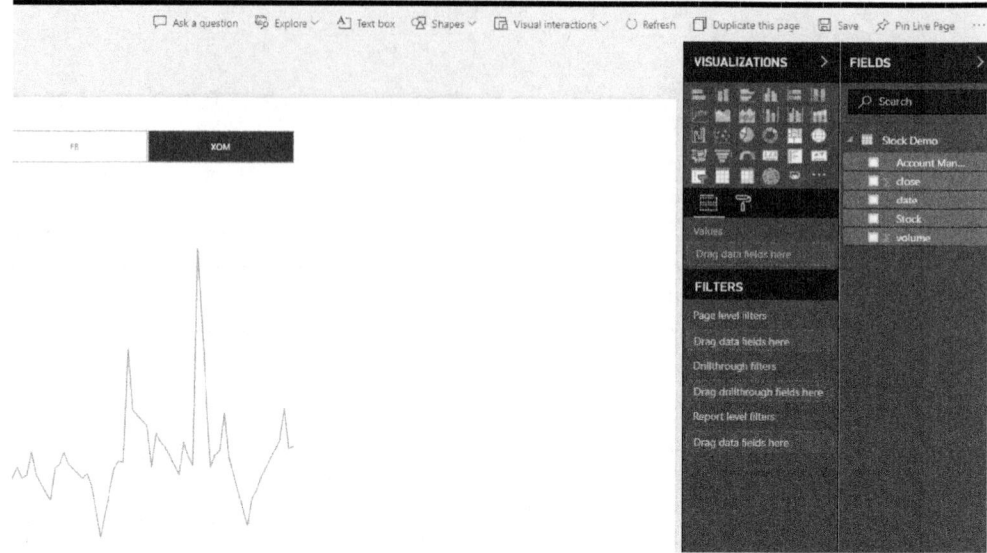

- Then select custom visual inside the power apps, drag the account manager then stock inside the power apps data field, and select **Create new.**
- The Power Apps visual provides an input area for the comment and to send emails to the account managers for each company. To store the comment, you can use a table inside Excel Spreadsheet.

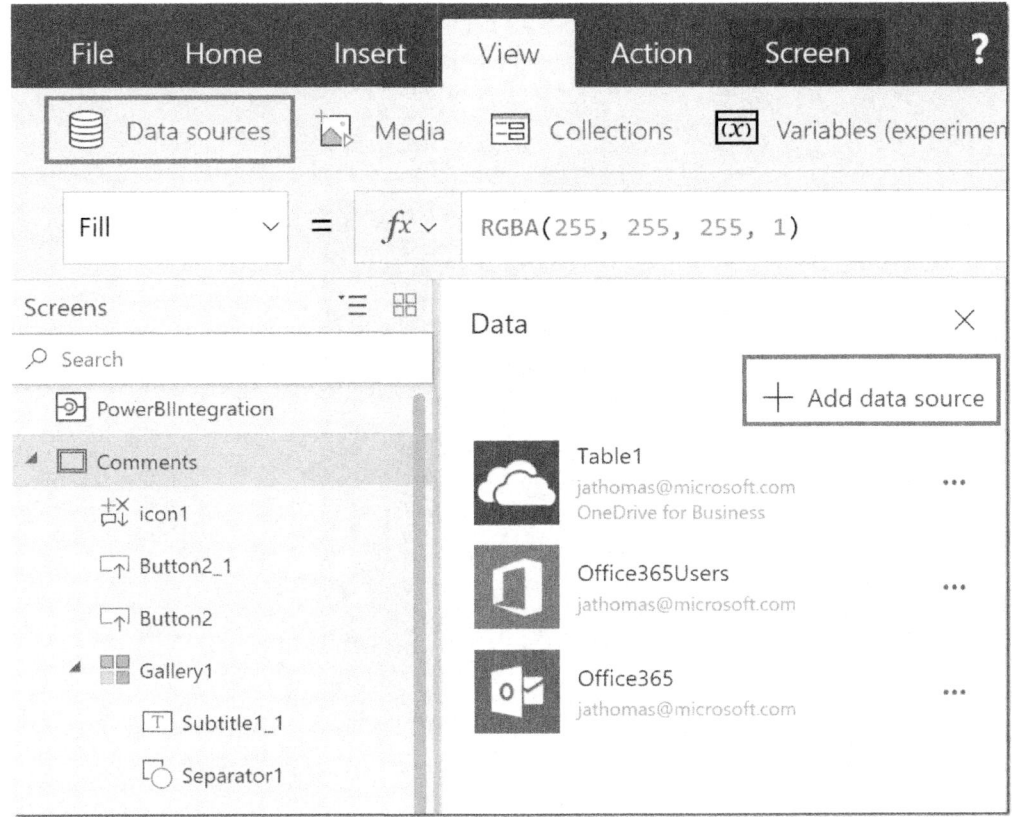

- Then you can start editing the comment page to get the following.

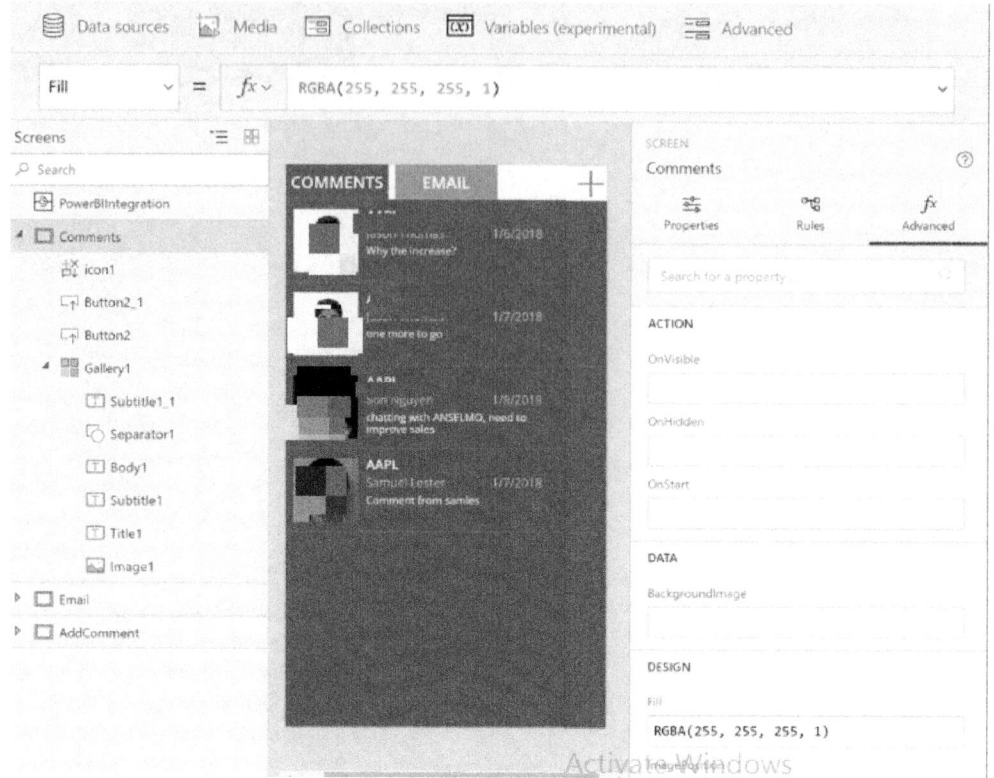

- Then on the next page which is the email page and is used when you want to share an email to the account manager without attaching comments.
- After the email page is the add **Comment page.** You can access the page when you select the plus icon inside the comments page and are used to add comments.

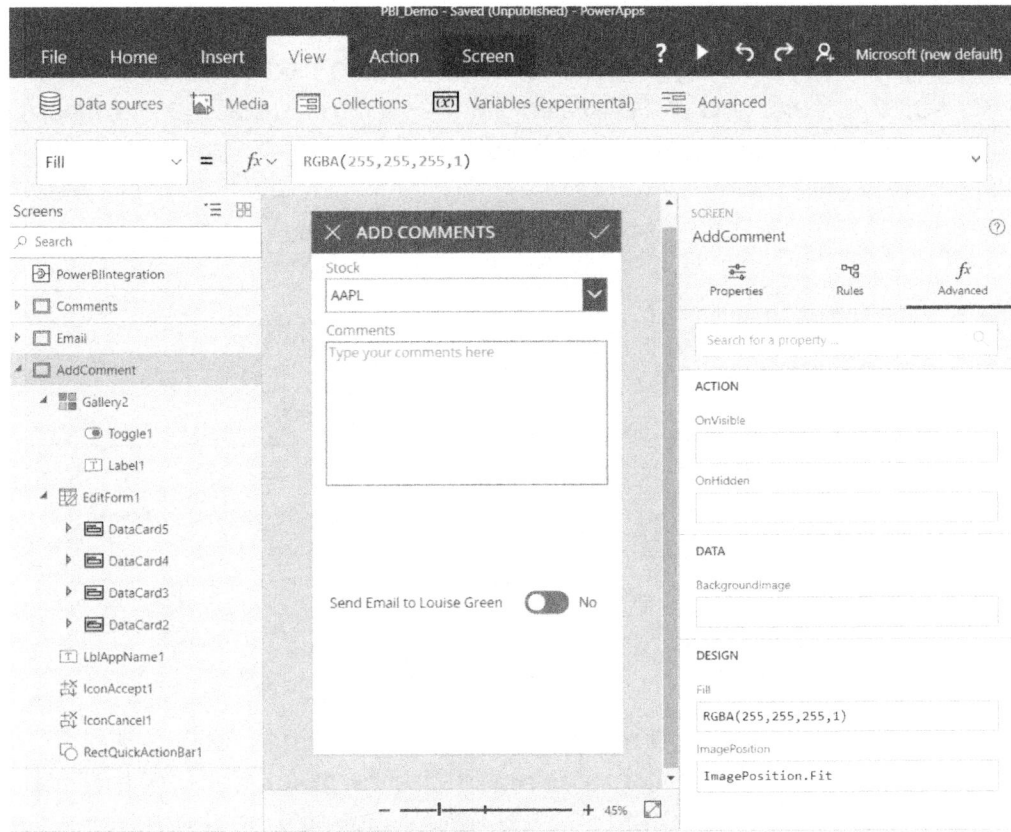

Working with variables

The approach you take to access variables on the power apps is a different approach from what is provided by other programming tools. Now when you build a canvas app you have to take the Excel approach.

Excel and Power App automatically configures formulas when the input data changes. This means that you do not need to create and update variables. This approach makes it easier to calculate, understand, and manage the app.

When you create an app with Power Apps, they work like they do with Excel. So you do not have to update the cells. What you do is add control to where you want them on the screen then name them so that you can use them in a formula.

Take, for example, you can just mimic the excel app behavior in an app first by adding a label control and two text input control. After you set the Text property of label1, this then sums the numbers in the TextInput1 and TextInput2 automatically.

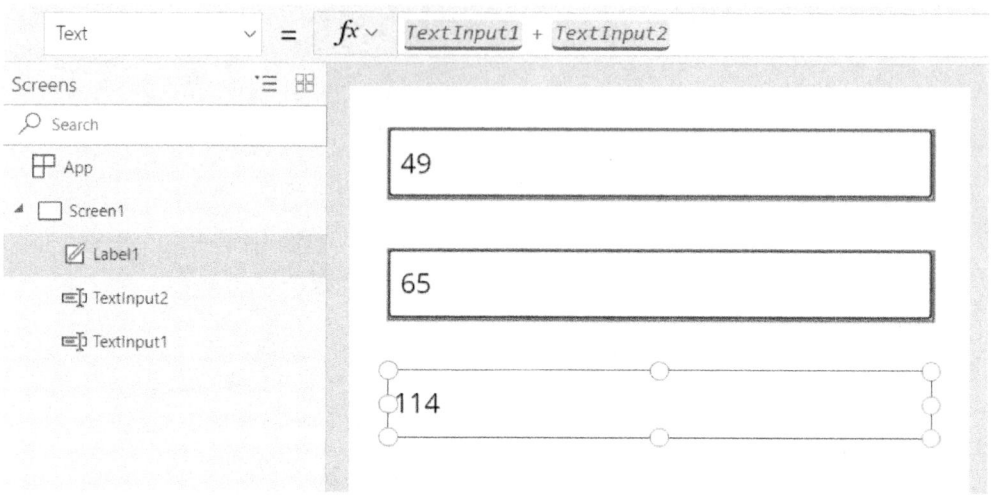

If you observed, you are going to see that when you select the label1, showing the Text formula inside the formula bar on the top of the screen. The Textinput1 + Textinput2 creates dependencies between the controls, the same way that you can create dependencies between cells in the workbook.

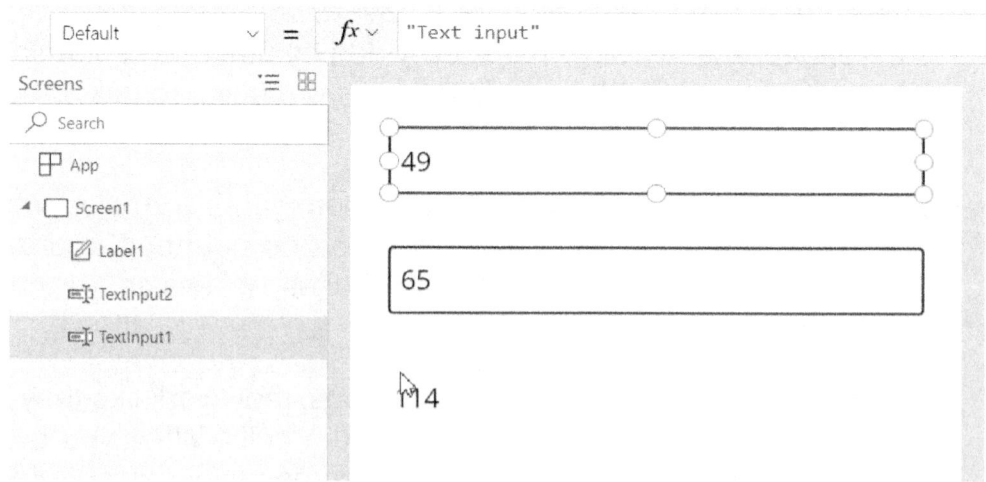

The formula for label 1 is reconfigured to show a new value.

You can make use of formulas in power apps to determine both the control's primary value and the properties like the formatting.

SETTING SCREEN VARIABLES

Setting Property Values from Code

The set property function simulates the interaction with the input control like the user entered or set values control. You will find this function when you write tests in the Power Apps test studio. You can set the following:

Setting global variables

So if we want to create an adding machine, we can use a variable to carry the running total and the best variable to work with inside the Power Apps are global variables.

We can rebuild an adding machine with the global variable:

1. Add a text input control and name it textinput1 and name two other buttons button1 and button2.
2. Then set the text property of the button1 to then add and set the text property of the button2 to clear.
3. If you want the running total updated when a user chooses the add button, set them **OnSelect** property to the formula.
4. If you want the running total to be 0 whenever the user chooses clear, set it **OnSelect** property to the formula.

5. Add a label control and set the text property to the running total.

6. Then preview the app.
7. Then to see the global variable value, choose a **File** from the menu and choose a **Variable** from the left-hand pane.

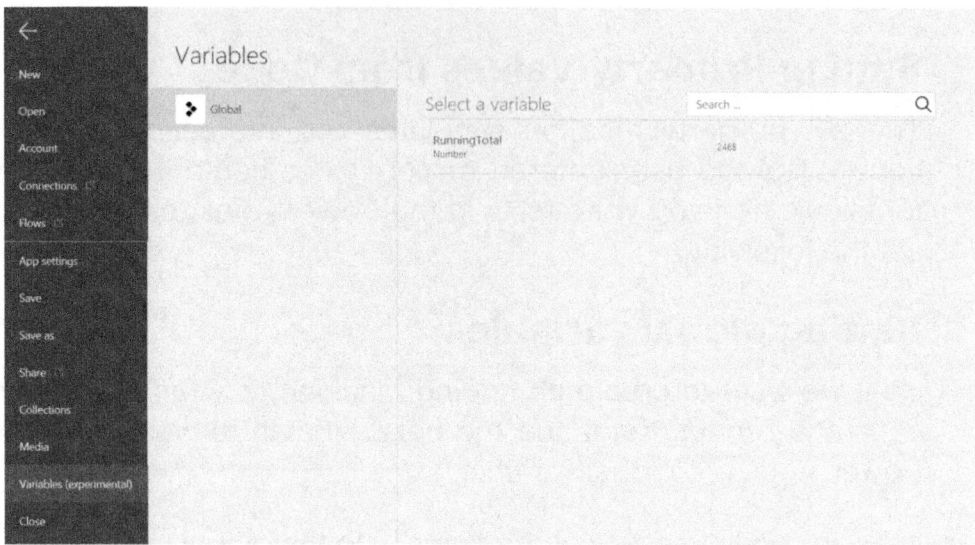

8. If you want to see all of the places where the variable has been defined and used, choose it.

Working with basic data types

There are three basic data types in power apps and we are going to be taking you through how to work with them.

Working with dates

You can use the text function to change values and formats that are original numbers or in dates and time to a text string with the TEXT function.

So it uses one of the following arguments to format numbers and times.

1. First, a predefined time/date format that you specify with the DATETIMEFORMAT number. This argument is the best because it just adjusts automatically the language and the region of the user.

2. A custom format that includes the placeholders that define if the numbers show the decimal separator and the dates also gives the month's full name, the month in abbreviation, or the number of the month.

Conditional statements and logic

The Power Apps IF function allows you to make a decision based on one or multiple conditions that you set.

The syntax for this Power App function is IF(condition1,thenresult1[,condition2,thenresult2,...[,defaultresult]])

The input parameters go as follows:

1. Condition1 (mandatory): refers to the condition that you want to evaluate. And must evaluate true or false
2. Thenresult1 (optional): here you are going to define what happens next when condition1 is true.
3. Condition2 (optional): this is for multiple conditions.
4. Then result2 (this is what happens to the second condition when it is true.
5. Defaultresult (optional) refers to what happens if the result of everything in the bracket is false.

The cell is going to be blank if the condition is matched.

Calling the switch function

The switch function is going to evaluate the conditions that you set and see if it is true or if the result of the formula matches the value in a set and also gives you a result while it executes actions.

The SWITCH function checks a formula and sees if the result of the formula matches the value that is in the sequence that you type. If there is a match then you are going to get a corresponding value and if there is no match you are going to get the default value. However, at the end of it, all the values that you get show a string showing formulas meant to evaluate some result.

Here is the switch formula Switch(Formula, Match1, Result1 [, Match2, Result2, ... [, DefaultResult]])

Color functions

When you use color enumeration, you can access those colors defined by the HTML cascading style sheets. When you type color.Green, you are going to get green.

There are three color functions:

colorvalue function gives you a color that is based on the strings within CSS and they take any of the following forms:

CSS color names, 6-digit hex value, and 8-digit hex value.

Then there is also the RGBA function that gives you the color based on red, green, and blue. And the function includes an alpha channel that you can use to mix colors.

The colorfade function will give you either bright versions of color or dark versions of the color. And the amount varies from -1 to 0 and 1 again.

Navigation function

In most apps, there are multiple screens. So you can use the back and the navigate functions to switch between the screens. Take, for example, you configure the **OnSelect** property of a button to formulas with the Navigate functions if you will like to show another screen when users choose that button.

In the formula, you can specify visual transitions like fade, to set the way a screen changes to another.

The **back** and **navigate** functions will only change the screens that are displayed. While the screens that are not displayed currently operate only behind the scenes. Furthermore, you can build a formula referring to the properties of controls that are on the other screens. As a user, for example, you can change the slider value on one screen then navigate to another that uses the values inside the formula, and set how it interacts with the new screens. The user can furthermore navigate to the original screen and then make the confirmation that the slider keeps its value.

For the navigate function, in the first argument, you need to specify the screen name that you want to display

And in the second argument, you need to specify the way that the old screen is going to change to the new screen

LAUNCHING WEBSITES AND APP

The launch function launches both web pages and canvas apps.

- You need the address, the parameters, and the target.
- The address refers to the webpage or the application ID
- The parameter is an optional argument that refers to the named values that you want to use to pass to the webpage or the canvas application. The canvas app reads parameters with the PARM function
- Then the target is also an optional argument and refers to the browser tab where the webpage or the canvas app is going to be launched

RETRIEVING STARTUP PARAMETERS

Exiting an app

When you use the exit function then you sign out from the app that is currently running and back to the list of apps. And the user can then choose another app that they want to open.

The exit function is then going to stop any evaluation of formulas.

The Syntax is exit([signout])

Managing errors

To manage the errors use the **iferror** function. This function evaluates the argument that you put in order and gives you the first one that is not an error.

You can use the **iferror**, to show to replace error values with valid values.

Review question

- How do you set up a screen variable?
- How do you retrieve the setup parameter?
- What is a conditional statement and Logic in Power App?

Summary

Functions in Power Apps work almost like they do in Power Apps. Sometimes, they are named the same way. So with a little bit of experience in Excel, you should be able to easily go about your way in the Power App.

PART TWO: WORKING WITH DATA

Now is the section where we are going to be taking you through how to work with the data.

CHAPTER SIX

SETTING UP SHAREPOINT, SETTING UP SHAREPOINT, SQL, AND MORE

SharePoint and SQL are some data sources that you can use for your application. We are going to be taking you through some of the steps to do to set all of these data sources with your power application.

What is the best data source?

As we have told you earlier. Your data source is stored in the cloud or specific applications. The popular form of the data source is a table. When you connect to a cloud or local data or connect to these data sources then you can read, edit and reformat the tables across the application. The most common power app data sources are. Microsoft Excel, Office 365 Apps, SharePoint, SQL, Microsoft Dynamics, and CRM databases.

USING A SHAREPOINT DATA SOURCE

In this section, we are going to be taking you through how to use the Share Point data source for the Power App.

Creating a SharePoint list

First, you want to create a connection by first signing into the power apps. Then choose **Data** and select **Connection** from the left navigation bar and choose the **New connection** on the left corner of the upper pane.

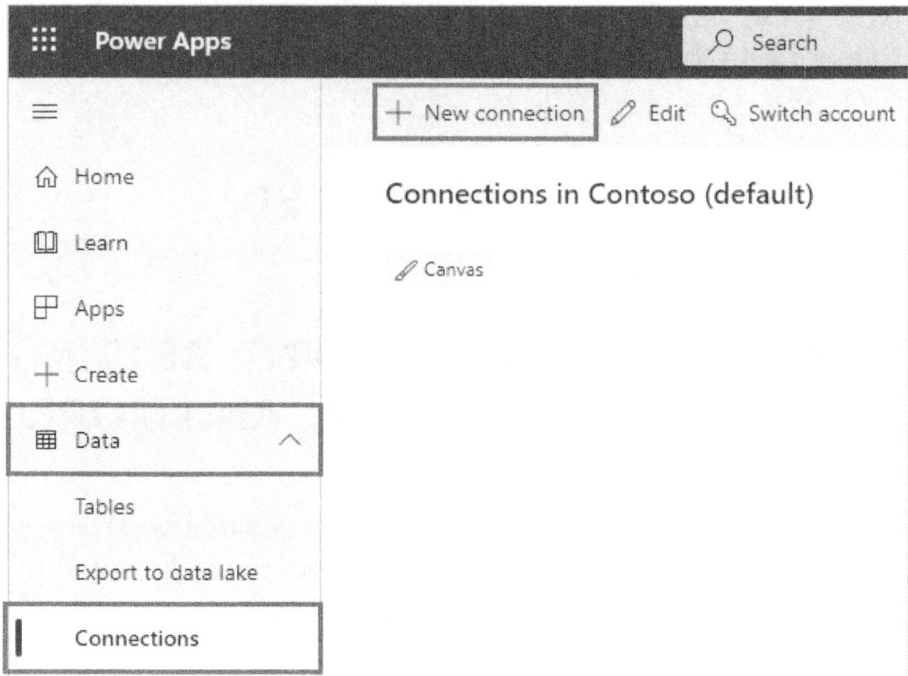

- Then choose **SharePoint** from the list.
- To then connect to SharePoint online, choose to **Connect directly and** then **Create.** Then add your credentials.

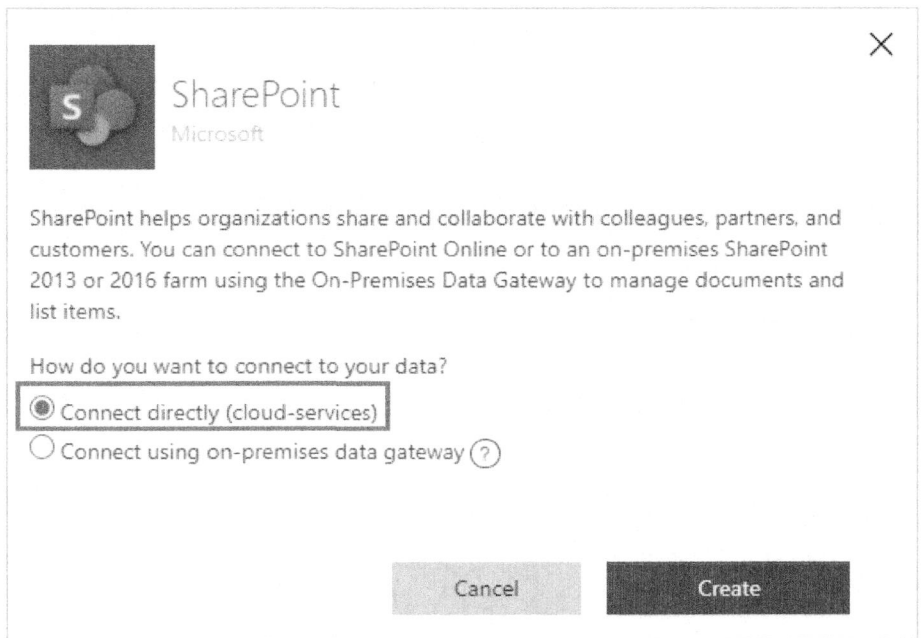

- If you want to connect to an on-premise site, select **Connect using the on-premises gateway**

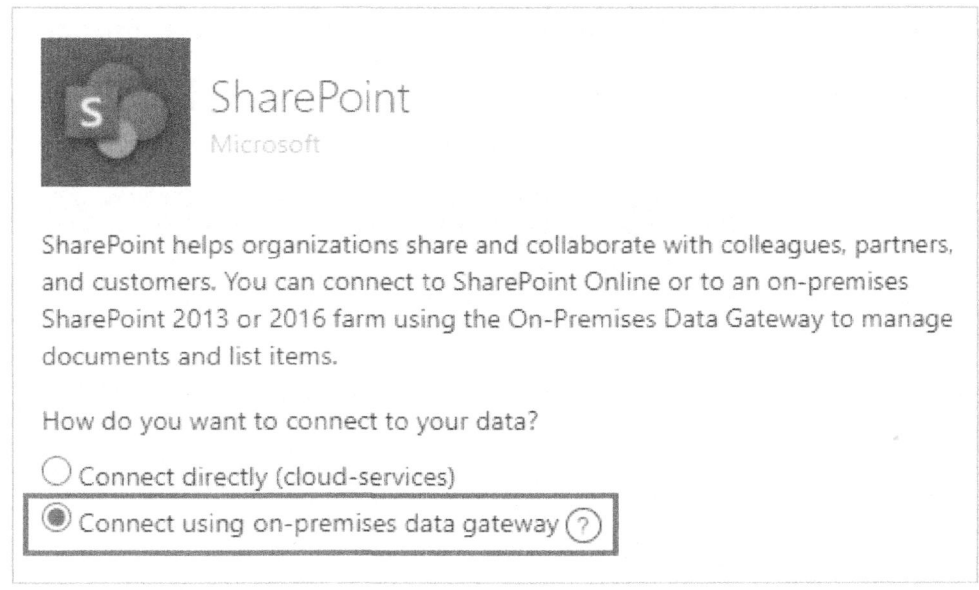

- Then make sure that you choose windows as the authentication type and make the specification of the credentials
- When you are in **Choose a gateway,** choose the gateway that you will like to use, and choose to **Create.**

UNDERSTANDING SHAREPOINT SPECIAL COLUMNS

Columns are characteristics or pieces of metadata that a user will like to manage for items in the list or content type where they added the column. One can **add columns** to the list, library, and sites and also reference them too.

The columns have three properties. They are the name, the data type, the detailed optional settings, and the column group to which the column also belongs.

SharePoint conflict management

There are times when you are going to see problems in your SharePoint workspace. There are ways that you can resolve these conflicts. There are three error or conflict types that you are going to see. They are: **Get Available Updates, Resolve Conflict or Error.**

You can use the resolve tab to then resolve the conflict whenever a document enters conflict or error mode.

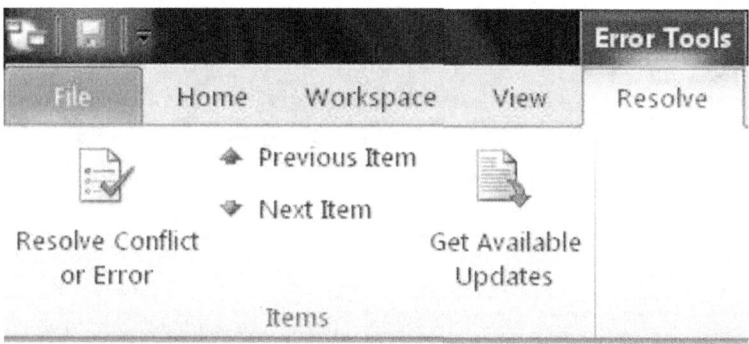

Connecting to SharePoint data source

Then you can add the data to an app that you create. Here is how to do it:

- Go first to the Power App studio and then open the app that you will like to update. Then choose **Data** from the left pane

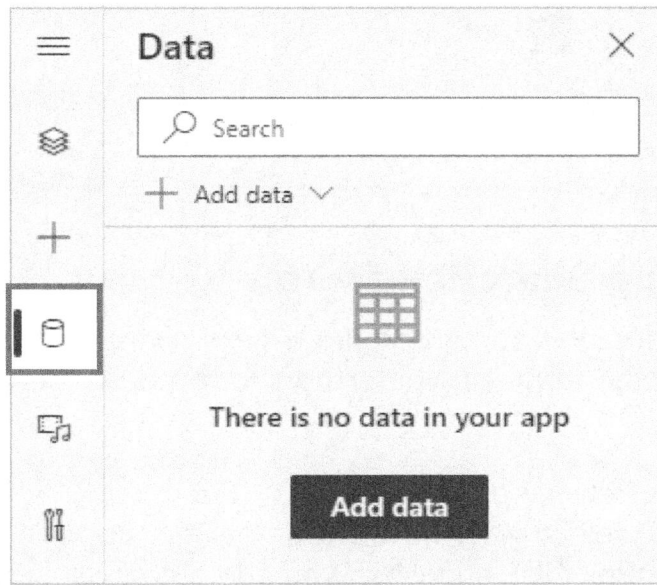

- Choose **Add data** then select **Connectors** and choose **SharePoint.**
- Then when you go to the **Connect to SharePoint site** quit the entry in **recent site connect.**
- From **Choose a list,** check the box that you will like to use, and **Connect**

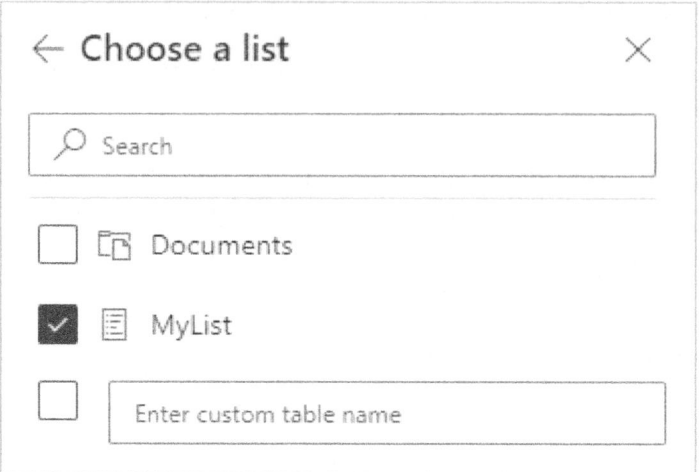

Building SharePoint forms

In SharePoint, you can create a form. Here is how. But before you manage the form list, you are going to need to edit the permissions first.

- Enter Power App.
- Then select a **New button** on the upper left corner of the SharePoint list. and when you add a new data column to the list, it is going to be replicated in the form

SQL SERVER

You can link up with the SQL Servers if you wanted to. You can do this through Azure or an On-premise data source. From this data source, you can then manage the data with the operations that are available there.

To use the SQL Servers, you need to sign up to the Power App and be signed in.

Then you need the name of the database, the server, a valid username and password, and the correct authentication that you need to connect to the data source.

When an on-premise database, you need to specify the data gateway shared with you.

SQL Server limitations

The SQL Server has the following limitations:

- It does not support SharePoint content types natively.
- You can only query 2000 items from a data source that is non-delegable
- You can only use one developer at a time through the canvas app
- Attachments cannot be saved to the SQL Server natively
- Only internal users can use the apps

Setting up SQL Azure

Here is how to automatically generate an app with the SQL Server

- After you signup, choose, **New** from the file menu on the left pane

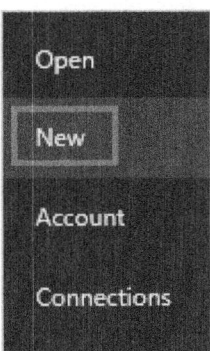

- Then go **Start with your data** and select the right arrow at the end of the row connectors
- If there is already a connection to the database that you will like to use, then the following step is not for you.
- Select the **New connection** and select **SQL Server.**

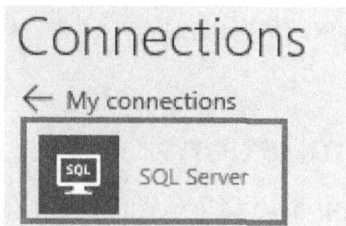

- Then you need to do any of the following: (1) Choose to **Connect directly (cloud services),** then you can type in the server base criteria like the name, the password, the username

How do you want to connect to your data?

- ⦿ Connect directly (cloud services)

- ○ Connect using on-premises data gateway ⓘ

SQL server name *

SQL database name *

Username *

Password *

* Required field

- However, when you choose **Connect using an on-premises data gateway,** then you need to specify the server name, the database's name, the user name, and the password, then select the authentication type and finally the gateway.

How do you want to connect to your data?

○ Connect directly (cloud services)

◉ Connect using on-premises data gateway ⑦

SQL server name *

[   ]

SQL database name *

[   ]

Authentication Type

[Windows   ⌄]

Username *

[   ]

Password *

[   ]

Choose a gateway *

[⌄] ↻ Refresh gateway list

If you don't see a gateway, or want a new one, you can install one now.

To see recently installed gateways, refresh this list.

Install a gateway

* Required field

- The select **Connect**
- And choose one of the options from **Choosing a dataset,** then select one of the options from **Choosing a table** and select **Connect.**
- Configure the application with the same steps that you would use to create applications from Excel.

Managing a SQL Database

With the SQL Database, You can create a database, list them, delete them and create users.

First, we are going to start by opening the database prompt with the socket/trust authentication.

If you are using ubuntu18.04, by default you can authenticate the root Mysql without the password with this command $sudo MySQL.

To create a database here is the command with the default settings configured.

Mysql > CREATE DATABASE database_name;

To list the database: by this we mean if you want to see all of the databases in the MTSQL or the MariaDB installation, here is the command.

Mysql > SHOW DATABASES;

To then delete the database: whether it is tables or data inside the data source, here is the command.

Mysql > DROP DATABASE IF EXISTS database;

SQL Database Views

The views in the database are something like virtual tables. They have rows and columns just like you will find them in actual tables and databases. To create a view, choose **Fields** from a single table or multiple tables inside the database. Furthermore, the views either have rows of tables or just specific rows that are based on some conditions.

To create a view, use the **Create view** statement. Here is the syntax CREATE VIEW view_name AS

SELECT column1, column2.....

FROM table_name

WHERE condition;

On-premises Data Gateway

The on-premise data gateway essentially works like some kind of bridge that gives you a quick and safe passage for your transfer of the on-premise data and different Microsoft cloud services. When you use a gateway, then you can have your database and another on-premise network there too.

INSTALLING THE GATEWAY

To use the gateway, you need to install them, then you need to configure the gateway based on the firewalls and some other network requirements.

Once you configure the settings, add the gateway admins, who can manage and administer the other network requirements.

But before you install the gateway, you need a minimum requirement of

- .NET Framework 4.7.2(for a gateway that was released before December 2020)
- .NET Framework 4.8 (for gateways that were released after February 2021)
- You need a 64-bit version for windows 8 or windows server 2012 and has a current TLS 1.2 and some cipher suites
- And there has to be a 4 GB disk space to monitor the performance. Here are the steps to download and install the standard gateway.
- The first thing to do is to **download the standard gateway**
- Then go to the gateway installer and maintain the default installation path, and review and accept the terms of use. Then choose **Install.**

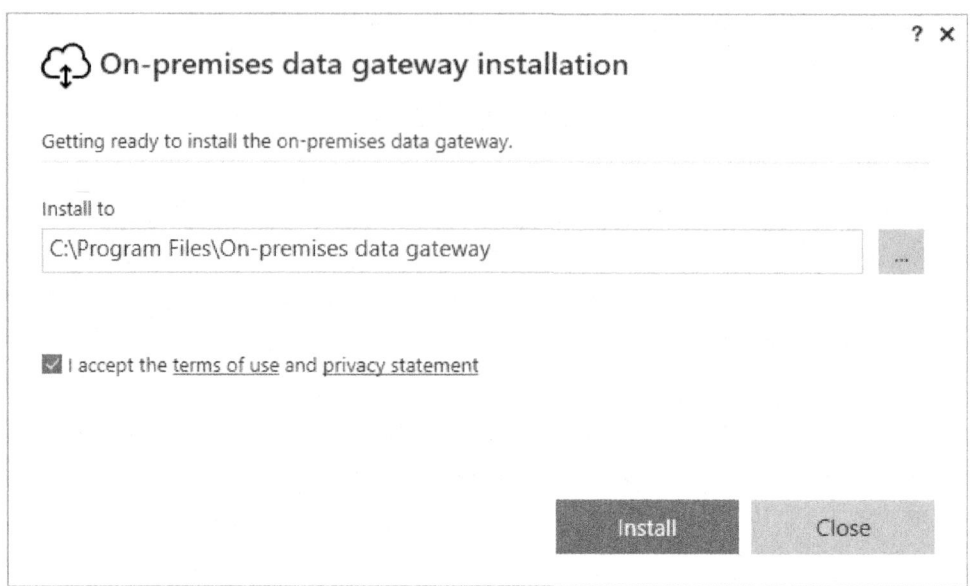

- Enter your office email for 365 organizations and click **Sign in.**

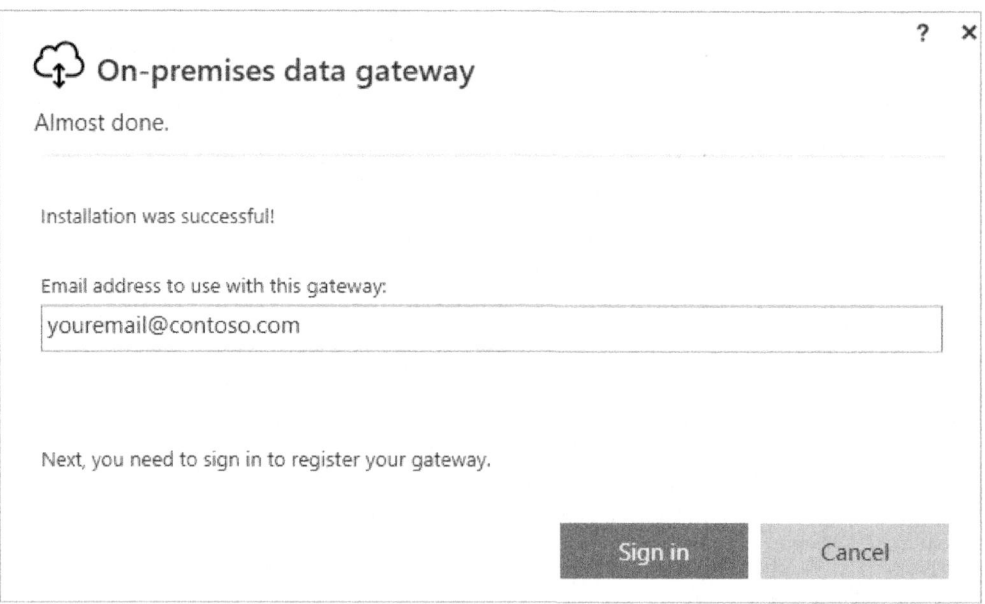

- Then choose **Register a new gateway on this computer** and choose **Next.**

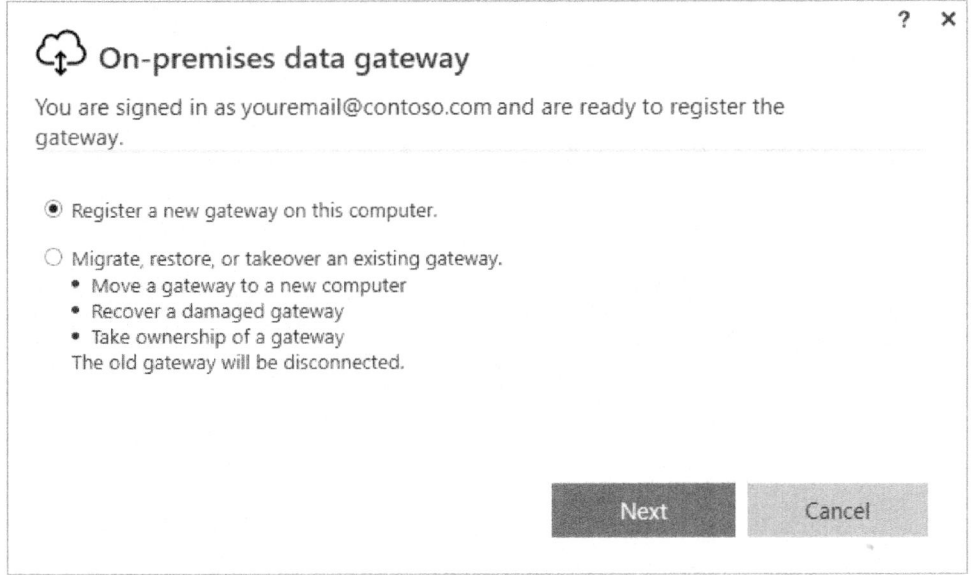

- Type a name for the gateway. Make sure that the name is unique and enter the recovery key. The recovery key is needed when later you want to move the gateway. Then pick **Configure.**
- Check out the information on the last window and choose **Close.**

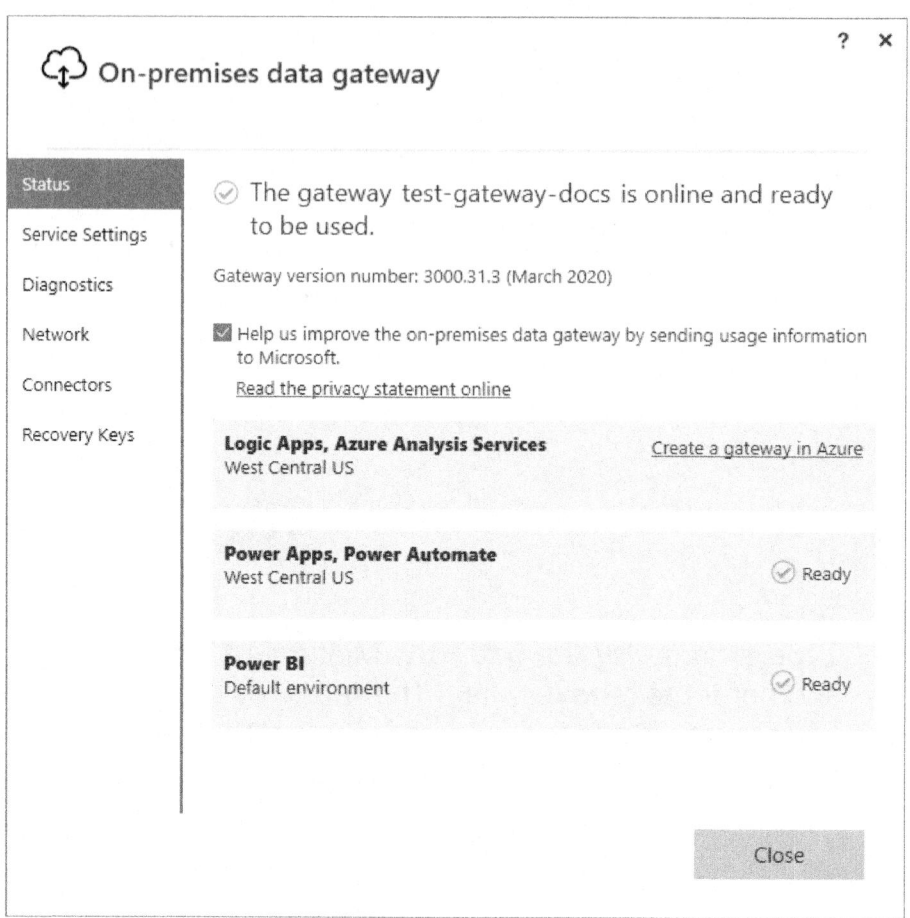

Starting the Gateway Service

After installing the gateway services, you can then quickly create and save data transfers between the Power Apps and the data sources that are not on the cloud.

If you want to see all of the gateways that have the administrative, manage, and connection permissions, enter **powerapps.com** and sign in with a work or a school account.

Then enter **Gateways** and **Manage** on the navigation menu.

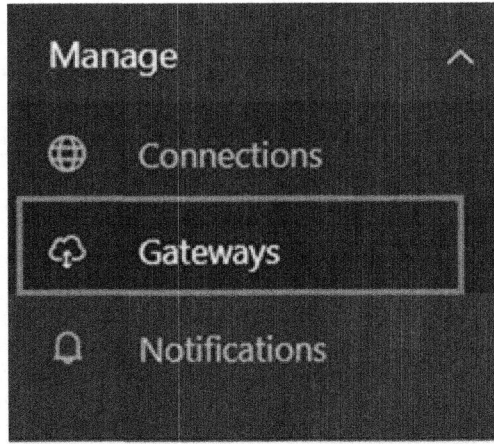

Then choose a gateway you will like to manage the permissions and the connections from. If there is no gateway, then you can install and create the gateway configurations.

To then remove or add a user from the gateway, go to **the users** tab, and from the drop-down, you can add a new user and make a specification of the level of permission. Furthermore, you can also specify the users that you will like to have the access to the gateway.

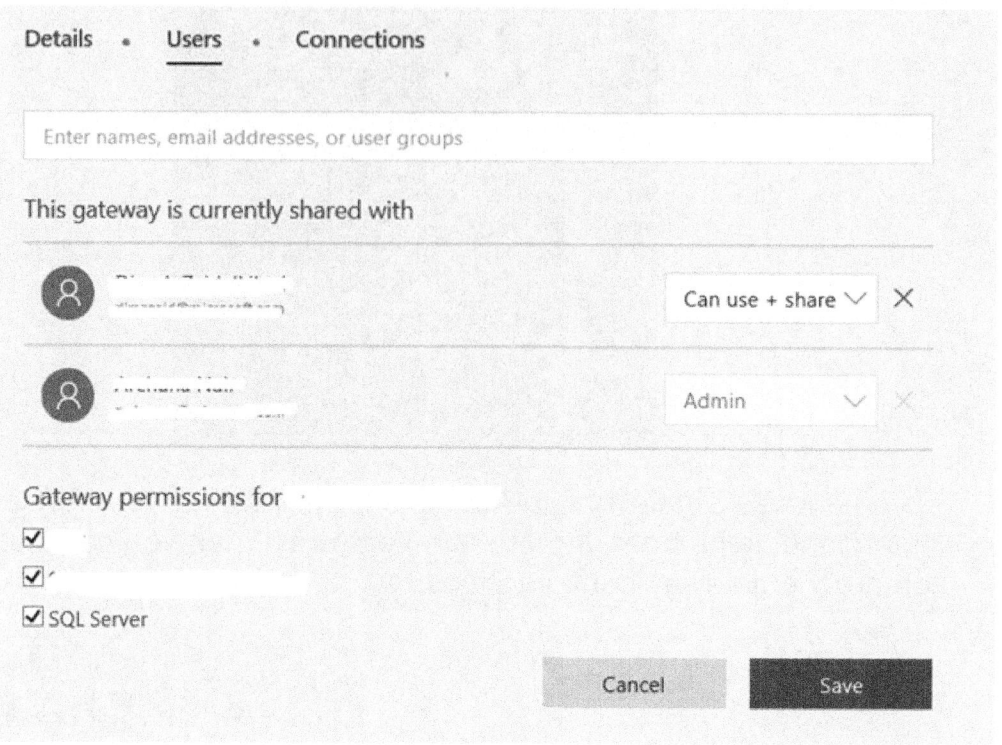

If you want to view the list of all of the connections from the gateway, go to the **Connections** tab. You need to be able to see all of the SQL connection that was created on this gateway.

Connecting to a Data Source

When you are connecting to SQL servers, you need a service account that you can share. Just choose the SQL connection then go to the **Share** tab so that you can see all of the users with the shared SQL connection

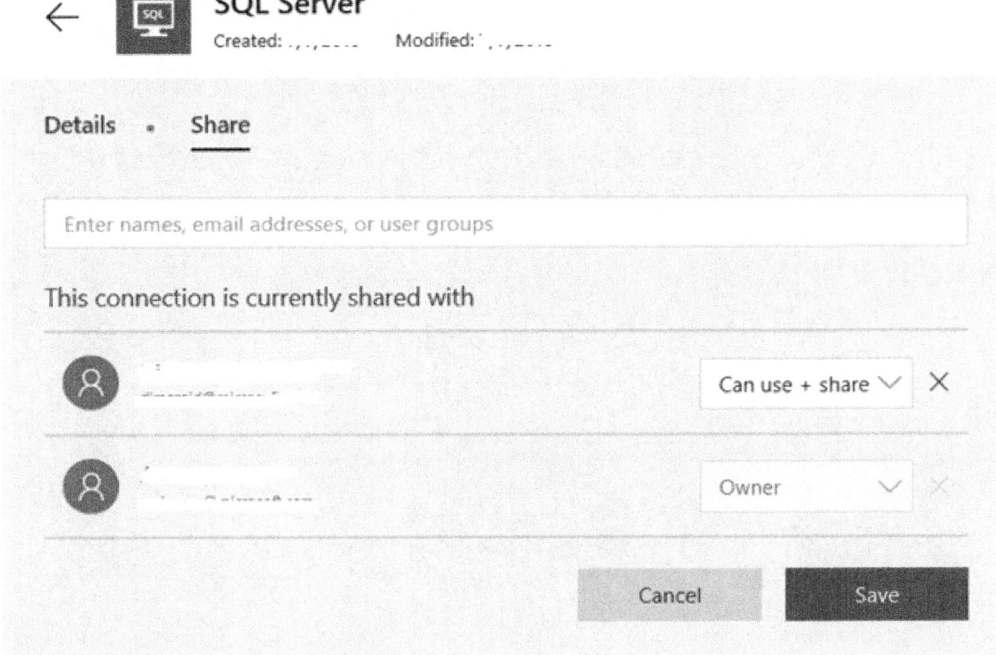

Uninstalling a gateway

To delete the gateway connection go to **powerapps.com** and go to the gateway name. Then you are going to see three dots. Select it and click **Remove.**

OTHER DATA SOURCES

Here are the other data sources in power apps.

Static Excel data

To load Excel in the form of static data, go to **View** and choose a **Data source.**

- Then look for Excel and choose **Import** from the options.

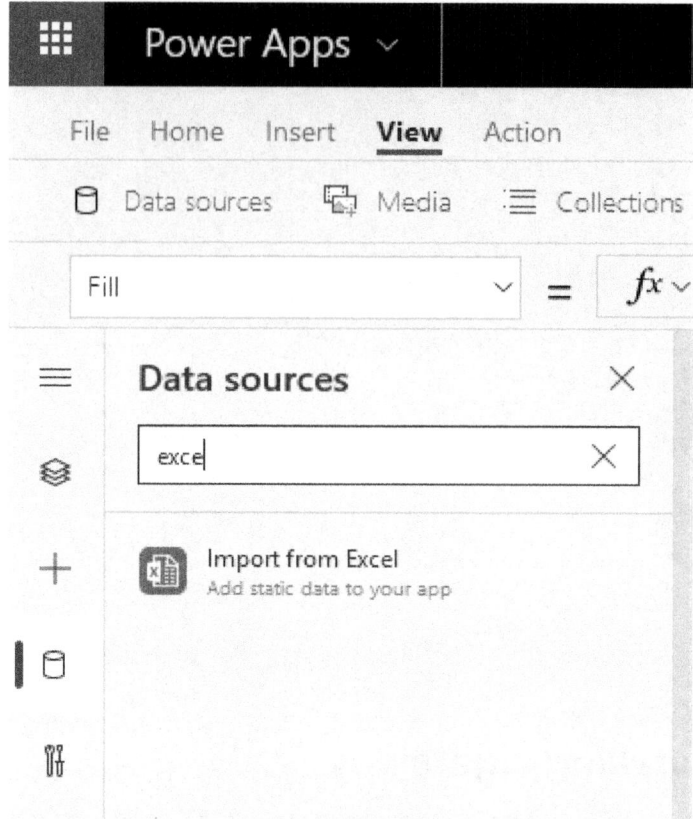

Microsoft Translator Data source

The Microsoft translator is also a data source for Power Apps.

To connect to one here is what to do:

- Create a canvas app.
- Then go to the left-hand pane and choose the **Data** tab and choose to **Add the data source.**
- Then click on **The New Connection** then click on **Microsoft Translator.**

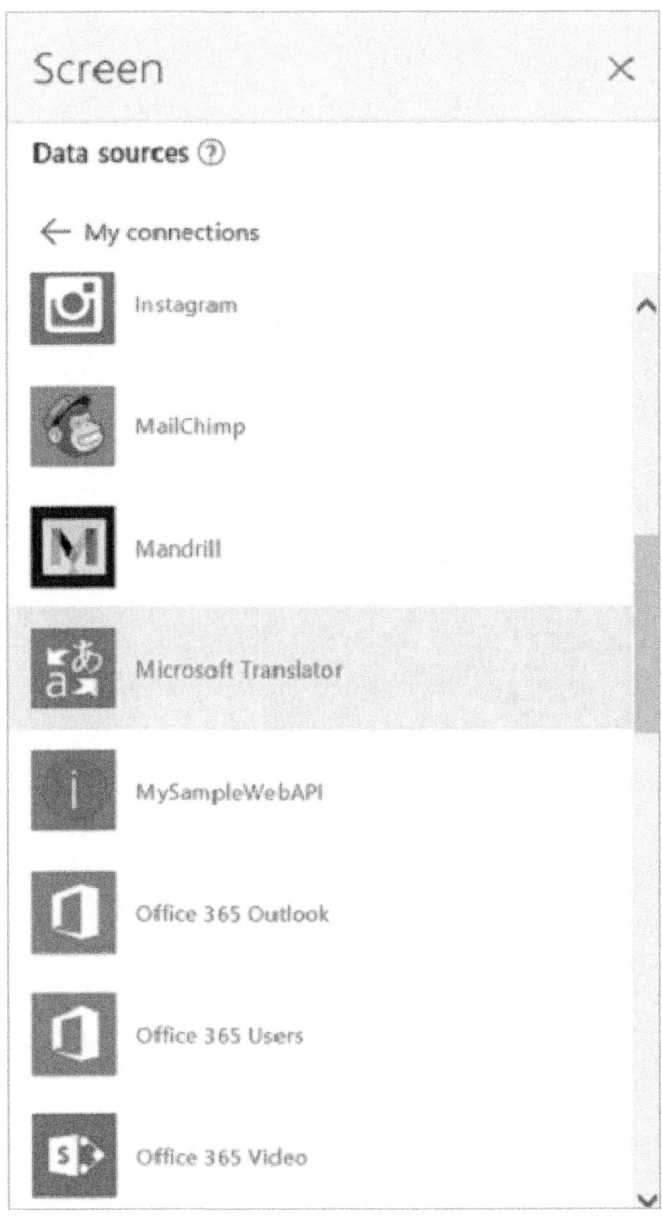

- Choose to **Connect.** This then brings a connection in **Data sources:**

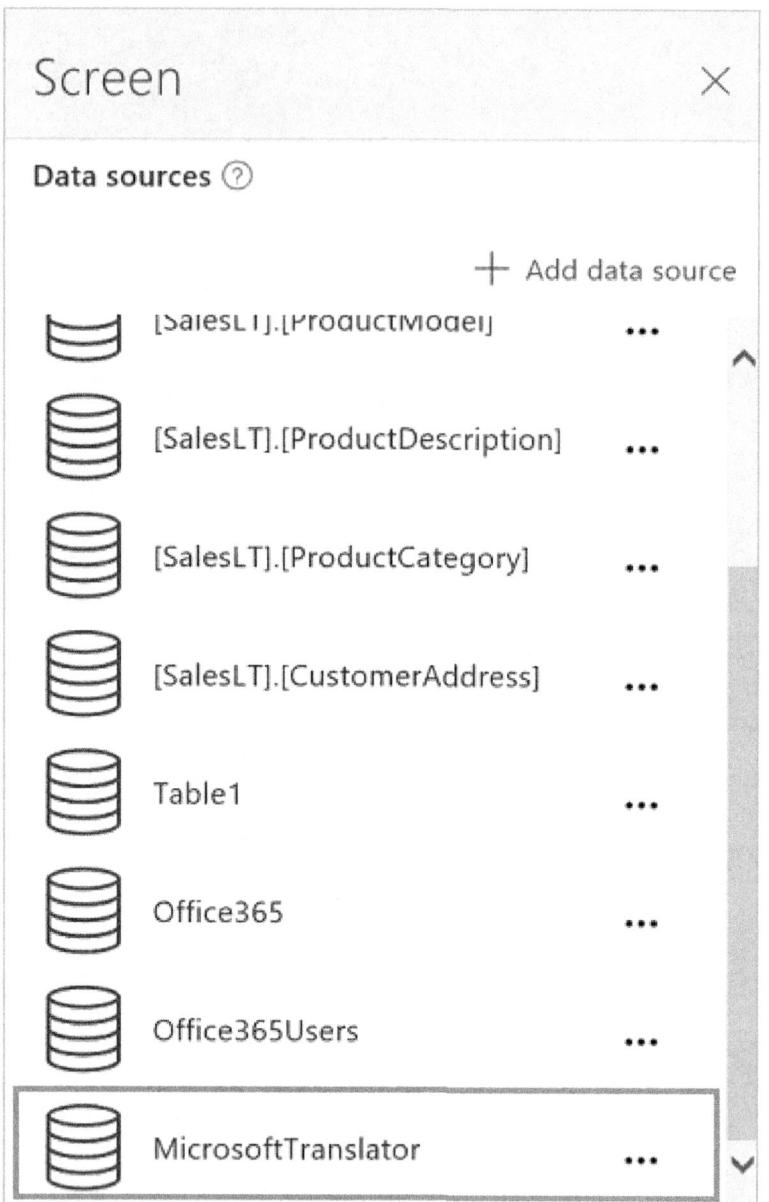

Microsoft MSN weather services

The Microsoft MSN weather service can give you the up-to-date weather forecast and are available as a connector with power apps.

Sending push notification

We are going to be using a sample app from the default case management app for this:

- The first thing to do is enter the app you will like to send a push notification.
- Then copy the ID for the application.
- Then go to the left pane and choose **Data,** then select **Connections.**
- Then **Edit the app.**
- Choose **View** and select **Data sources.**
- Then choose to **Add a data source.**
- Click on a **New Connection.**
- Click on the **Power App notification.**

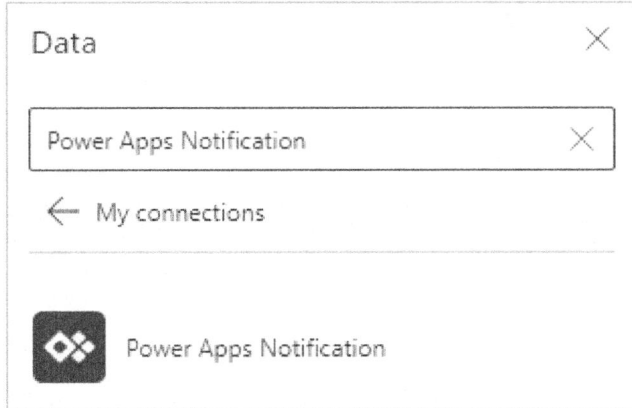

- The app id that you copied previously needs to paste text here.

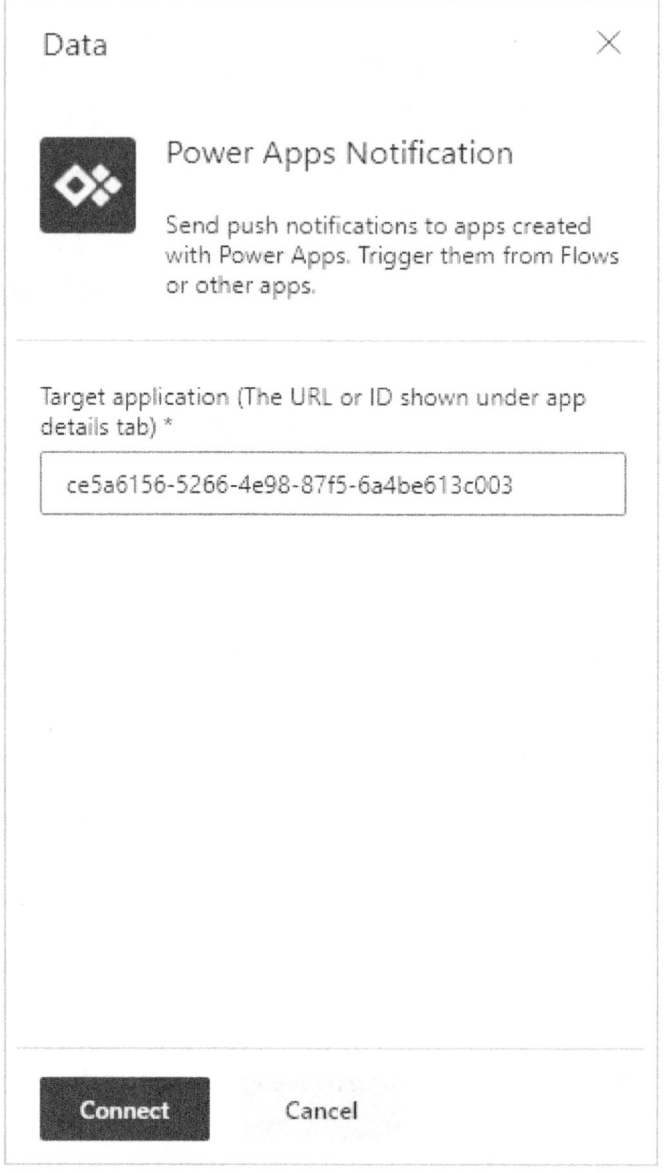

- Then choose to **Connect.**
- Then add a push notification connection to trigger apps with similar steps.

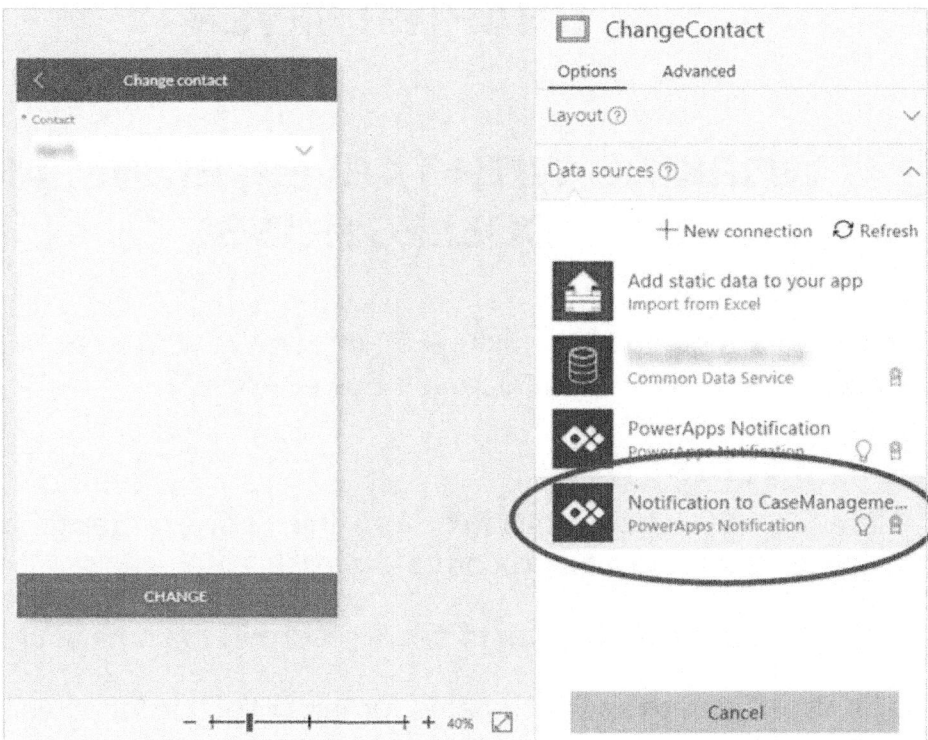

- Then go to the push notification and call **send push notification.**

Review Question

- How do you connect to a SharePoint data source?
- How do you install a gateway?
- How do you send a push notification in Power App

Summary

The database is an important part of any work you will be doing on the power app. You need a place to secure your data and access them easily. We have given you all of the steps that you need here.

CHAPTER SEVEN

WORKING WITH TABLES, ROWS, AND COLLECTIONS

Here we are going to be taking you through how to work, with tables, collections, and rows on Microsoft Power Apps.

Basic syntax

Here is the basic syntax for the power apps collection. Collect(CollectionName, record(s))

Here, **Collection** helps you to add a record to the data source.

Then you need to specify a name for the collection when you create it and that is what the **collectionname** represents.

Records- this refers to the record: it can be a single value, an item, or a table.

OVERVIEW OF COLLECTIONS AND FUNCTIONS

We are going to briefly brush through what a collection is in Power Apps.

Collections are means that a group of items or an array that aids in storing data into the Power App's memory.

Working with collections

From the Power Apps collection, you can save the data and share it to data sources like SharePoint Online and on an Excel spreadsheet.

Setting up a demo app

The first thing to do is to go to web.powerapps.com

- Then go to the **App** area on the left pane.
- Then select **Create an application.**

Adding a single row

In adding rows to Power Apps, here is what to do.

So since we have a gallery that repeats tables in a team's Power Apps. In the first image, the rows are blank.

And in this image the rows we have one unsaved item.

Then in the last image, we have added a row and saved the item

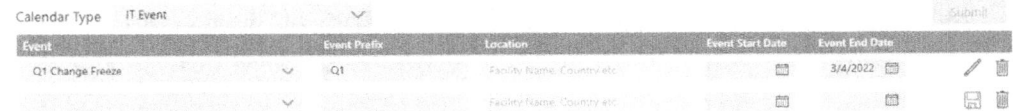

Working with data source

So far we have been talking about saving a data source. It is about time that we talked about other Power Apps.

Using for-all to build HTML

One of the best ways to see data when you are working with power apps is with the HTML template. You can use it to create a report and send emails with the app.

So we are going to be working with HTML. So let us assume that you have created a conference app. When users register to the app, they are going to get confirmation emails and details of the conference.

If the data is already represented in the context variable. So we are going to be working with this sample verbal and call it to template 1

```
"<h4><strong>Hello " & User().FullName & ",</strong></h4>
<p>Your registration for " & Session.Title & " Session has been confirmed.<br /></p>
<p><span style='text-decoration: underline'><strong>Session Details</strong></span></p>
<p>Dates: " & Session.DateFrom & " - " & Session.DateTo & "</p>
<p>Presenters: " & Session.Speaker_FullName & "</p>
<p>Location: " & Session.Venue & "</p>"
```

So when we work with this, we are going to be hardcoding the data to correspond with the HTML template. The maintenance after all is going to be harder as when you make any changes then you also have to modify the template at the same time.

To solve this, we can store placeholders in line with the HTML template and not the hardcoded application. The placeholders will be in the format of "I" which is the index of the placeholder that is about to be replaced. So we can call it template2.

You can then store the index and also the application data values in a local collection. Make use of the **for-all** loop and switch the placeholders with the values from the local collection.

```
<h4><strong>Hello {0},</strong></h4>
<p>Your registration for {1} Session has been confirmed.<br /></p>
<p><span style='text-decoration: underline'><strong>Session Details</strong></span></p>
<p>Dates: {2} - {3} </p>
<p>Presenters: {4}</p>
<p>Location: {5}</p>
```

Then when you want to work with it the first thing to do, is to create an external source to store templates. You can connect from any data source.

Name	Value
	`<h4><strong>Hello {0},</strong></h4>`
	`<p>Your registration for {1} Session has been confirmed. </p>`
	`<p><span style='text-decoration: underline'><strong>Session Details</strong></span></p>`
	`<p>Dates: {2} - {3} </p>`
	`<p>Presenters: {4} </p>`
HTMLTemplate	`<p>Location: {5} </p>`

If you then have another source with the actual conference data, name it.

Title	SessionId	DateFrom	DateTo	Speaker_FullName	Venue
PowerApps & Flow App In A Day	1	5/21/2018	23-May	Vasavi Setty	Orlando, Florida

Here are the steps to follow:

Enter the on the visible event of the confirmation screen. Then create session info with the values that are from the selected session.

```
ClearCollect(SessionInfo, {i:0, value:User().FullName}, {i:1, value:Session.Title},
{i:2, value:Text(Session.DateFrom,ShortDate)},
{i:3, value:Text(Session.DateTo,ShortDate)},
{i:4, value:Session.Speaker_FullName},{i:5, value:Session.Venue})
```

Gather the settings and place them in the local collection named **Appsettings.** We do not want to make a modification to the original template and then store it locally.

```
ClearCollect(AppSettings, Settings);
```

The next thing to do is to update the template using placeholders in other to then embed the screen details inline. For this to work, loop through the indices inside the session info, in each of the indexes, then look for the placeholders inside the template, then replace the placeholder index with the value that is associated.

Then you now have the HTML template that has application data that is embedded inline. This confirmation message can then be part of the email.

GROUPING, COUNTING, AND AGGREGATING RECORDS

Creating sequences

You can make use of the sequence functions in power apps to create sequences. What it does is it creates on column table of sequential numbers. The column is named value and sequence (4) is equal to 1,2,3,4.

When you use Sequence with the **forall** function, then it iterates the number of times. Furthermore, the forall function can also be sued to change the values in other data types and give you a new table. take, for example, this formula will give you a formula for the next 10 days ForAll(Sequence(10), DateAdd(Today(), Value, Days))

The syntax is Sequence(Records [, Start [, Step]])

With record representing the number of records to generate.

Start represents the number for the sequence

The step represents the increment for any successive number within the sequence.

Counting records

You can use the count function to count the records with numbers within a single-column table

The COUNTA function will count the filled records within a single-column table.

The COUNTIF function counts the number of records within a table that is true with a logical formula.

And when you use the COUNTROWS function then you are counting the records inside a table.

They all express a number.

Before it works you need to first set up the enhanced delegation for the Microsoft Dataverse. Here is how:

- Go to the app that you want to use the function in.
- And go to **Setting** then enter **Upcoming features** and select **Previews**
- Then turn the **Enhanced delegation for Microsoft Data verse** on.

Aggregate math's

Since the Power Apps version 680, there is one new feature and that is the delegation of the aggregation function. Here delegation means that you are taking a data operation to the source. So, as you know you need data to work with Power Apps. However, if you go about downloading them one by one it is going to take too long. And no one has time for that. So instead of wasting your time, all that you have to do is just take your work to the cloud or an on-premise server where it is all easily accessible.

There are a few things that you can do. You can work with the sum, average, the min, and the max through the SQL Server.

So here is how it works. So all you have to do is connect to the SQL Server that you want to work with and run with this script

```
CREATE TABLE LongTable ( LongNumber BIGINT IDENTITY
(1,1) PRIMARY KEY, ShortNumber BIGINT );

INSERT INTO LongTable ( ShortNumber ) VALUES ( 1 );

DECLARE @i INT; SET @i = 1; WHILE @i <= 20
BEGIN
     INSERT INTO LongTable SELECT LongNumber AS
ShortNumber              FROM              LongTable
          SET       @i      =      @i      +      1
END;
```

So what this script does is to double the table 20 times repeatedly till the 2^{20} rows.

And the long number column then provides you with something that you can then aggregate.

Then connect to the table with Power Apps then combine a label control that has text property with the following. Sum('[dbo].[LongTable]', LongNumber)

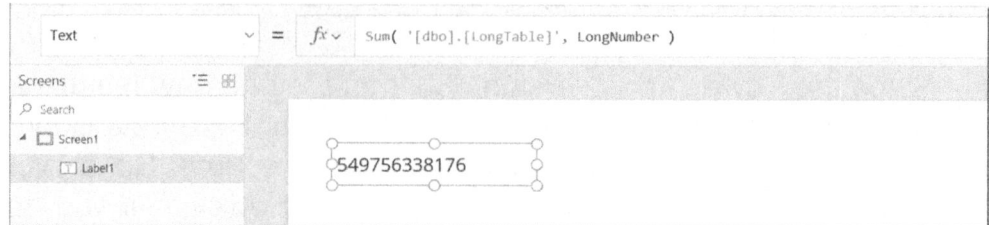

The aggregate function not only works with whole tables. You can also use a sum and a filter so that you can work with a part of the table that you choose. So if you want the application to skip the first row, here is the formula.

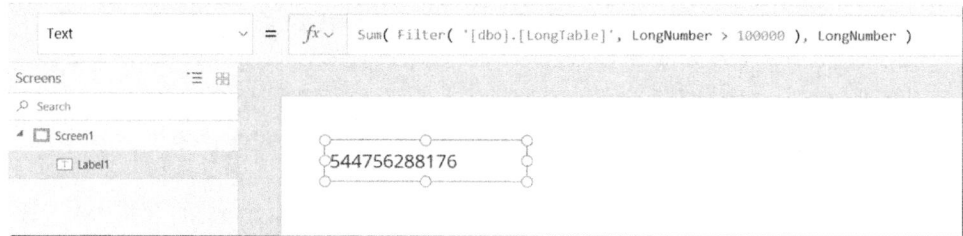

Looking at the formula that we created, the sum of the number 100,000 is 5,000,050,000. Then if you then remove this from the result that we got earlier, here is the answer that we are going to get. 544,756,288,176

The returning min and max records

The min and max functions in power apps, both find you the minimum and maximum values respectively.

The values for these functions can both be provided as:

1. A separate argument
2. A table and formula that you can operate over the table. then the aggregate is going to be calculated on the values of the formula for each of the records

You can only use these functions on numeric values at this time. Furthermore, you can delegate them. The syntax for the min and the max is as follows MIN/MAX (NumericalFormula1, [NumericalFormula2, ...]) that is if you are working with a separate argument

And when you are working with the tables here is the function MIN/MAX (Table, NumericalFormula)

Grouping and aggregating values

So you can use the group by function so that you can get a table that has its record group based on the values from either a single or multiple columns. When the record is in the same group, they will be placed on record and there is going to be another column added to hold the nested table of all of the remaining columns.

Then when you use the **ungroup** function, you are going to get the reversal of the **group by** function.

Furthermore, you can then aggregate a result that you have grouped using any of these

- The **group by**
- With the **add column** function with the sum, average, and the other aggregate function
- Then you can also use the **drop columns** function in other to drop a group table.

The syntax for the group by function is as follows GroupBy(Table, ColumnName1 [, ColumnName2, ...], GroupColumnName)

With **table** referring to the table that you want to group

The **column name(s)** refer to the column names inside the table where you want to group the records

The **groupcolumnname** is the column name to store the record data that is not inside the column name(s).

Ungrouping records

The syntax to ungroup is as follows:

Ungroup(Table, GroupColumnName)

- Table refers to the table that you want to ungroup.
- And the groupcolumnname refers to the column with the record data that was created with the **group by the** function.

Combining rows

You can make use of the CONCAT function in other to combine the strings without using the separators.

Make use of the **MATCHALL** function on the other hand to then split strings with regular expression.

Splitting text into rows

So you can use a split function to break text strings down to tables with substrings. You can make use of the split in other to break the comma delimited lists, or dates with a slash between the parts and also in other situations where a delimiter is used.

Here is the syntax to split text strings.

SPLIT(text,separator)

The text refers to the text that you want to split.

And the separator refers to the separator that you want to use to split the sting. You can use a character from zero.

Splitting and concatenating rows

The **concatenate** function concatenates a mix of individual strings and also one column table of strings. When you make use of this function in individual strings, it is just like using the & operator.

On the other hand, the CONCAT function concatenates the results of a formula that you apply across all of the records in a table, which then gives you a string.

Use the following syntax when using CONCAT:

Concat(Table, Formula, separator)

Here, the table refers to the table that you want to operate on

The formula represents the formula that you want to be applied to all the records within the table

The separator refers to the text value that you want to insert between the concatenated rows of the table.

On the other hand, the concatenate function is as follows:

Concatenate(String1 [, String2, ...])

Strings here refer to the mix of either individual strings or also a column table of strings.

Building comma-separated strings

Here is a combo box with a CSV list of chosen items in a table.

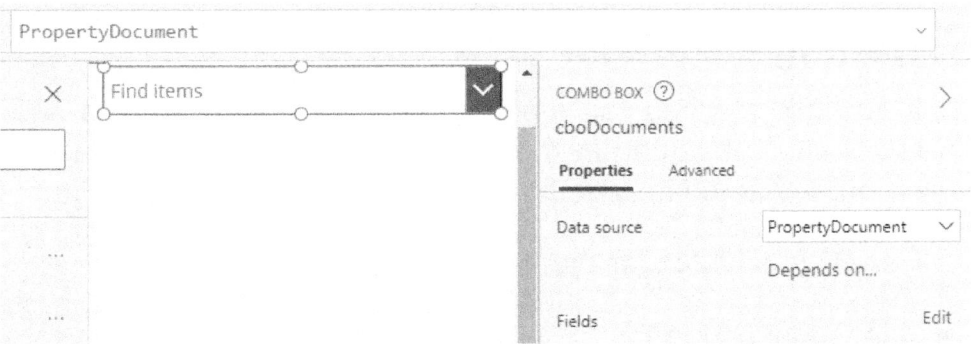

Then we entered the following syntax to work with the image above

With({concatResult:Concat(cboDocuments.SelectedItems,   this record.Title & ", ")},

    Left(concatResult, Len(concatResult)-2)

)

In the image below, there is a combo box that has three items chosen: which are the tenancy agreement, the energy certificate, and the inventory checklist. And in the label under the combo box, you will see the CSV list of chosen items.

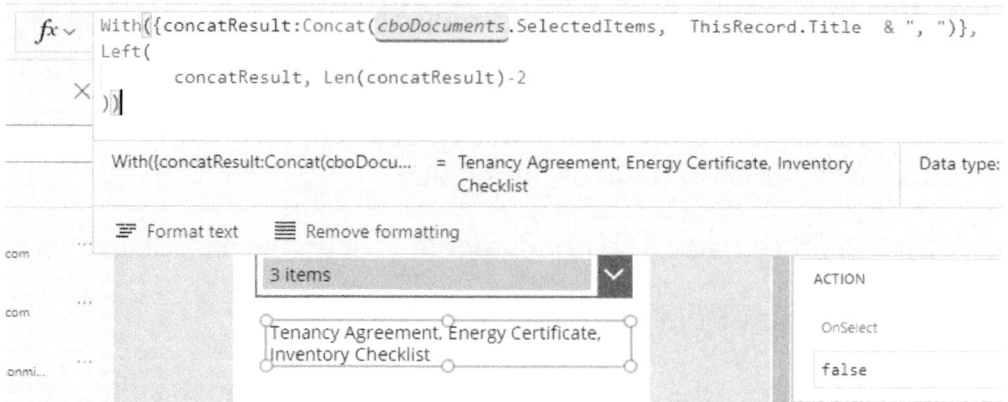

The Concat function takes two arguments, which are the data source and the output so that it can then produce for each of the rows within the data source. So here we built an expression that returns the title field and we followed it with a comma and space.

Getting hashtags.

If you use the hashtag function, you are going to get a one-column table with a hashtag in the string. And if there is no hashtag in the string, the function is going to give you an empty one-column table

Here is the syntax for the hashtag:

HashTags(String)

Here the strings refer to the strings that you want to scan for hashtags.

Review Question

- So a small business owner with a log of information about your product that is updated once there is a new business. It is virtually impossible to input the items for oneself and it can be time-consuming too. So build a Power App that logs new items and changes the item's data in line on the same screen and in sync with the data source.
- How do you delete multiple rows?
- What are collections in Power App?

Summary.

So from tables to rows, Power Apps is beginning to look a lot like Excel. But do not let that fool you. There is much more required.

CHAPTER EIGHT

SEARCHING AND RETRIEVING DATA

Now we are going to be taking you through the basic process of searching a retrieving data within Power Apps.

Basic behavior

There are some basic things that you need to understand and we are going to be taking you through some of them.

Understanding delegation

Delegation simply has to do with working with data directly from the data source. Instead of going through the time-consuming process of working with the app locally, you can work with the app in the data source.

However, there is a problem as it is not everything that you can express in the power apps formula can also be delegated to every data source.

So if you are working with a large data source, then you might need a data source and a formula that you can delegate. This is the best way for your application to perform well and the users also have access to the information that they require.

So you have to also be on the lookout for the warnings concerned with the delegation, especially in the places where they tell you that delegation cannot be possible.

Now when the data source you are working with on the other hand is a small one then it is fine to use the data source and formula since the app can also be processed locally even though the formula cannot be delegated

Increasing the data row limit

Power Apps has a default delegation limit of 500 entries. Data sets with fewer than 500 records are exempt from delegation; they will operate without any problems. Additionally, this restriction may be raised to a maximum of 2000 records.

- Launch your app.
- Navigate to **File** > **App Settings.**
- Go to **Advanced Settings**.
- The "Data row limit for non-delegable queries" parameter may be set to a maximum of 2000 records.

HOW TO MANAGE LARGE QUANTITIES OF DATA

In this section, we are going to be going through how to manage large quantities of data.

Searching data

First, we are going to be taking you through the search functions in Excel.

Basic search function

The Power Apps function is going to give you the columns that are in the table you are using the search function on.

The table should have columns that also have text or string values. It won't accept any other column values, such as Number, Choice, Picture, Hyperlink, etc., besides a Text value.

Here is the syntax for the Power Apps search function Search(Table, SearchString, Column1 [, Column2, ...])

The search parameter represents the Power Apps function for searching.

The table represents the table name that you want to use to search.

You need to specify the string that you want to search for in the area for the **search string.**

Columns represent the column names that you want to search from the table. Whatever columns you pass should be Text columns, and the column names should be strings included in double-quotes. The column name supplied should be static and cannot be calculated using a formula.

Sorting data by multiple columns

Here we are going to be taking you through how to sort data with multiple columns. It can be important that once in a while you view multiple columns. Take for example that you want to show active account views. The viewer can then sort by either country, city, or zip/postal code. This works well when there are different accounts and they all have the same city and the same country.

You can go to the dynamic 365 classic user interface and customize the sorting for the specific view however there are only two columns that need to be added for sorting.

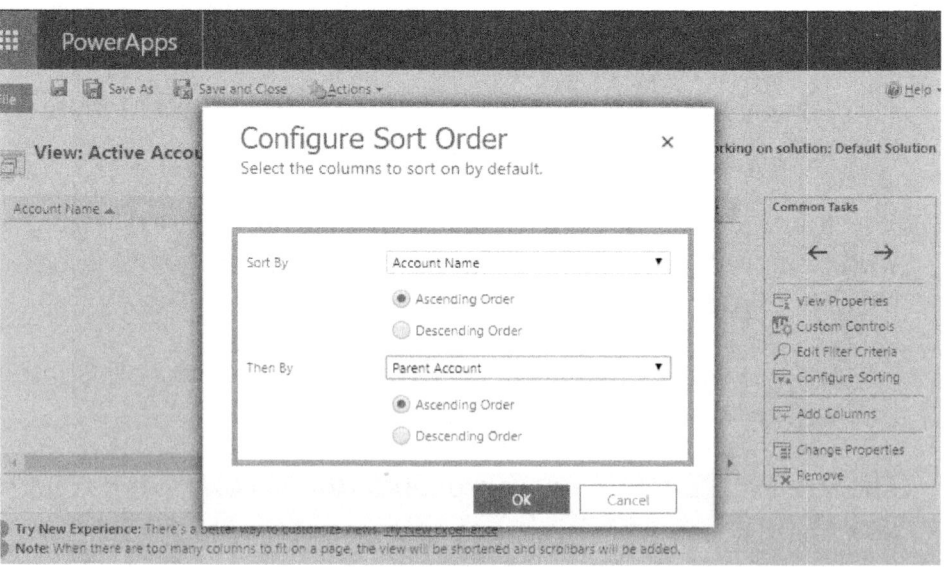

There are CRM modifications that can also be used to sort multiple columns for CRM displays. In this article, we will walk you through the procedures required to configure the view with sorting on several columns.

Please follow the instructions below to configure sorting with multiple columns for view:

1. Log in to PowerApps by visiting web.powerapps.com.

2. Select the Solutions tab.

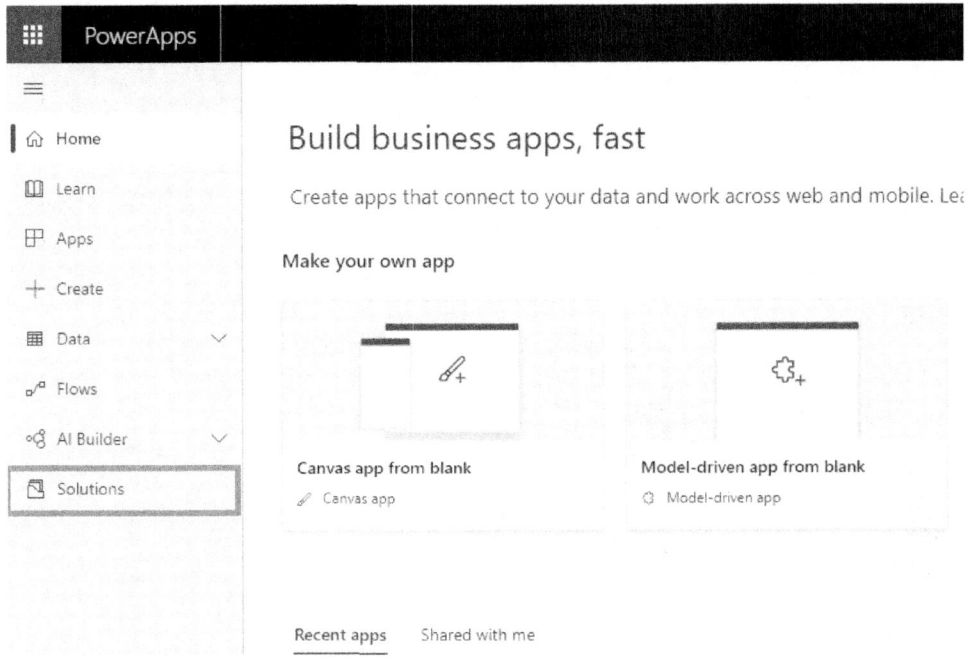

3. Then you can pick a solution. Go to **Account** entity and choose the **Active accounts.** Then it brings the below window.

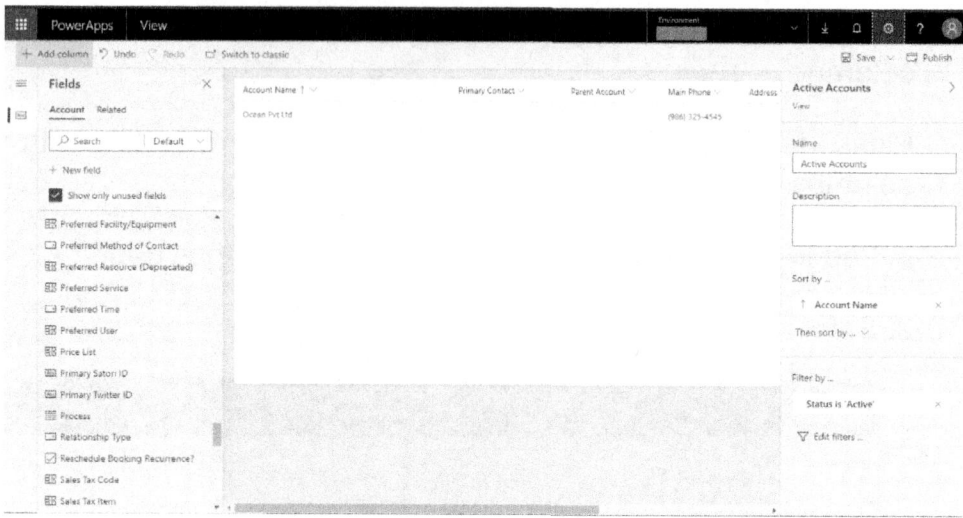

4. To then sort multiple columns, then you need to choose the columns from the **sort by** drop down.

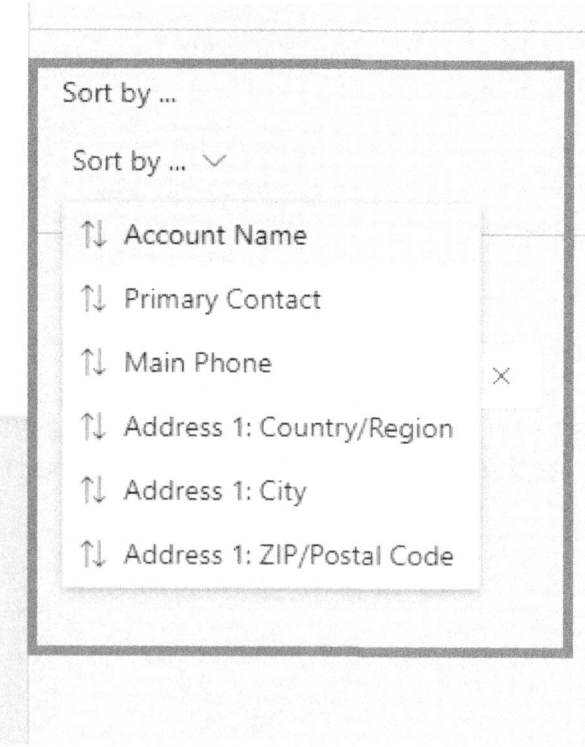

The arrow beside the field can also be used to sort the column in an ascending or descending order. Here is the screenshot below.

6. The next thing to do is to **Save** then **Publish** the changes that you made
7. Then open an active account view so that you can see the changes that you made.

Join Date

We are going to be taking you through how to join operations in power apps. There are going to be times when we need to, for example, combine data from two different lists and then put them in one single gallery. So here we are going to be taking you through how the process works.

JOINING RECORDS: SHOWING RELATED RECORDS

In Microsoft Dataverse, the Relate function connects two records via a one-to-many or many-to-many relationship. On the other hand, the **unrelate** function runs the operation backward and eliminates the link.

In terms of the one-to-many relationship, the many tables contain a field for foreign keys which gives you the direction of where the record of one table is. The relate function sets the field by pointing to the specific record inside the one table. On the other hand, the unrelated function is going to leave that field blank. When you use the related function and the field is already set then the old link is going to be replaced with a new one. You can also set this field with the patch function or the edit form control. In this instance, then the related function is not needed.

In the many-to-many relationships, on the one hand, the system connecting the records will keep the join tables hidden. You cannot access the join table directly. You can only set it as 'read only' with one too many projections with the **relate** and the **unrelate** function. The two related tables have no foreign key.

Here is the syntax for the relate function

=Relate(Table1RelatedTable, Table2Record)

Table1relatedtable is required and in the record for table1, a record from Table1 is connected to a record from Table2 via a one-to-many or many-to-many connection.

Table2record. Is important and refers to the table 2 record that needs to be added to the relationship.

=Unrelate(Table1RelatedTable, Table2Record)

Table1relatedtable is required and in the record for table1, a record from Table1 is connected to a record from Table2 via a one-to-many or many-to-many connection.

Table2record. Is important and refers to the table 2 record that needs to be added to the relationship.

Matching against a list of data

The IsMatch function determines if a text string fits a pattern, which might be made up of random letters, preset patterns, or a regular expression. The Match and MatchAll methods return the contents of the match, including sub-matches.

IsMatch will validate a user enters into a Text input control. For example, you will know if a user submitted a valid email address before saving the result to your data source. If the entry does not meet your requirements, include additional buttons that ask the user to modify it.

Match returns the first text string that matches a pattern, whereas MatchAll returns all text strings that match. Sub-matches can also be extracted to parse complicated strings.

Here is the syntax

Match(Text, Pattern [, Options])

= MatchAll(Text, Pattern [, Options])

=IsMatch(Text, Pattern [, Options])

The text refers to the text string that you want to test

The pattern refers to the pattern that you want to test as a text string. The preset concatenate patterns provided by the Match enum or specify a regular expression. The pattern must be a constant formula that does not contain variables, data sources, or dynamic references that changes when the app is running.

The option is optional and it refers to the text string combination for the match option enum values. The **matchoptions.complete** is used automatically.

Matching blank fields

Isblank helps you to find fields with no value or unknown value If the user hasn't made a selection, the Selected property of a Combo box control, for example, is empty. Many data sources can store and gives you NULL values, which are shown as blank in Power Apps.

So that the app that you are making is easier to make, you can use the Isblank and coalesce functions to look for blank values and empty strings. By empty strings, we mean strings that have no characters.

Here is the syntax

=Coalesce(Value1 [, Value2, ...])

The value refers to the value that you want to test.

=IsBlank(Value)

The value here refers to the test for blank values or empty strings

IsEmpty(Table)

The table here refers to the table that you want to test for records.

Returning distinct records

The Distinct function applies a formula to each record in a table and provides a one-column table with the results with no duplicate values. Her column is referred to as the result

The formula has access to the fields of the current record being processed. Use the ThisRecord operator or just refer to fields by name, just like any other value. furthermore, the As operator may also be used to name the record processed, which can assist in making the formula more understandable and allow you to access nested data.

This function cannot be delegated when used with a data source. The function will be applied after retrieving only the initial piece of the data source. Sometimes you are not going to get a result with the full story. Then you are going to be reminded of any limitations if there are any.

Here is the syntax

=Distinct(table,formula)

Resolving delegation issues

We are going to be taking you through the process of resolving delegation issues.

SharePoint

You can get a delegation warning shown with the 'IN' operator here is how to work around this

The first thing first is that The Delegation warning is not a mistake; it simply implies that you were unable to delegate the Data process from your app to your data source. Instead, data could only be processed locally. And you could only process up to 2000 records locally.

If you want to remove the Delegation warning prompt and your SP List does not exceed 2000, I believe the collection will meet your needs. Here is what to do:

Set the **onstart** property's as follows: ClearCollect(RecordsCollection, Approvals)

Then go to modify the formula Filter(

RecordsCollection,

Title = Gallery_approvals_list.Selected.Result,

User().Email in Concat(Approver, Email & ";"))

Then you can check the power app again to see if the problem persists.

Chapter Activity/Review Question

- Update the power apps 500 record limit according to your needs.
- What is delegation in Power App?
- How do you sort data by multiple columns in Power App?

Summary

We have talked a lot about records and gone to records and data.

PART THREE: DEVELOPING CANVAS APPS

In this section, we are going to be going through the steps of designing a canvas app.

CHAPTER NINE

CANVAS APP DESIGN

First, here are the basics of the canvas application design.

Using Screen Predefined Layouts

There is an orientation attribute on the screen that tells you the current orientation that the device is on. They are Layout.Horizontal or Layout.Vertical.

These predefined layouts can be used to improve your experience with the app. So, when you go through each orientation. So if you want to manage the top half of the screen on the device using portrait mode, you can just change the screen properties with the following formulas.

X: 0

Y: 0

Width: Parent.Width * If(Parent.Orientation=Layout.Vertical, 1.0, 0.5)

Height: Parent.Height * If(Parent.Orientation=Layout.Vertical, 0.5, 1.0)

Scrollable Screen Template

You can also create a screen that makes use of a screen scroll to navigate through items. For example, you can create a phone app with data in different charts that users can see if they scroll through.

After you add different controls in a section, then the controls will have a relative position within the section. However when you are using a phone app or tablet app. The orientation and the screen size are factors that affect the section arrangement.

To create a scrolling screen, here are the steps.

1. Choose the **New screen** under the pane
2. And choose **Scrollable**

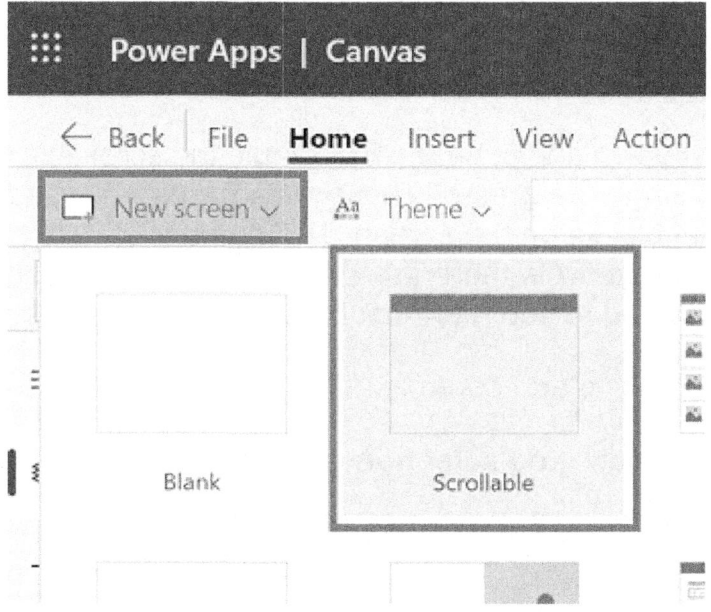

3. Then you are going to see the new scrollable screen.

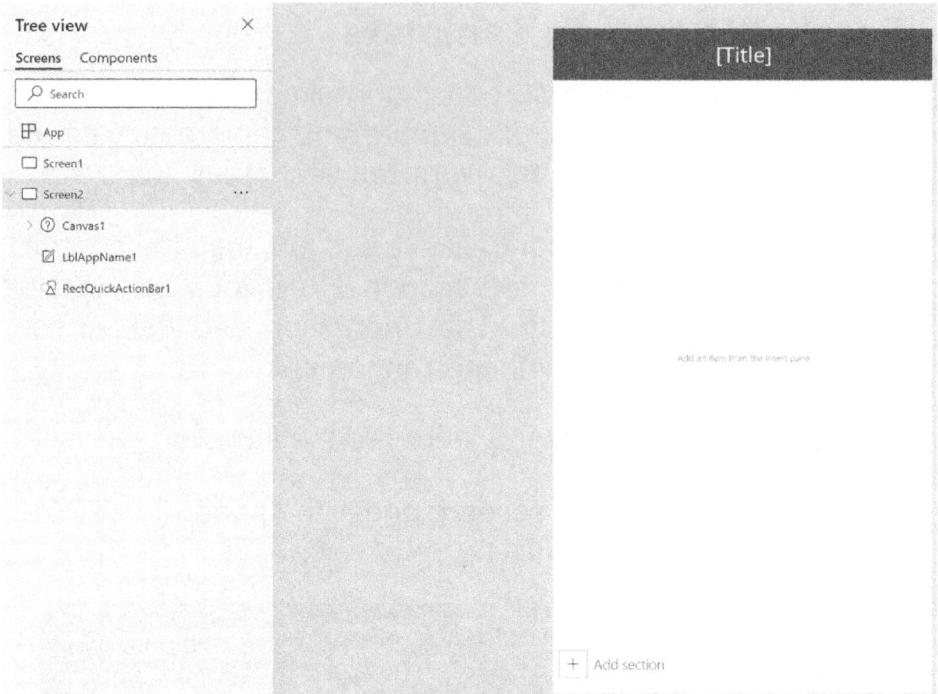

Then you can add controls. By default, the scrollable screen has a grid with a single data card. These data cards are used to separate the building blocks on the screen. The number of data cards there is and the more controls there are determine how scrollable the screen is. So you need to add more controls to meet your needs.

Here is how to add controls:

- First select **Add selection** under the scrollable screen.

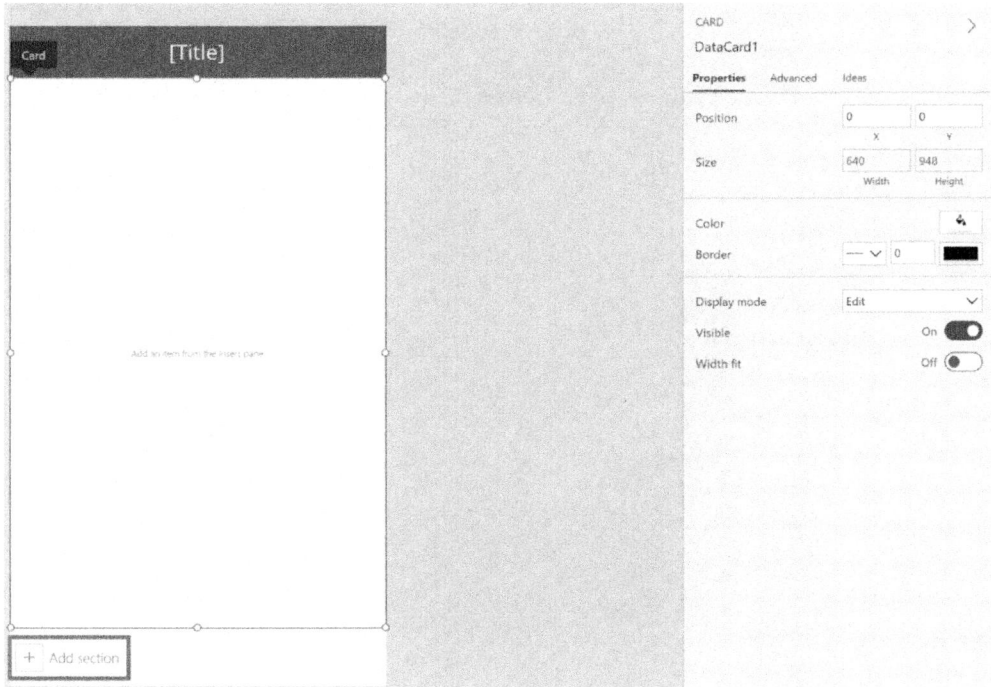

- First, start by adding controls to the data card that is provided by default with the scrollable screen, and then create a new section that adds another data card. Once a new data card is available, we will put another control within it.
- Then the two data cards and controls inside the data card increase the screen's default length, thereby making the screen scrolling more functional.
- So choose the plus icon or **Insert it** from the left pane.
- Then increase the chart size and choose the **Column chart.**
- Resize the chart that you added to the screen so that you can work with two-thirds of the screen.
- Reduce the data card size to the added chart size.

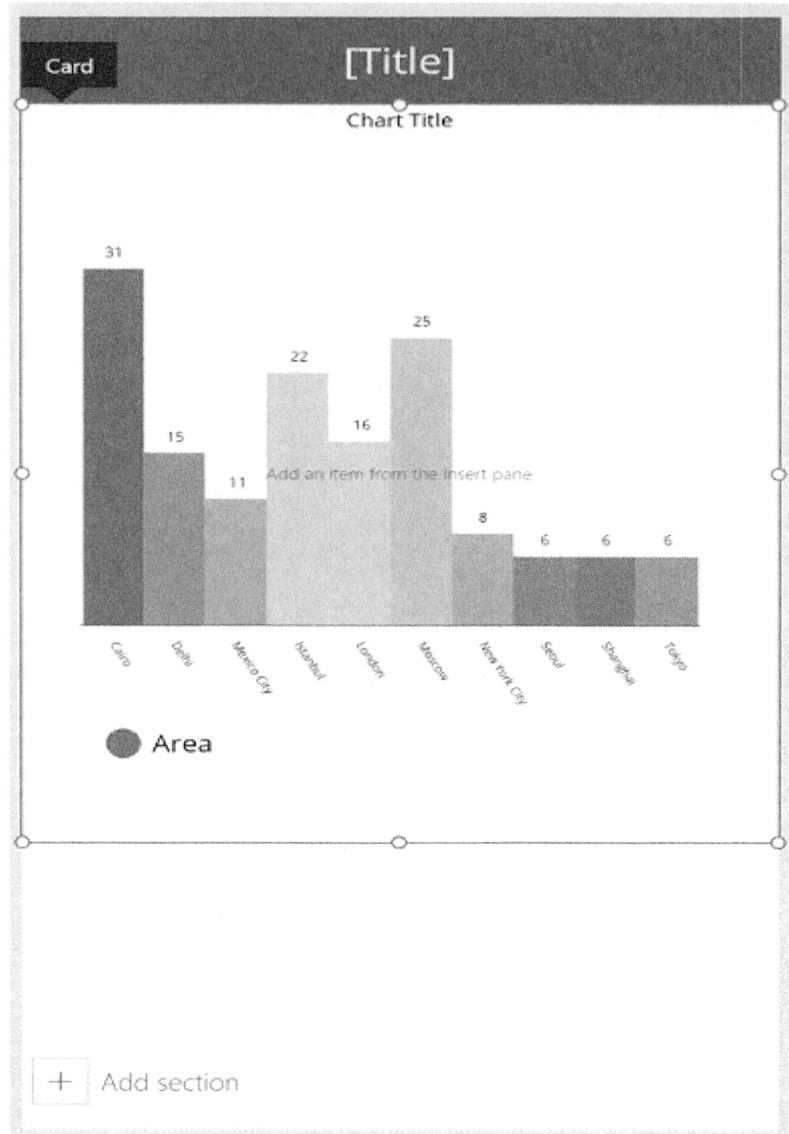

- Choose to **Add section** so that you can add another section

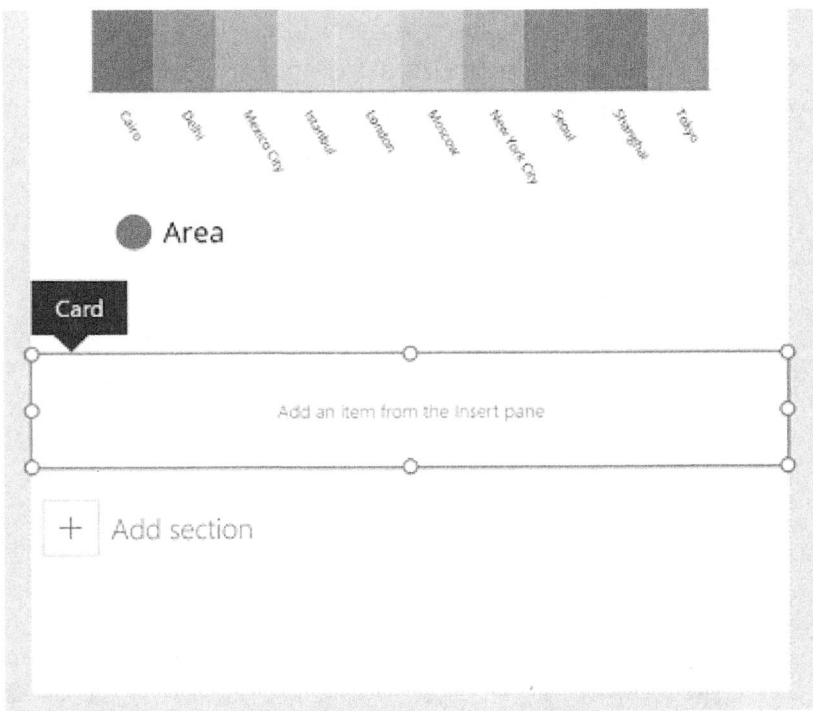

- Choose **Insert > Charts > Line chart** from the menu.

- To add a third data card, scroll down the screen using the scroll bar on the right side of the screen, and then click Add section.
- Choose **Insert > Input > Pen input** from the menu.
- Increase the width of the data card to resize the Pen   input control.

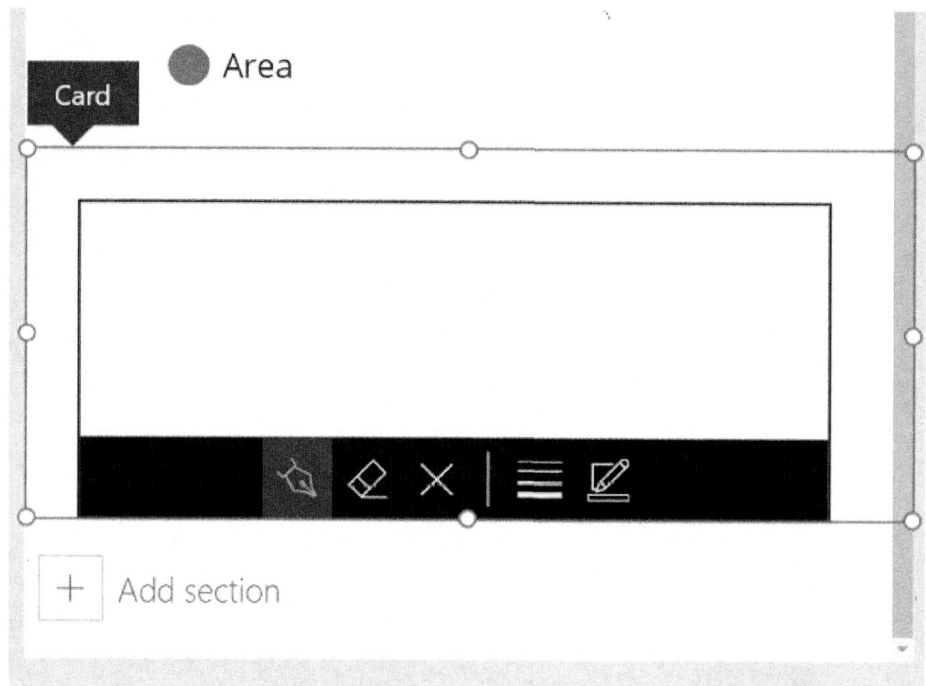

- To preview the app, press F5 on the keyboard. Scroll down to the bottom of the screen by using the scroll bar.

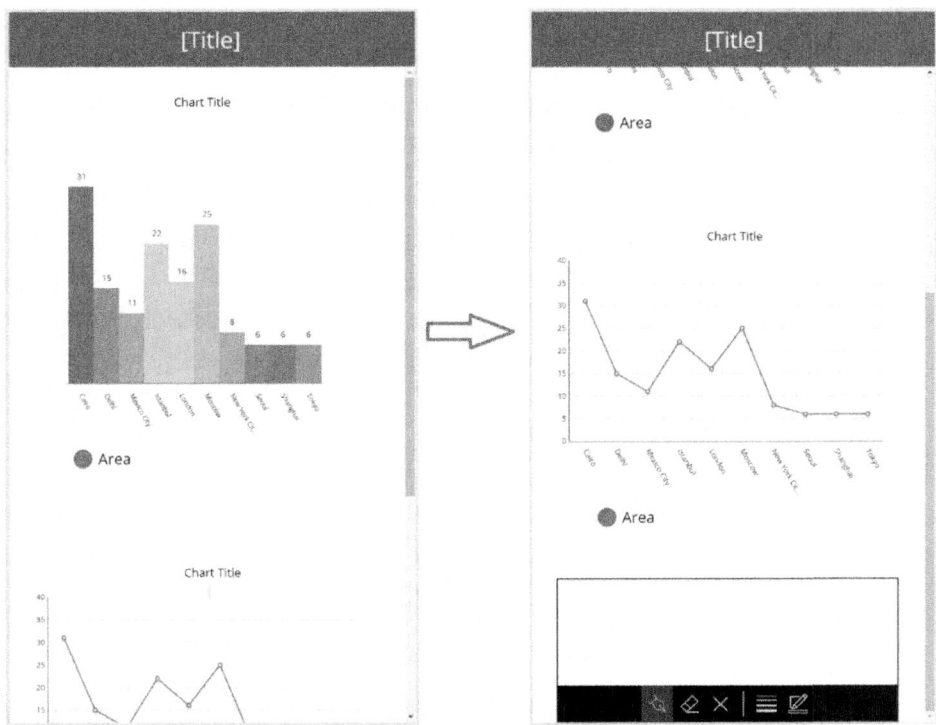

TUTORIAL SCREEN TEMPLATES

Office 365 Screen Templates

It is now very easy and quick to add some of the features of Microsoft Office to the custom apps. First, select one of the new screens, then it adds all of the required components, data source, and expression.

So there are new screens that you can add including email, people, and meetings. Calendar, tutorial, success.

Icons and Shapes

And now, we are going to be working with icons and shapes.

Using Icons and Shapes as Buttons

The buttons we are talking about here are arrows, geometric shapes, action icons, and symbols with attributes like fill, size, and placement. Furthermore, you can set their OnSelect attribute to have the app react when the user picks the control.

Here are the key properties of the icons and shapes

- **Fill**: refers to the background color of the control.
- **OnSelect**: refers to the action that you want to perform after you choose a control.

Using Themes

When you enter power apps, the **Enable basic theme** is disabled. However, you can turn the feature on to then use the default themes. Furthermore, copies of these themes can be used for additional customization.

Here is how to enable basic themes in the existing portals

- First sign in to the **Power Apps.**
- Then choose the **Apps** on the left navigation pane and choose a **Portal**

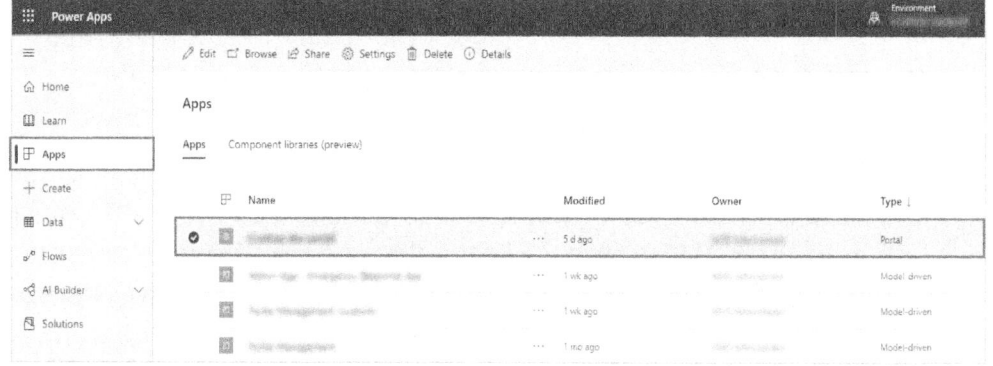

- Then choose **More commands** and choose **Edit.**

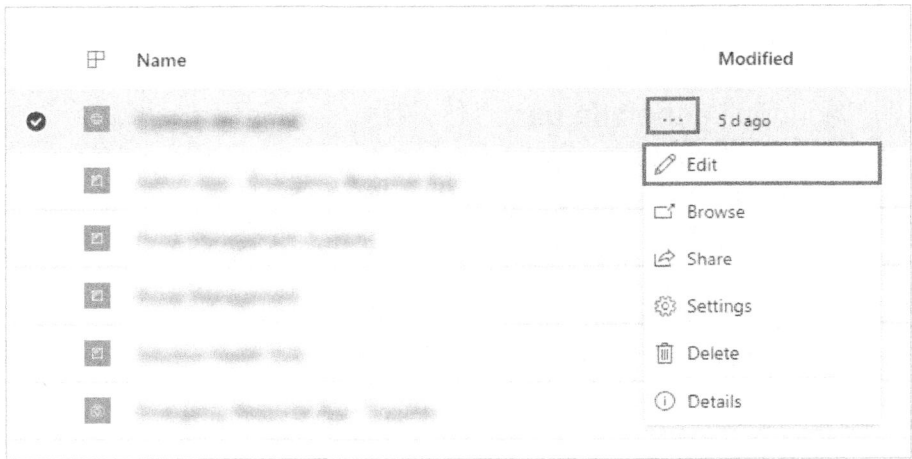

- Then **Enable the basic theme** and choose the left navigation pane.

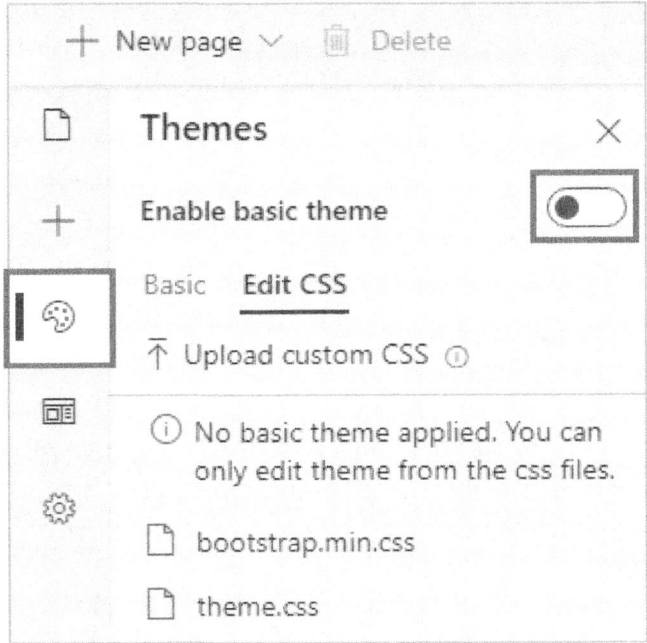

Building a list and details screen

To create a list and details screen in power apps, the first thing to do is install a northwind traders database. Then create the **Order** gallery and then the summary form.

Then create another title bar.

- Go to the top of the screen and copy and paste the **Label** control acting like the title bar.
- Then adjust the size and move that copy below the summary form
- Then you can remove the text from the copy either by double click on the text to choose it and select **Delete**
- Then set the label's text property to empty strings

Then **add a Gallery**

Here is how:

- Pick a gallery control that has a blank layout.

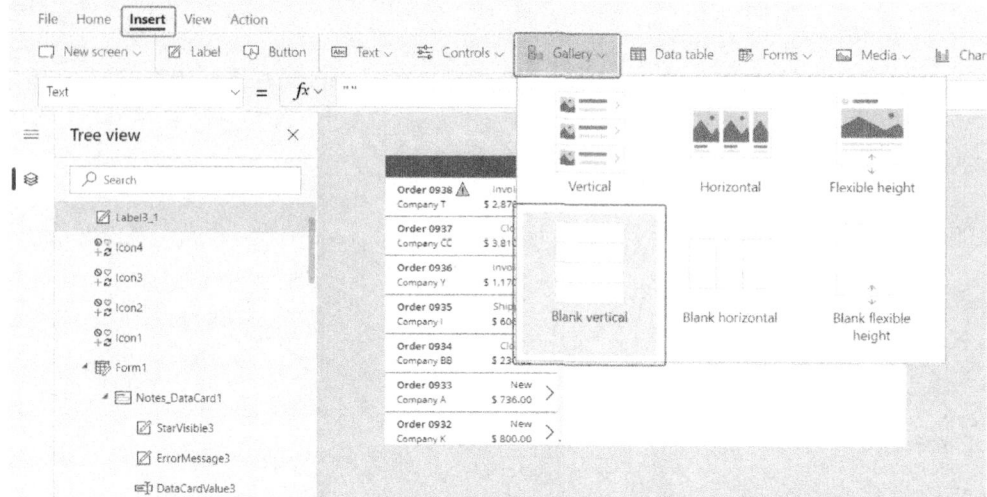

- Then the new gallery with the order details will be on the top left.
- Then close the flyout data source dialog box, and adjust and take the detailed gallery into the lower right corner just under the new title bar.

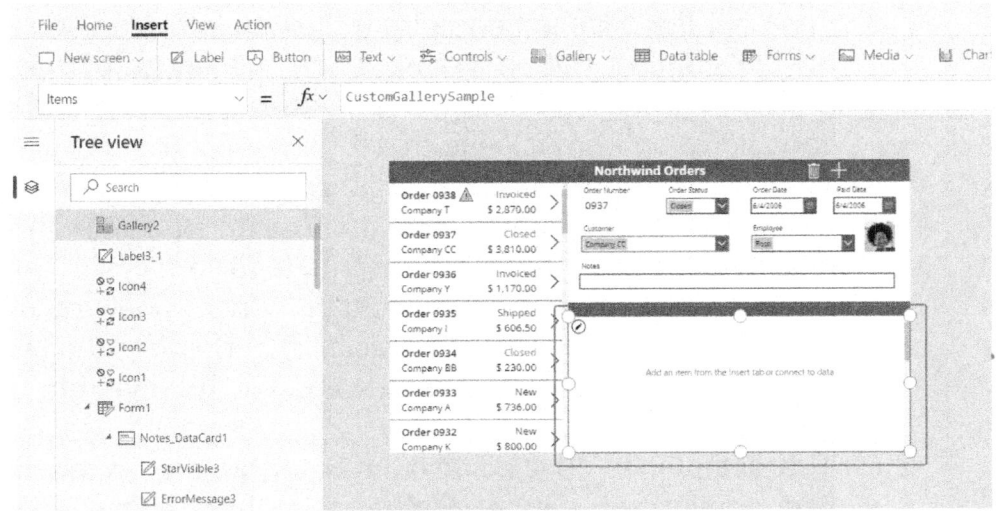

- Then configure the item property to the following formula. Gallery1.Selected.'Order Details.
- If you find an error, make sure that you name the ordering gallery as Gallery 1. And if the gallery has another name, then you need to rename it "**Gallery 1**".

  You have now connected the two galleries. When a user chooses an order from the ordering gallery, it identifies a record in the Orders table.

Displaying a delete confirmation screen

So after you create an app with the power apps and you do not see the delete button or when you delete it is too easy, you can set this stuff.

Here is what to do:

1. The first thing to do is to build a Boolean variable that will be used to show or hide buttons. Go to the left side pane of the screen and Click on the screen that has the Delete button. Then, in the OnVisible property, then enter the following: UpdateContext({isVisible: false}

2. You can then add the confirmation and cancel icons. Then go to the insert ribbon to add the two icons to the screen. Then add another label on top for 'are you sure?'

3. Then cut the onselect code from the delete button and paste it on the confirm button then change the code for the delete button to UpdateContext({isVisible: true}) to then change the variable value from false to true.
4. Then copy the following 'reverse' code to the OnSelect on the cancel button UpdateContext({isVisible: false}). This then changes any false variable from true to false
5. Because you don't want the icons to appear until you click the delete button, then modify the visibility attribute of the two icons and the label. Then the default value for the **Isvisible** variable changes.
6. The last thing to do is disable the other buttons so that the user can confirm or cancel **Delete.** To then finish, adjust the expression when you go to the **Display mode** property of the **Delete** and **Edit** button. Then you need to add isVisible to the if function. So that is more visible, and the buttons are disabled, then you need to change the disabled font color to grey.

Building a tab control screen

Here is how to create a tab in Power Apps after you create a canvas app:

- Then go to the **Insert** tab and insert a button. If you want the button in the text and not in the button, then type in the text that you will like the tab to say.
- Then on the insert tab again go to the section for **form** and choose **Edit** form and add it under the buttons.
- Then if you want to add background color to the form go to the home tab and select **Fill** and select a color.
- Then choose the buttons and enter the **Advanced** pane to the right. Then set the radius top left as 20 and the radiustopright as 20. It creates a curved tab.
- When you right-click on each of the buttons, select **Reorder,** then **send back.**
- Choose each of the tabs and choose **OnSelect** property. If the forms have three tabs for example, OnSelect of Tab1 - Set(Tab1,true);Set(Tab2,false);Set(Tab3,false)

OnSelect of Tab2 - Set(Tab2,true);Set(Tab1,false);Set(Tab3,false)
OnSelect of Tab3 -Set(Tab3,true);Set(Tab2,false);Set(Tab1,false)

- If the tab is active and you want to change the tab color, choose the file property from the advance pane.

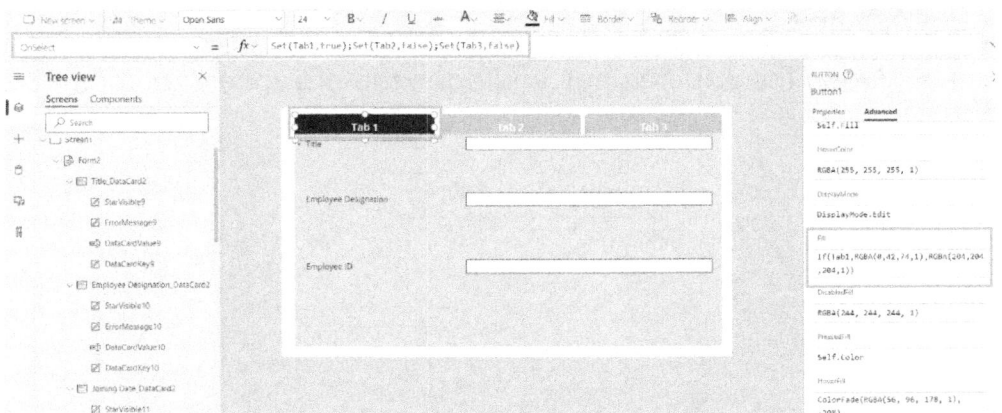

- Then add the content to the respective tab by choosing the data card to be brought under tab 1 then switch the visible property of the Datacard to tab1, then the same applies for the two tab content.

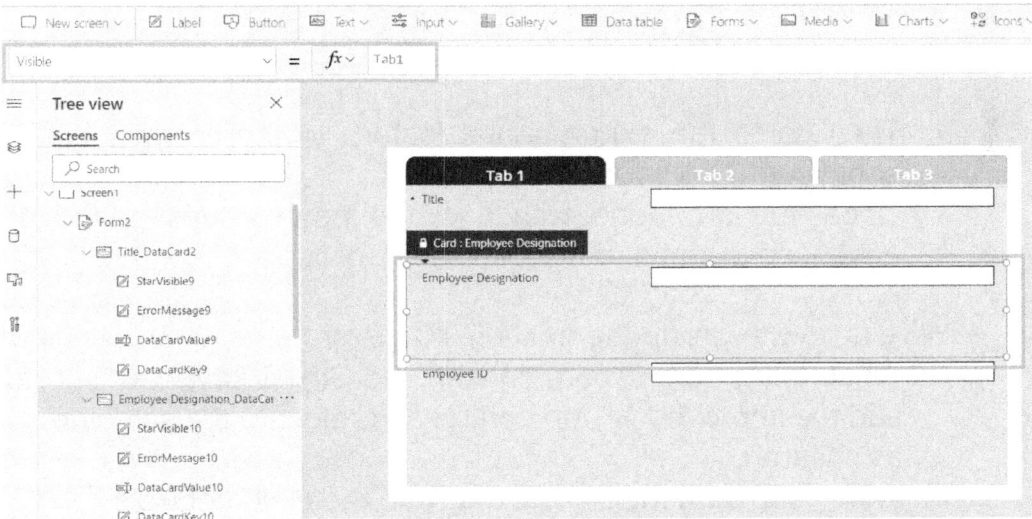

ORGANIZING CONTROLS

Grouping controls

Here are the steps to start with the new behavior to enable enhanced groups

- Open the app settings and open the advanced settings

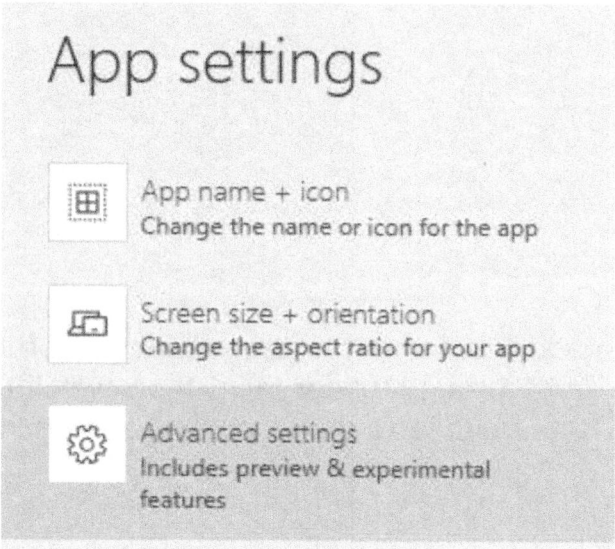

- Then go to the experimental feature to then toggle the 'try the enhanced group control' and switch
- Once you are done with this, the new groups added are the enhanced group and not the classic group

Here is how to group the multiple controls:
- When many controls are chosen, the Ctrl+G keyboard shortcut will add the improved Group control and relocate the selected controls as children.
- With a subsequent Ctrl+G, ungroup the child controls.
- The group and ungroup commands may also be found in the Home > Group menu.

- To convert an existing traditional Group control into an upgraded Group control, use the Ungroup and Group commands. Multiple controls have been chosen in the image below.

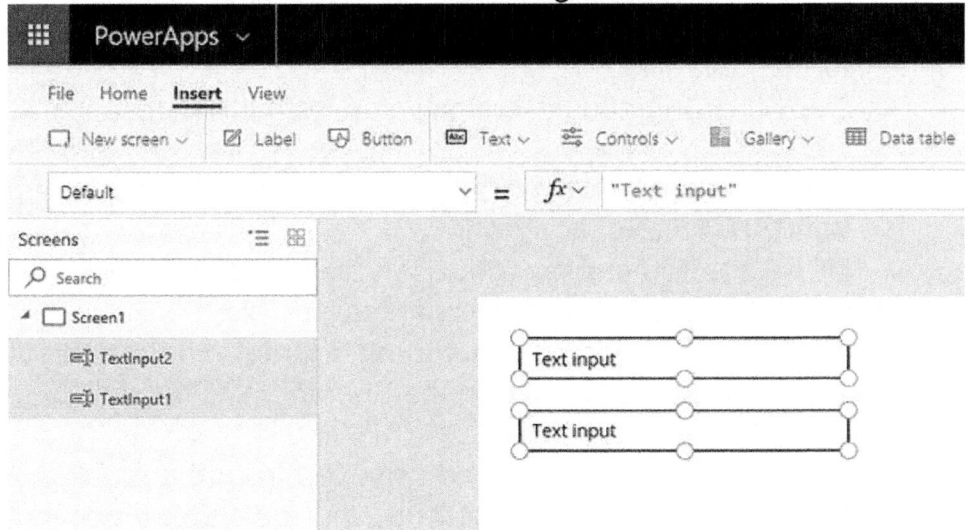

You can group the control using Ctrl+G or using the menu command.

Applying a consistent appearance

Phone Vs. tablet apps

After creating a Power App, you have to choose the layout that you want to use. Many times, after you've produced a PowerApp in one layout, you can then decide to switch it up. At the moment there is no other way for you to achieve this. When PowerApps incorporate a lot of functionality and interactions with other systems, they might take several hours to design. You don't want to start again with the complete PowerApp. So here is what you ought to do

- Export the mobile layout.
- Make a new tablet layout.
- Export the tablet layout PowerApp.
- Rename the .msapp files with the.zip extension.
- Extract the mobile export file to a single directory.
- Extract the tablet export file to a different location.
- Open the properties.json file from the mobile export directory.

- Open the properties.json file in the tablet's export directory.
- Up the tablet properties.json file, fill in the Name element with a value. This is the name of PowerApp.
- Copy the LocalConnectionReferences element from the mobile file to the tablet file.
- Copy the OriginatingVersion value from the mobile file to the tablet file.
- Open the mobile export.zip file in an archive program such as WinRAR, WinZip, or similar.
- DRAG the tablet properties.json file into the mobile export.zip file to replace the archive's properties.json file.
- It is important to note that you must drag and drop the file into the archive; zipping the files in the directory will not work.
- Close the archiver.
- The.zip extension should be removed from the mobile export file.
- Launch PowerApps Studio from your desktop or web browser.
- Click the **Open** button.
- Select **Browse**.
- Choose the .**map file** for mobile export.
- Select **OK**.
- Tap **App Settings**.
- Select **Screen size + orientation**.
- Select 3:2 in the Size radio button.
- Click the Apply button.
- Save the file.
- Select **16:9** in the Size radio option.
- Click the **Apply** button.
- Save the file.
  When you are done, you can then start to reposition the apps.

Designing a responsive app

The first thing that you want to do when building a Power App is to specify if the app should be in a phone or tablet layout. The decision that you make is what determines what the size and the shape of the canvas are going to be like.

After you've made that decision, go to **Settings > Display** to make a couple more. You may select portrait or landscape orientation as well as screen size (tablet only). You may also lock or unlock the aspect ratio and also if you want the app to support rotation too.

These choices are the most important when you are designing the screen layout. If you launch your app on a different device or the web, your whole layout adapts to match the screen on which the program is running. When a phone app runs in a wide browser window, for example, it adjusts to adapt and seems huge for its space. The program cannot make use of the extra pixels by displaying more controls or information.

Existing Formulas

So instead of using coordinate values, you can create a design that is responsive to formulas and not coordinate values. The formula expresses the control position based on the size of the screen or the relative positions of the other screen.

The Parent operator is used in these calculations. Parent refers to the screen when control is put directly on it. The control appears in the upper-left corner of the screen (0, 0) and has the same Width and Height as the screen with these property values.

Alternatively, the control might take up only the top half of the screen. Set the Height property to Parent. Height / 2 and leave the other formulae alone to get this effect.

There are two other approaches to follow if you want another control for the bottom half of the screen

Control	Property	Formula
Upper	X	0
Upper	Y	0

Upper	Width	Parent.Width
Upper	Height	Parent.Height / 2
Lower	X	0
Lower	Y	Parent.Height / 2
Lower	Width	Parent.Width
Lower	Height	Parent.Height / 2

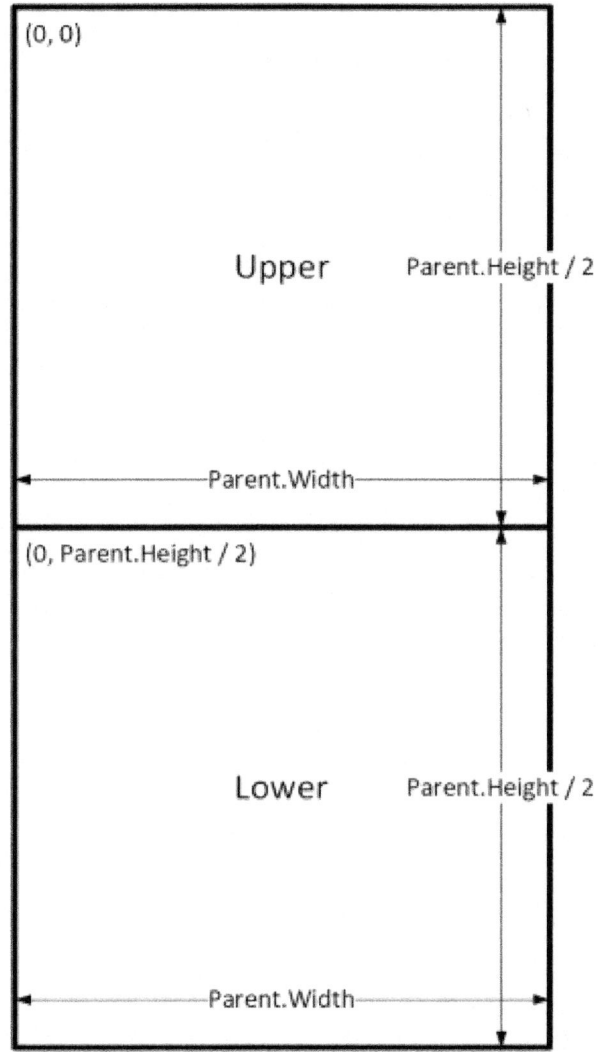

For the effect that you want the configuration that we have here is just enough but it is going to need a few edits to each of the formulas if you want to configure the relative size of the controls.

So if you want to determine if the top control should take up just one-third of the screen, while the bottom control takes up the other two-thirds.

To get that effect, you'd need to modify the Upper control's Height property as well as the Lower control's Y and Height values. Instead, consider putting the Lower control formulae in terms of the Upper control (and itself),

Control	Property	Formula
Upper	X	0
Upper	Y	0
Upper	Width	Parent.Width
Upper	Height	Parent.Height / 3
Lower	X	0
Lower	Y	Upper.Y + Upper.Height
Lower	Width	Parent.Width
Lower	Height	Parent.Height - Lower.Y

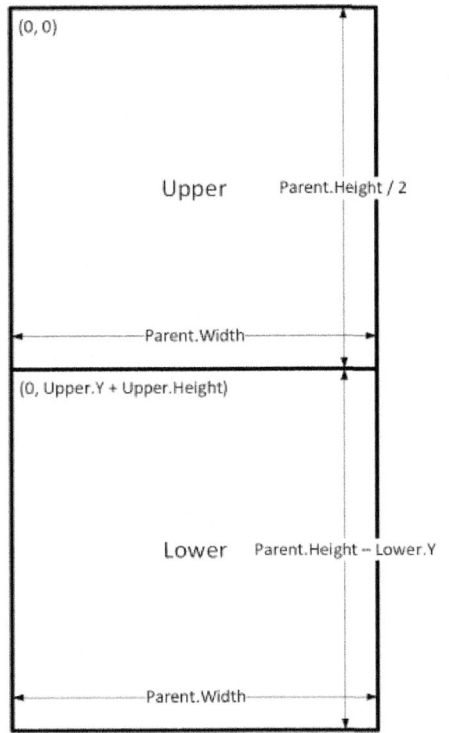 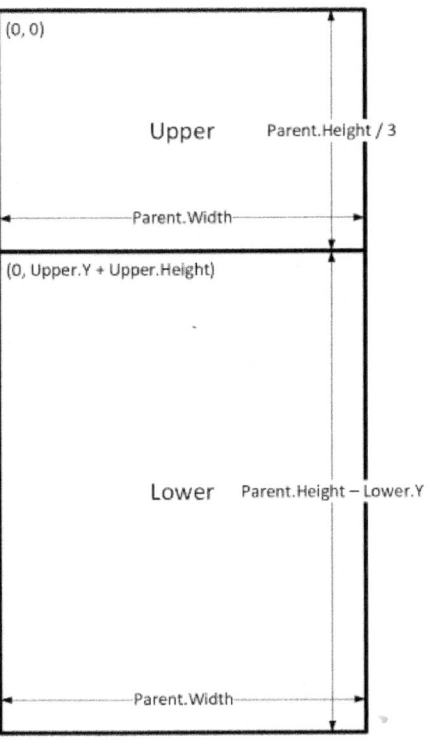

Then if you are using these formulas you might then have to change the height property of the upper control so that you can express a distinct fraction of the screen height. These move the lower control and then it adjusts to adapt to the changes made.

Building a responsive app

The first thing that you can do is disable the scale to fit.

This means that you set the screen to make the layout just adapt to the space the application is running by.

Turn off the app's **Scale to fit** to activate responsiveness. As you turn that off, also turn off the **Lock aspect ratio** since there is no specific screen shape.

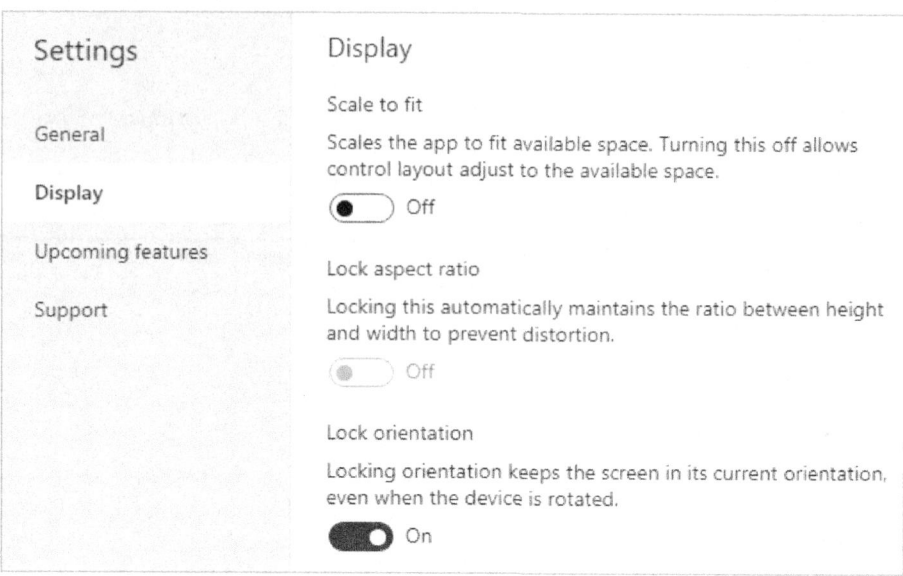

There are other steps to take for a responsive app, but here is the first thing to do

Using the timer control

The first thing to do is log in to the Power Apps:

Then create a canvas app.

To add the timer control, go to the **Insert** tab and select **Input,** then select **Timer.**

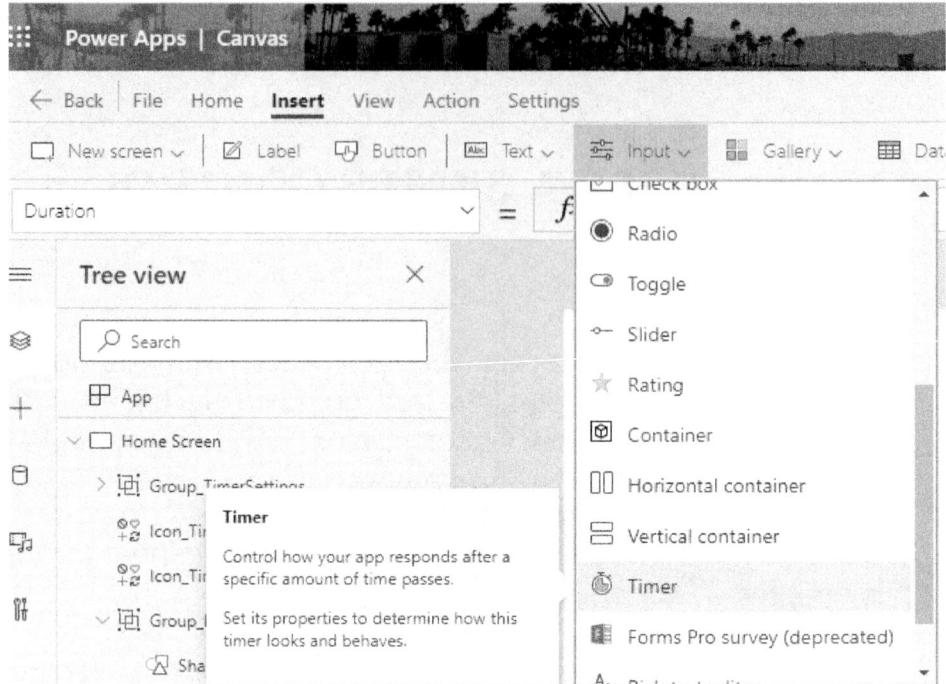

Review Question

- How do you design a responsive app?
- How do you create a scrollable screen template?
- How do you group controls in Power App?
- What are the formulas used in Power App?

Summary

Here we have talked about creating a responsive app and adapting them to layouts. This makes the app that you are working with not just efficient but also easy to work with.

CHAPTER TEN

USES A SIMPLE CONTROL

Chapter overview

With control, you can interact with applications and properly design an application. In this chapter, we are going to be taking you through controls that edit ad show singular values. And they include rich text, radio, toggle, rating, slider, and others.

We are going to be referencing the below spreadsheet throughout this chapter.

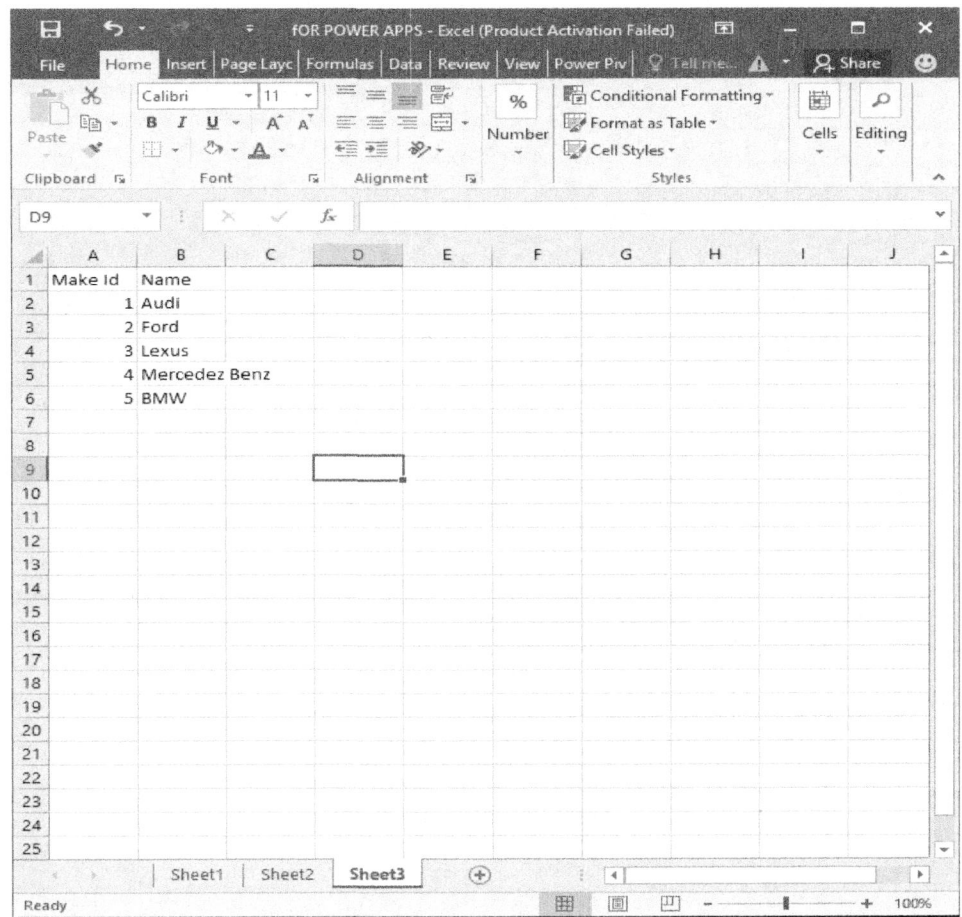

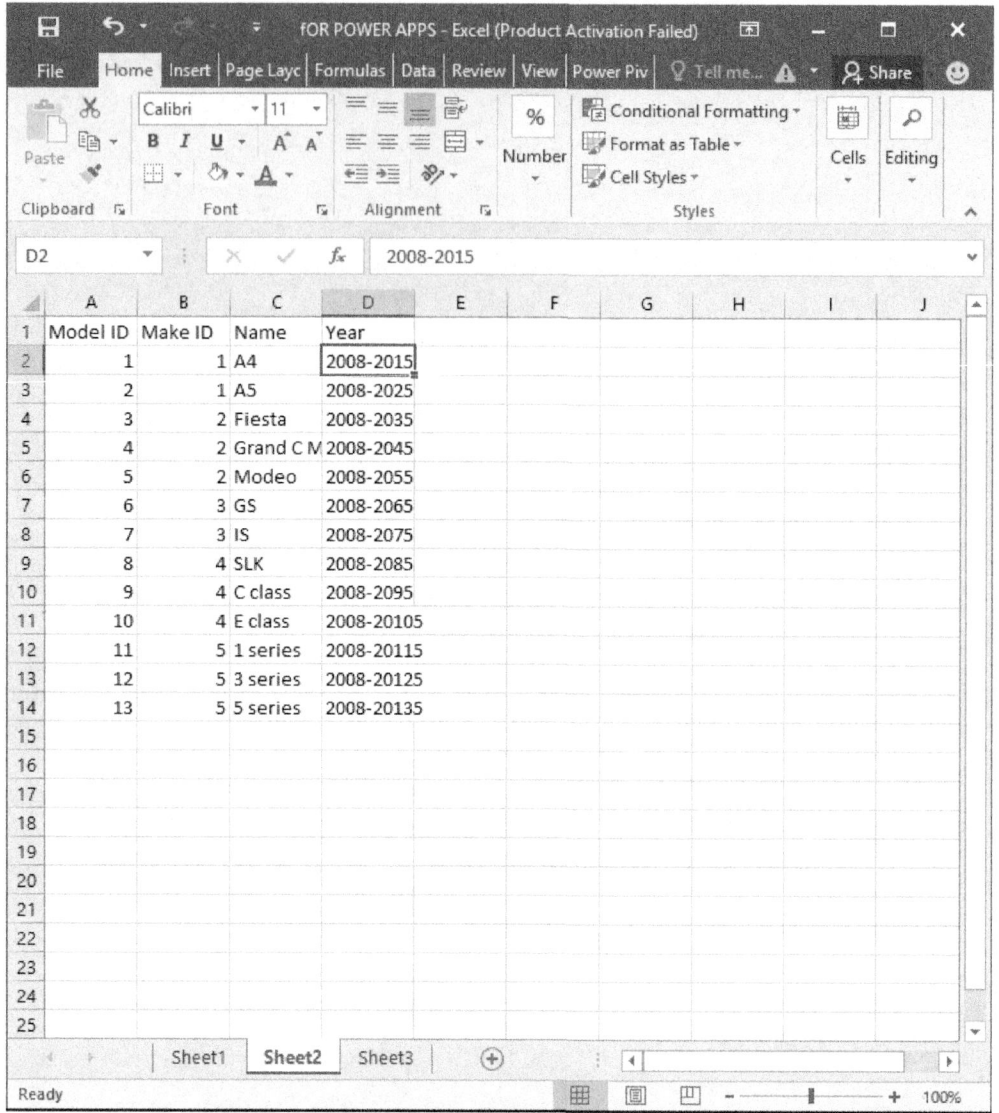

Model ID	Make ID	Name	Year
1	1	A4	2008-2015
2	1	A5	2008-2025
3	2	Fiesta	2008-2035
4	2	Grand C M	2008-2045
5	2	Modeo	2008-2055
6	3	GS	2008-2065
7	3	IS	2008-2075
8	4	SLK	2008-2085
9	4	C class	2008-2095
10	4	E class	2008-20105
11	5	1 series	2008-20115
12	5	3 series	2008-20125
13	5	5 series	2008-20135

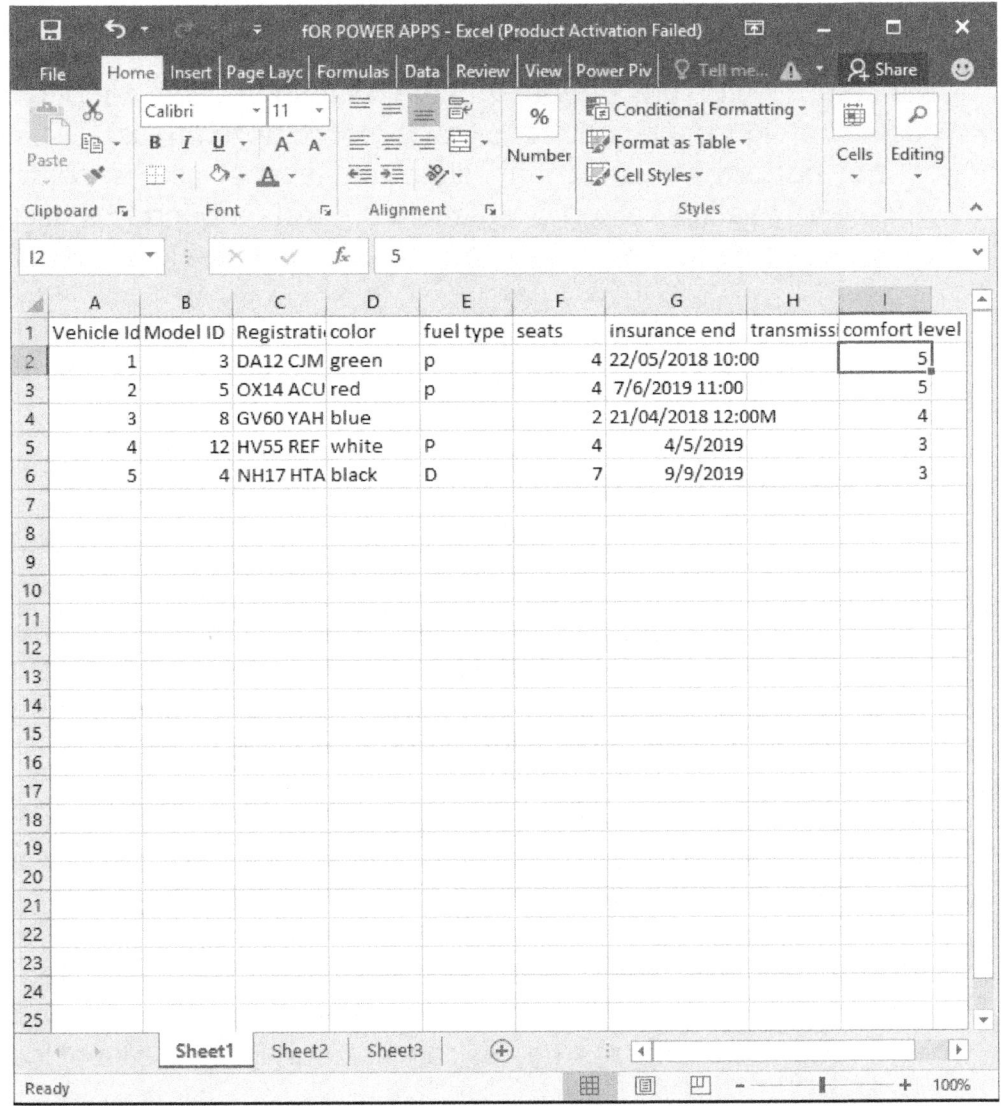

	Vehicle Id	Model ID	Registrati	color	fuel type	seats	insurance end	transmissi	comfort level
1									
2	1	3	DA12 CJM	green	p		4	22/05/2018 10:00	5
3	2	5	OX14 ACU	red	p		4	7/6/2019 11:00	5
4	3	8	GV60 YAH	blue			2	21/04/2018 12:00M	4
5	4	12	HV55 REF	white	P		4	4/5/2019	3
6	5	4	NH17 HTA	black	D		7	9/9/2019	3

Building data structures to support controls

So, the first thing to imagine is an excel spreadsheet with, for example, details of vehicles like registration number, and the color of the model.

Then the model idle field stores the model number which corresponds with a value that is held in a model table. These table sets reflect a common data structure found in a relational database.

Displaying data

But before we go any deeper into the data control, we need to find out how to configure the control so that it responds to the user. The button control performs this job and also, and almost all the controls are capable of this kind of job. To make a control respond to a user tap or click, we would add a formula to the control's OnSelect attribute.

You can use the buttons on the action menu to build an OnSelect formula and also to go to a new screen and remove items from collections.

The label control

The label control only shows the simple text, while the Home menu gives you the choice of format. You are going to see controls to change the font type, size, and color of a label, just like in the image below Text styles like bold, italics, underline, and strikethrough can also be used. By altering the vertical and horizontal text alignment, we can better match our label with neighboring controls.

The Text attribute specifies the text that displays in the label and can include multiline text. We can enter a line break by typing it into the formula bar.

We may set the label height to adjust automatically based on its content. This is enabled via the AutoHeight parameter. When you set the Overflow attribute to true, we can also configure the label to display scrollbars.

However, on the other hand, there are only a handful of available fonts that you can use.

The HTML text control

When you are using the HTML control you can then display HTML content. HTML allows us significantly more flexibility over text formatting. Unlike the label control, we may use HTML to change the colors and styles of specific words in a phrase.

After you add an HTML text control to the screen the text property is going to give you an example markup so that you can format the basic HTML. This also shows how you can also set the text style to bold using the <b> tag, and also hot to configure the text color to blue with the tag <font color=blu.

When we wish to show characters that are not available in plain text, we can utilize the HTML text control. This includes superscript letters in chemical symbols, mathematical symbols, and even musical symbols. CO_2 (COsup>2/ sup>), (∞), and B (B ♭ are some examples of symbols and their associated HTML tags.

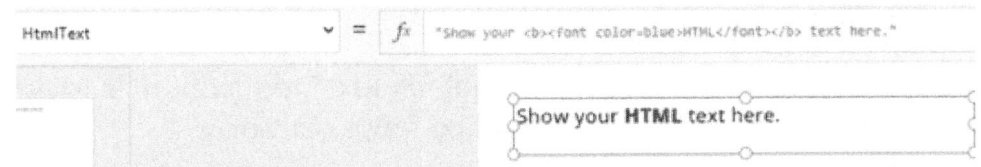

USING SIMPLE DATA ENTRY CONTROLS

Text to input controls

This is the default text that you are going to see on the edit form. What it does is receives text input from the user and also some other features to work with.

The control has a mode attribute that we may change to one of three values to limit the data that users can enter: MultiLine, SingleLine, or Password. The MultiLine and SingleLine attributes govern multiline text insertion. In password mode, the control replaces each character entered by the user with an asterisk.

We may utilize the maximum length parameter to limit the amount of text that a user can enter. The control also has a format attribute that may be adjusted to either text or numeric. If we set the control's format attribute to a number, it will only take numeric input from the user.

Additionally, there are two more features to aid the user. They are the **tooltip** property and the **hint text** property. The tooltip property refers to when a user hovers the mouse over a control, it displays help text.

Because mobile devices lack the idea of a mouse, the hint attribute comes into play. When the text input control is empty, it displays the hint text. Once the user then enters text to the control, it deactivates the hint text and only shows the text the user inputs.

Radio controls

In the radio control, the user can select from the list. We'll replace the fuel type text input control in our edit form with radio control to show how to utilize this control. In this example, we'll configure the radio control to save one of three values in the spreadsheet. P, D, or E will be the values stored in the 'fuel type' field (to denote petrol, diesel, or electric).

The first step in replacing the default text input control is to unlock the 'fuel type' card and delete the text input control.

The designer will display two warnings when we delete a text input control from a card. The first is about the card's now-invalid Update attribute, and the second is about a formula that generates the y-position coordinate of an error warning label. This formula must be modified to refer to our new control rather than the old text input control name. Because the remaining examples in this section follow the same structure, these instructions will also apply to them.

The following step is to add a radio control and call it RadioFuelType. Set the Items property to the following value to determine the items that display in the radio control: Table({FuelId:"P", FuelDesc:"Petrol"}, {FuelId:"D", FuelDesc:"Diesel"},

{FuelId:"E", FuelDesc:"Electric"})

This formula creates a table with the columns FuelID and FuelDesc. The FuelID field represents a single character code, whereas the FuelDesc field provides a nice description of the fuel type. Set the value property to FuelDesc to configure the radio control to display the friendly description.

When a user saves a record, the card is configured to use the selected radio item to update the 'fuel type' column. To do this, pick the parent card control and set the Update property to the following formula: RadioFuelType.Selected.FuelId.

To finish this example, modify the radio control to display the right item when a user opens an existing record. The selected radio option is defined by the default property, and in our case, we need to give a nice description because this is what the control displays. As a result, we require a formula that translates P to Petrol, D to Diesel, and E to Electric. Here is the formula for setting the Default property: If(Parent.Default="P", "Petrol",If(Parent.Default="D", "Diesel",If(Parent.Default="E", "Electric","))).

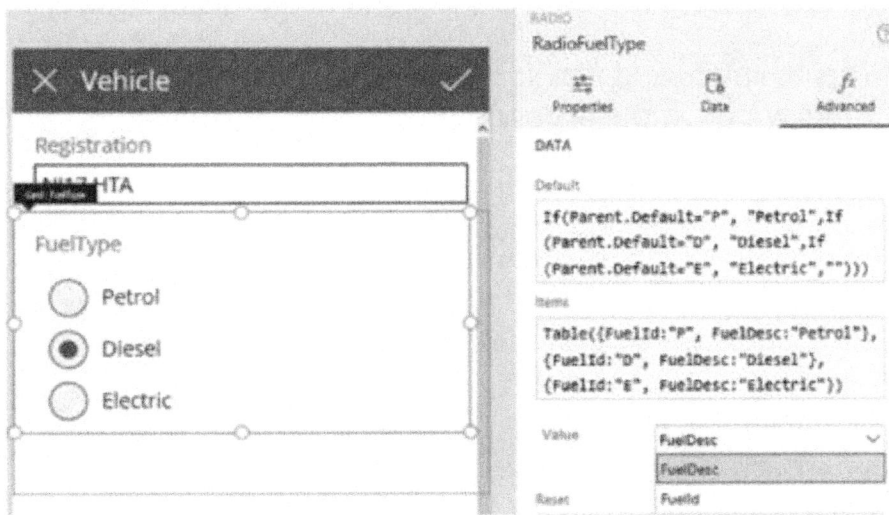

Toggle and checkbox controls

Two controls allow the user to enter yes/no or true/false answers. The toggle and checkbox controls are examples of this. Both of these controls operate identically, so for the sake of brevity, we'll simply look at the toggle control. The toggle control is similar to the checkbox control in that the user changes the state of the control by sliding a button rather than clicking a checkbox with a mouse.

To show this control, we'll add a toggle control to our screen that allows users to select a vehicle's gearbox type. The spreadsheet's transmission field will contain the values A or M. (to denote automatic or manual transmission). A toggle control's state can be true or false. In our app, true will represent an automated car and false will represent a manual vehicle.

Slider controls

This way you can enter the numeric values between a minimum and a maximum value. Here is how to for example add the slider control to the edit form so that we can set the number of seats that are in a vehicle.

First, remove the text box from the text box and unlock the seat card. Resolve any mistakes that arise, same as in the previous example. Insert a slider control and give it the name SliderSeats.

The minimum and maximum values are two helpful characteristics that we may put on the slider control.

The lowest value can be negative, and the maximum value can be as high as the maximum value.

JavaScript's maximum amount of variables. The size of the slider bar and button are also used variables.

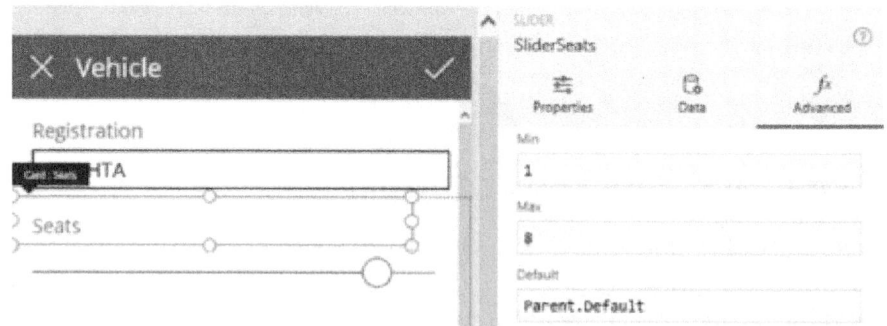

Then you are going to have to set the card so that they work with the slider value then you can update the field for seats after users save the record. To accomplish this, you need to choose the parent card control and then configure the Update property. SliderSeats.Value

Finally, you want to see the correct value after you open existing records. For that, then set the default property as **parent.Default**.

Then you can use the slider control to set the number of seats.

Rating controls

Finally, concerning the rating control, it sets and also returns numeric values. This way, the user can just use stars to set the rating.

For example, if you want to use the rating control for the level of comfort that a vehicle provides. What you are going to have to do first is to unlock the level of comfort and then delete the text input control. Then when you enter a rating control, name it.

Then you can set the maximum value the control can accept.

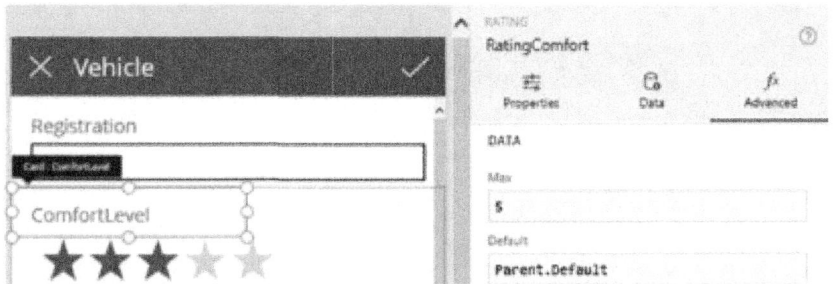

Then you need to design the card such that when a user saves a record, the rating control updates the comfort rating field. Set the Update attribute of the parent card control to RatingComfort.Value

When a user opens an existing record, the rating control should reflect the right value.

Set the Default property to parent.default to do this.

Then open the software and use the rating control to select the comfort level of a car. Sometimes, especially with people who use iOS, there are complaints that they might have to hold a click before their control is registered. So that is something that you want to mind.

Working with dates

In this section, we are going to be taking you through the dates. We are going to be walking with the date picker control. You might encounter problems sometimes, considering during time conversion the app might then be saved and show a different date entirely. So, we are going to be taking you through the steps to go avoid any of these kinds of problems.

Data picker controls

PowerApps has a date picker for users to enter dates. Here is the date picker widget in action.

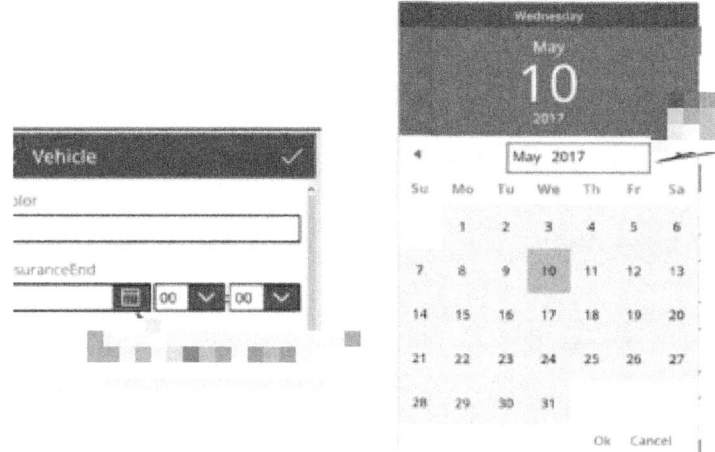

The following are the highlights of this control. The control initially appears on a single line and displays the date in a short date format. The control uses the short date format associated with the device's or browsers regional settings, and there is no option to provide an alternative format. When a user selects the control, a calendar view appears, allowing them to pick a date.

To browse across the months, the calendar that we have above includes forward and backward icons. Users may rapidly modify the year and month values with the labels, which may be overlooked. It is very easy to miss that feature so that means that work is harder and more frustrating when the date set is significantly different from the current date with the backward and the forward navigation icons.

The start year attribute is an essential one to be aware of. This is set to 1970 by default, and users cannot choose a year earlier. If we wish to allow older dates, we must lower this number.

When using Excel data sources, we must first upload sample data to a spreadsheet before attempting to develop an auto-generated program. The designer cannot discover the data types of any of the fields if we construct an auto-generated app with a spreadsheet that just has table heads. In this case, all of the auto-generated cards will include text input controls.

UNDERSTANDING TIME ZONES

Saving dates in year-month-day format

It is a difficult task to create an app that writes time values for them to be placed consistently throughout the app that you create. Now, when you use the UTC adjustments then you increase the likelihood of entering incorrect data becomes more because there are going to be dependencies that you cannot control.

One common problem that an app developer might have is that when using applications that link to SharePoint, the timings entered by users do not match the values that display in SharePoint. We have two reasons why this is so. Firstly, the client device's or browser's regional settings may be wrong. Alternatively, the administrator may never have configured the SharePoint site's regional settings.

These issues are almost certainly going to be tough to diagnose. To ensure consistent dates, one easy method is to save our date and time data as strings in the format yyyymmddhhmm.

To display dates in apps, you need to first format the date. This brings a benefit which means that we can then sort the date value either in ascending or descending order.

To then amend the so that you can store the insurance end date value in the format of yyymmmdddhhmm. Here is the formula. Text(DateValue1.SelectedDate, "yyyymmddhhmm")

Datevalue1 means date picker control.

Then you can set the default property for the date picker control so that you can get a valid date after one opens a record. The developer has to work with the DateTime value function and also add an input string with the format yyyy-mm-dd-hh-mm.

DateTimeValue(Left(Parent.Default, 4) & "-" & Mid(Parent.Default, 5,2) & "-" & Mid(Parent. Default, 7,2) & " " & Mid(Parent.Default, 9,2) & ":" & Mid(Parent.Default, 11,2))

That formula produces the following error since in the first spreadsheet, the data type of the insurance end area is a date and then we modify the field in other to store the text value too.

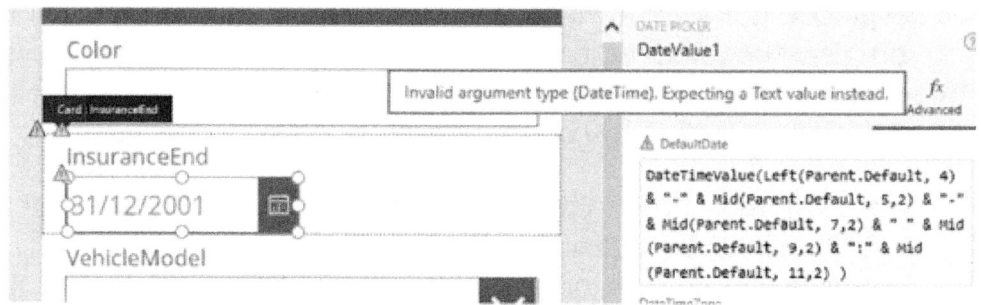

If you do not want this error to appear, here is what to do.

First, change the **date value** form the excel spreadsheet so that it is in the format yyyymmddhhmm. It is important that if you are working with excel you enter the values using single quotes.

Then you need to convert the cell format to text just the way we have it here.

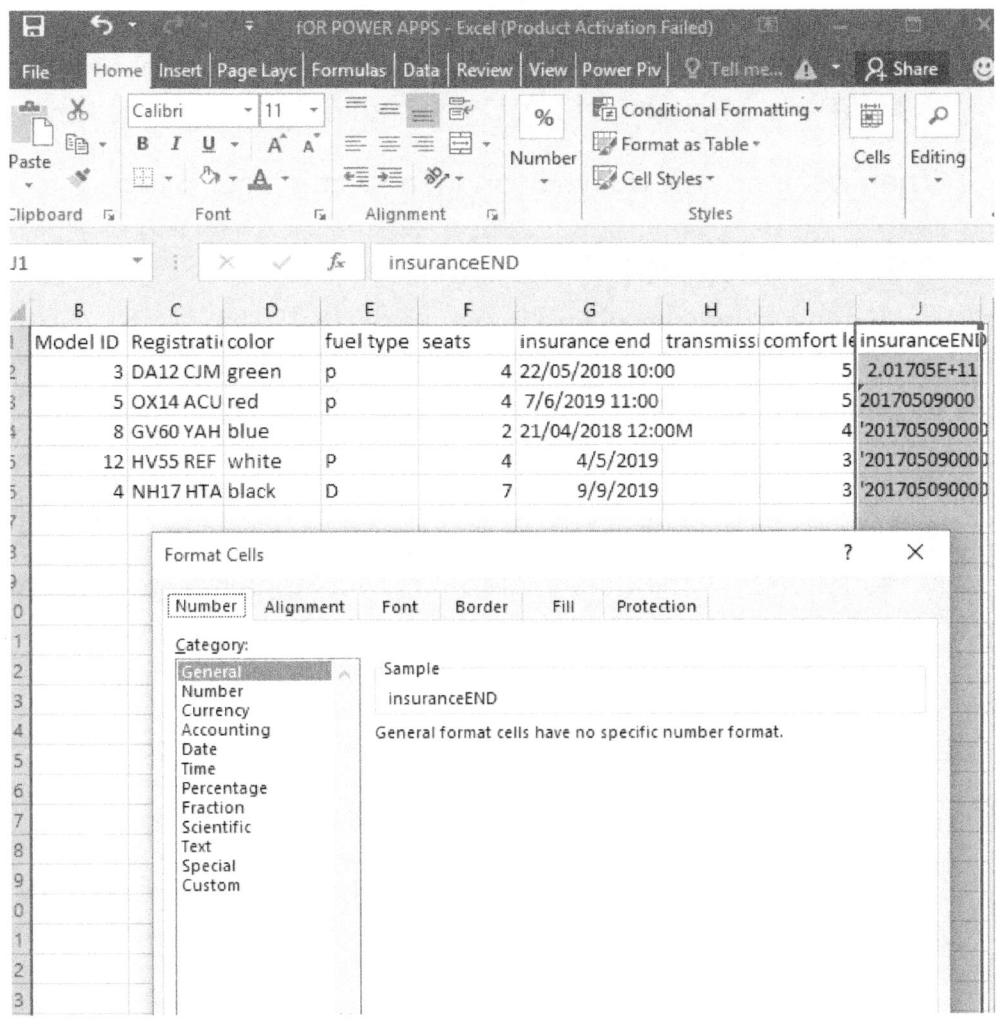

Then go to the power apps and then refresh the data source simply by selecting insert and go to the data sources. When you use the right-click refresh option for the data source then you are not going to see the error anymore.

The next step is to make any controls that show the 'insurance termination date' data more legible. This would have to be done on the detail form in the auto-generated app. To display the date in a long date time format, we may use a formula, as shown below.

Text(DateValue(Left(Parent.Default, 4) & "-" & Mid(Parent.Default, 5,2) & "-" & Mid(Parent. Default, 7,2) & " " & Mid(Parent.Default, 9,2) & ":" & Mid(Parent.Default, 11,2)), DateTimeFormat.LongDateTime)

Then we are done. So, you can then run the application.

Review Question

- Explain briefly how time is stored on the Power App?
- What is a slider control in Power App?
- How do you build data structures that support control?

Summary

We have accomplished a lot in this chapter. We hope that you understand how the data values in Power Apps are stored and how to use slider and action controls.

CHAPTER ELEVEN

USES TABLE/RECORD RATE CONTROLS

In this section, we are going to be discussing tables and record rate controls in Power Apps.

Chapter overview

In this chapter, we are going to be discussing the drop-down controls, the data entry control, layout forms, and some important table controls.

Data entry control

Dropdown control

A drop-down control saves screen space, especially when there are a lot of options. Unless the user chooses more options, the control takes up only one line. The control can display up to 500 items.

Setting lookup values

Here we are going to be going through how to use the drop-down and list box controls. Since the controls help us to limit the values that a user can input this control is very important.

To showcase the drop-down control, we'll add it to two fields in our auto-generated app's edit form: the color field and the model id field. You can evaluate the structure of our data by referring to Figures 8-2 and 8-3.

Customizing the drop-down display value

You can replace the text input control using the down list of hard-coded color values. The first thing to do is open the **Edit form** and look for the card that is connected to the color field. You can switch the control type as allowed values then you can unlock the card.

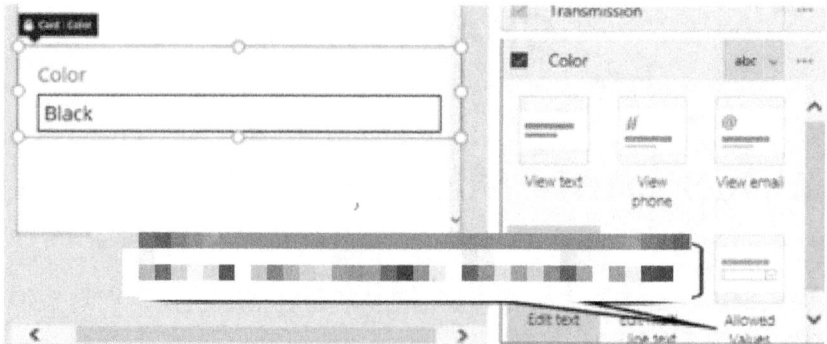

Then choose the drop-down control from the card then configure the item property inside this formula ["Red", "Green", "Blue", "Yellow", "Orange", "Purple", "Pink", " Brown" ," White"," Black"]

In this section, we are going to be seeing how the setting then displays. Then you can run the app with the drop-down to then set the color field for the vehicle

Nestling drop-down controls

We can nest groups of drop-down controls together so that things are easier for customization. So to demonstrate we are going to be adding a make drop down into the edit form so that we can then set the vehicle model to drop down to the show values that also match the specific vehicle make.

Here is the vehicle make:

	A	B	C
1	Make Id	Name	
2	1	Audi	
3	2	Ford	
4	3	Lexus	
5	4	Mercedez Benz	
6	5	BMW	
7			
8			
9			
10			

To create this, choose the card with the vehicle model then inject the drop-down control just above the vehicle model drop-down. Then you are going to have to name the control as dropdown makes then choose the items property as vehicle make

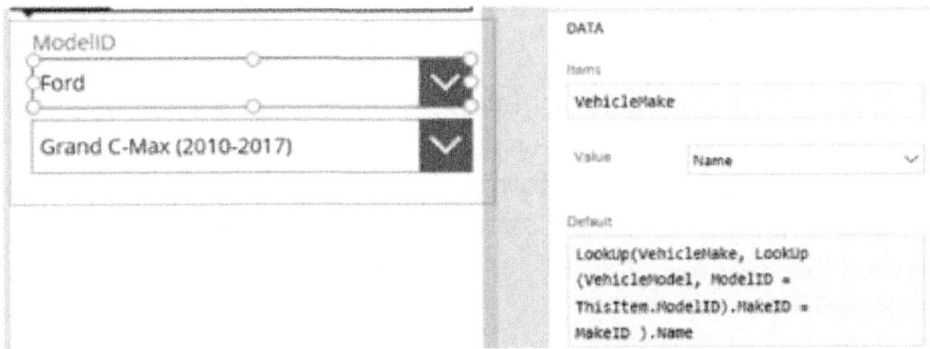

When the card loads an existing vehicle record, it must display the vehicle make that matches the record's vehicle model. To accomplish so, set the DropdownMakes control's Default attribute to the following formula: LookUp(VehicleMake, LookUp(VehicleModel, ModelID = ThisItem.ModelID).MakeID = MakeID).Name

This formula includes a series of nested lookups. The innermost lookup returns the MakeID associated with the vehicle record's ModelID. It does the lookup using the VehicleModel table.

The name field of the made record that matches the MakeID value from the inner lookup is returned by the outermost lookup.

Filter(AddColumns(VehicleModel, "ModelAndYear", Name & " (" & Year & ")"), MakeID =DropdownMakes.Selected.MakeID)

We may now run our screen and choose a vehicle manufacturer. When this occurs, the car model drop-down will only display vehicle models corresponding with the specified vehicle manufacturer.

Data display controls

List box control

With the list box control, the user can choose multiple items. It works just like the drop-down control and the only thing that sets it apart from the drop-down control is that you will always see the data items.

The Items attribute specifies the control's data source. If the data source has many columns, the value attribute specifies which one to show.

The select multiple attributes determine whether the user may choose several items or not. May only choose a single item. To access the chosen items using a formula, we may utilize the Selected Items property. If you want to see all of the items that you chose, you can use the Concat method to create a string that displays the items chosen.

The syntax looks like this Concat(ListBoxDefects.SelectedItems, Description & " ")

The Concat function takes two arguments: a data source and a formula. This function runs the algorithm on each row in the data source and aggregates the results into a single output value.

The list box control's default attribute indicates the chosen item. This would be set to the text of the item to be selected. However, one significant drawback is that we can only choose one thing at a time, preventing us from utilizing this control to display many objects connected with a record.

Displaying tables of data

Then here we are going to be taking you through those controls that show data in tabular form. Here is how to add the control.

- Select **Data table** from **Insert** menu.
- You can then use the item property to find the data source.
- Then you can set the columns inside the table when you enable the cards

The table control is read-only and does not provide cell-level editing, like Excel. Because it retains track of the chosen row, this control works similarly to the gallery control. A common design pattern is to place an edit form next to the table control and set the edit form's data source to the selected item in the data table. This enables users to choose and modify a record on the same screen.

Working with gallery controls

A Gallery control can display many records from a data source, each of which can include different sorts of data. Use Gallery control. If you want to display many contacts, each item displays contact information like as the name, address, and phone number of each contact.

You will see data fields in different control inside the gallery control. You can set these controls with templates. You will see the template as the first item inside the gallery

Choosing a gallery type

You will find them here:

- In horizontal/landscape orientation, on the left border of a Gallery control.
- Also, at the top of a vertical/portrait Gallery control.

Any modifications you make to the template are mirrored in the Gallery control. There are predefined templates for displaying photos and text in a gallery, as well as a gallery for variable-height objects.

Applying layouts

The gallery has two layouts and they are

1. **List**: when you choose the list from the gallery layout section, you will notice seven types and they include, Blank; Title; Title and Subtitle; Title, subtitle, and body; Image and title; Image, title, and subtitle; and the image, title, subtitle, and body
2. Then there is the **gallery:** when you choose the gallery layout, you are going to notice four different layouts. They are the 2 columns, the 3 columns, Title and subtitle, and Title and subtitle on overlay.

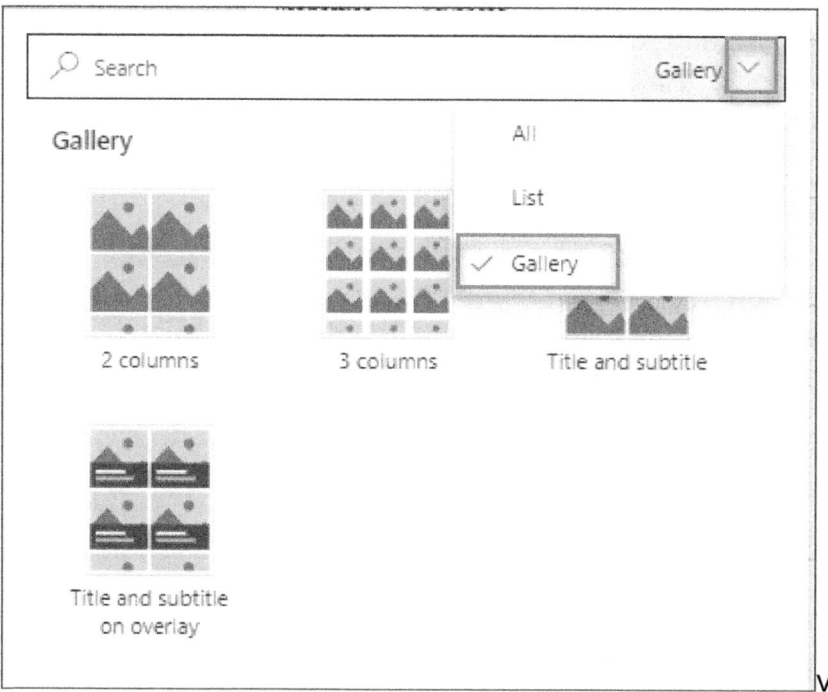

Setting properties

The properties include, items, default, selected all items, border color, delay item loading, display mode, fill, item accessible label, loading spinner, loading spinner color, navigation step, selectable, show navigation, show scrollbar, template fill, template size, transition, visible and the wrap count.

Incorporating data entry controls

Working with forms

A form is made up of a collection of card items. Text boxes (or other controls) are used on each card to show the data values. The hierarchy of controls here is not very easy to understand. However, do not be discouraged. You can add a textbox to the screen directly and it might feel a little redundant to add a complex structure that needs us to connect text boxes to cards and the cards to forms.

The point of this is that you can build screens quicker and reduces the time spent writing codes to access data.

The figure above shows the design view of **EDITFORM1**. The items under the Fields header are the auto-generated cards that appear in the form.

They are called auto-generated cards because, as a designer, you can automatically create cards based on the fields that are in the data source.

The card list responds to the data source in real-time. If we added a new column to our Excel table (for example, phone number), the designer would produce a phone number card as soon as we refreshed our data source.

If you want to hide a card, uncheck the checkbox next to the card you wish to hide. In the image below we are going to be depicting how the form looks with the 'active' card concealed. As you can see, when the card is concealed, the designer displays a grayed-out version of it. Simply click the button to re-enable the card to reinstate it.

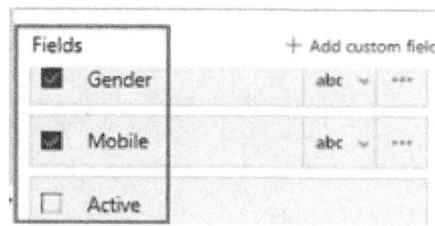

Resetting form controls

- You can reset the form controls with the ResetForm function.
- The syntax is reset form(form name)
- The form name here refers to the form that you want to reset.

Validating form values

It is important to do data validation. Ensuring that information is received in the correct format saves less effort later to standardize it. When developing trustworthy reports, data accuracy is also critical. The most pleasant aspect, however, is that when done correctly, data validation may improve the user experience by providing immediate feedback.

You can use the logical expression for data validation and you are going to get true or false.

Retrieving validation rules

If you want to make use of the power app validation, you have to first create an app for the SharePoint list. The first thing is to enter the **Power Apps** tab and then choose to **Create an app.**

- Then name the app and select the create button
- You are going to see the detail screen, the edit screen, and the edit screen
- The validation works on the edit screen.
- Then you need to unlock the data card value and rename the field. To unlock the data card, enter **Advanced** and select the **Lock icon**
- Any mandatory field is marked with asterisks. To do this field the way it is, first chooses the specific **Data cards** and you are going to use this formula.Required = true

Review Question

- What is a drop-down control?
- How do you apply Layouts?
- How do you retrieve validation rules?

Summary

In this section, we talked about Power Apps and control and how to input text controls, etc.

PART FOUR: DEVELOPING MODEL-DRIVEN AND PORTAL APPS

CHAPTER TWELVE

BUILDING A DATAVERSE DATABASE

In this section, we are going to be going through how to build a data verse database using the power apps.

Why use dataverse?

Data verse integrates data from numerous sources into a central store, which can subsequently be used in Power Apps, Power Automate, Power BI, and Power Virtual Agents with data from Dynamics 365 apps.

The common data model

It is time-consuming to carry data from multiple systems and apps. Since you cannot share and easily understand the data, the apps or the data integration project needs custom implementation.

How much can we store?

The data verse database can hold up to 3GB of data. Also, you can choose an environment with 0GB and then enter the environment capacity analytics to view what it consumes.

The Common Data Model is a reference architecture designed to expedite this process by offering a standard data language for usage by business and analytics programs. The metadata system of the Common Data Model allows data and its meaning to be shared across apps and business processes like Power Apps, Power BI, Dynamics 365, and Azure.

The Common Data Model is a collection of standardized, extendable data schemas. Tables, attributes, semantic information, and relationships are among the predefined schemas in this collection. To facilitate data production, aggregation, and analysis, the schemas describe regularly used concepts and actions such as Account and Campaign.

The schemas of the Common Data Model can be used to guide the development of tables in Data verse. The tables that result will then be interoperable with apps and analytics that use this Common Data Model standard.

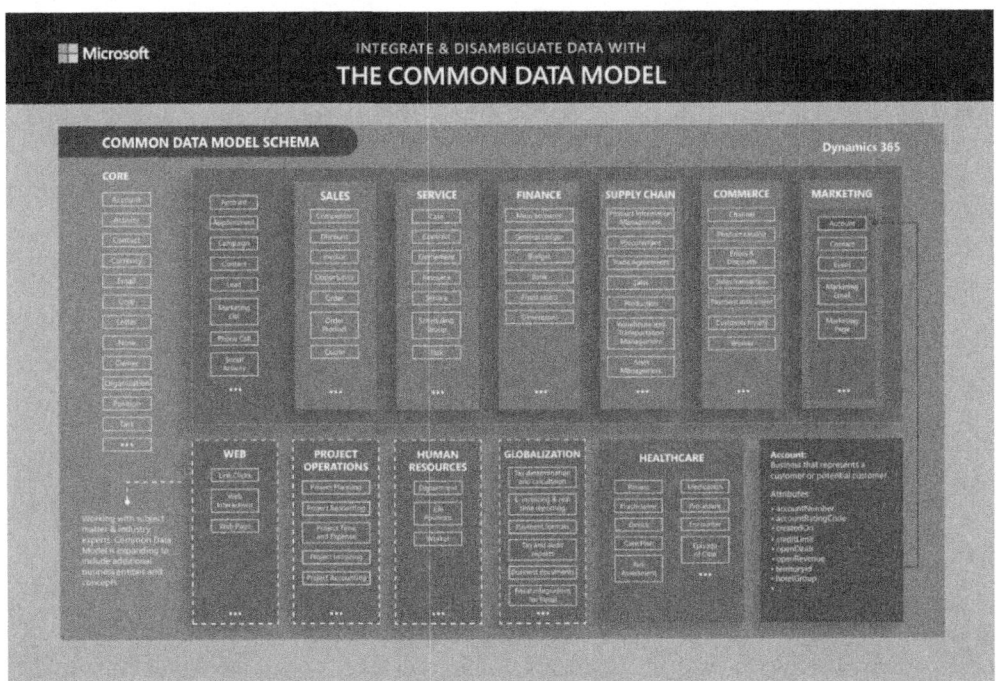

Creating a dataverse database

- Select **Environments** from the admin center's left navigation pane.
- Choose the environment to which the database will be added.
- Choose **+Add** database.
- Create a database.
- Enter the following information, like Language, currency, enable dynamics 365 apps, deploy sample apps and data, and security groups then click Add.

Listing tables

Tables are used in Dataverse to model and manage business data. Dataverse contains a collection of tables called standard tables to boost productivity. These tables are meant to capture the most typical ideas and circumstances inside a company, following best practices. The common data model is followed by the standard tables.

Standard tables are a set of tables that are regularly used across sectors, such as User and Team, and are included in Dataverse. These pre-built tables may easily be altered by adding more columns. Furthermore, Dataverse allows you to simply design your tables.

Editing tables

We are going to be taking you through the steps of editing tables in power apps dataverse.

Creating a custom table

Here is how to create a custom table

- Access make.powerapps.com.
- Select your surroundings
- Go to **Dataverse >Tables > Table Update**
- Fill in the Display Name, Plural Name, and Primary Field Name fields.
- Please enable Notes and Attachments by checking the box.

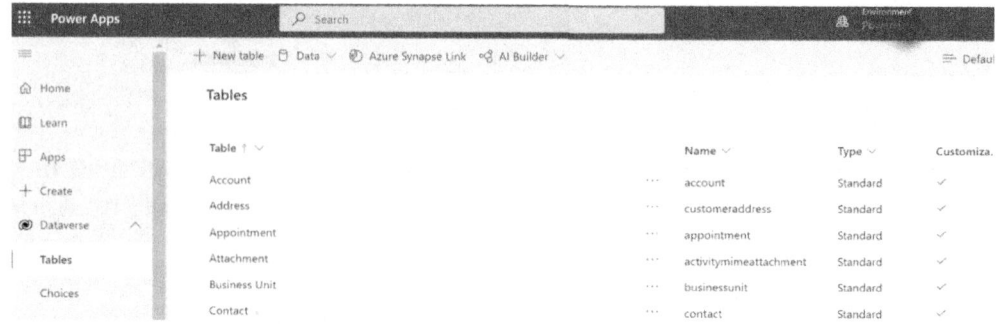

- Then choose more settings to then complete the description, the table type, and collaboration, and then create and update the settings.

Table settings

Adding a new column

Columns are separate data pieces that can be stored in a table. Developers may refer to fields as attributes. Columns in a table portraying a university course may include "Name," "Location," "Department," "Registered Students," and so on.

Columns may include several forms of data, such as numbers, strings, digital data, photos, and files. There is no need to artificially divide relational and non-relational data if they are part of the same business process or flow. Dataverse saves data in the optimum storage type for the model that was constructed.

Each of these columns can be associated with one of Dataverse's various data types.

Here is how to create a columns:

- Go to data on the left pane and choose tables.
- Choose the table that you want to add
- Then select **Add column**

Defining relationships

Data found in one table typically define the ways that the rows can be related in the diverse model.

Dataverse gives simple visual designers for defining many sorts of linkages from one table to another (or between a table and itself). Each table can have several relationships with other tables, and each table can have multiple relationships with itself.

We are going to be taking you through some of the relationship types in the upcoming section.

Setting up a one to many relationships

The most prevalent type of connection is a one-to-many relationship. A row in table A may have multiple matching rows in table B in this type of connection. However, a row in table B can only have one corresponding row in table A. The "Publishers" and "Titles" tables, for example, have a one-to-many link. That is, each publisher creates a large number of titles. However, each title is published by a single company.

If just one of the associated columns is a primary key or has a unique constraint, a one-to-many connection is formed.

The main key side of a one-to-many connection is marked by a number 1 in Access's relationship pane. An infinity symbol represents the foreign key side of a connection.

Setting up many too many relationships

A row in table A can have many matching rows in table B in a many-to-many connection, and vice versa. You define such a relationship by defining a junction table, which is the third table. The junction table's main key is made up of the foreign keys from both tables A and B. The "Authors" and "Titles" tables, for example, have a many-to-many relationship defined by a one-to-many relationship from each of these tables to the "TitleAuthors" table. The primary key of the "TitleAuthors" table is the combination of the au ID column (the main key of the "Authors" dataset) and the title ID column (the primary key of the "Titles" table).

Storing dates

You can format the dates with the date value. Here is how to do that

- Insert a Text input control called ArrivalDate and enter a date (for example, 5/10/85).
- Create a Label control called FormatDate and add its Text attribute to the following formula:

DateValue(ArrivalDate.Text)

FormatDate displays the date you typed, with the year shown as four numbers.

- Set the FormatDate Text property to this formula:

DateValue (ArrivalDate.Text, "fr")

FormatDate displays the day before the month, as expected by a French user.

- Set the Text property of FormatDate to this formula to utilize one of many built-in formats:

DateValue(ArrivalDate.Text),   DateTimeFormat.LongDate)
Text(DateValue(ArrivalDate.Text), DateTimeFormat.LongDate)

FormatDate displays the current weekday, month, day, and year.

- Set the Text property of FormatDate to this formula to use a custom format:

("yy/mm/dd") Text(DateValue(ArrivalDate.Text), ("yy/mm/dd")

Then you are going to see the date in the format that you choose.

Storing auto numbers

We are then going through auto numbers in power apps.

Log in to make.powerapps.com and open the solution you're working on. Insert the table component and the table component within the table component. Create a new field with the data type "Auto Number."

After you choose Auto Number as a data type, we may choose between text prefix, date prefix, custom prefix, counter pattern, and suffix of the numbering format.

Let us select String Prefix. Give the prefix CUST, imagine the counter has a minimum of 5 digits and a seed value of 10000.

Now, choose Done, Save Table, and Publish Solution. When you create a record for the object, the field value will be auto-populated.

Setting up a self-relationships

Assume we're establishing new student records. We will need two forms to generate a student record as well as that student's data: frmStudents (FormMode set to New) for the student's table and frmPersonalDetails (FormMode set to New) for the personal details table. The forms can be structured such that they seem to end users as a single form.

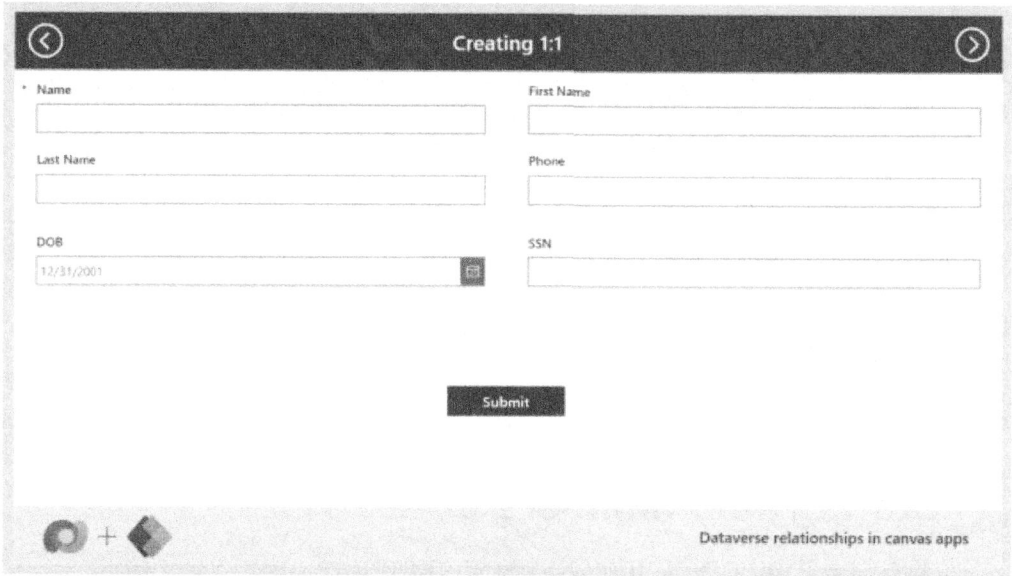

Dataverse relationships in canvas apps

- To begin, fill out frmStudents to create a new student record.
- Make use of frmStudents.LastSubmit to save the newly created student record.
- Submit frmPersonalDetails to generate a new personal detail record.
- Make use of frmPersonalDetails.
- With the frmPersonalDetails.LastSubmit to save the newly produced personal information record
- After that, join the newly established student record with the newly created personal detail record.

- Finally, link the newly formed personal detail record to the newly established student record.

Defining keys

With the Power App, there is now an easy way to see and create a table alternate key using Microsoft dataverse. Power Apps allows you to configure the most popular choices, however, certain options can only be adjusted through the solution explorer.

First, you have to view the alternate keys:

- Log into the power apps and enter **data** then choose **tables** then select the table you will like to see
- Then choose the keys so that you can see the list of all of the alternate keys defined

Choices

The Choices function returns a table containing all of the potential values for a lookup column.

Use the Choices function to provide a list of options for your user to choose from. In edit forms, this feature is frequently used with the Combo box control.

Creating sets of choices

- Log In to the power then go to the **data** section. Then choose **tables** from the left navigation table.

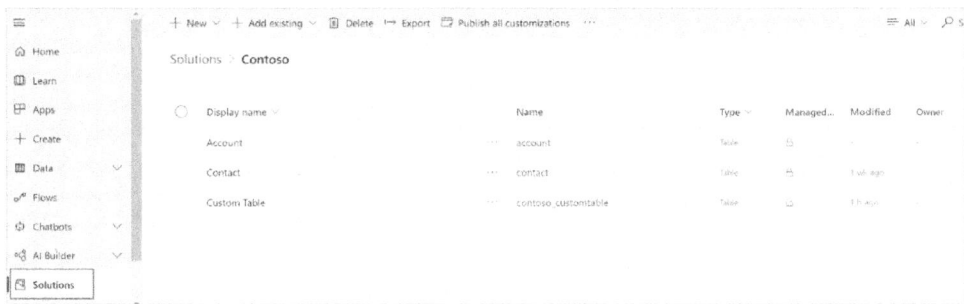

- Select an existing table by clicking or tapping it, or Make a new table.
- By choosing Add column, you may add a new column to your table.
- Enter the Display name for your column in the new column panel; the Name will be auto-populated and used as the unique name for your column. While showing this column to your customers, the Display name is utilized; the Name is used when creating your app, in expressions and formulae.
- Select Choice or Multi Select Choice from the Data type drop-down menu.

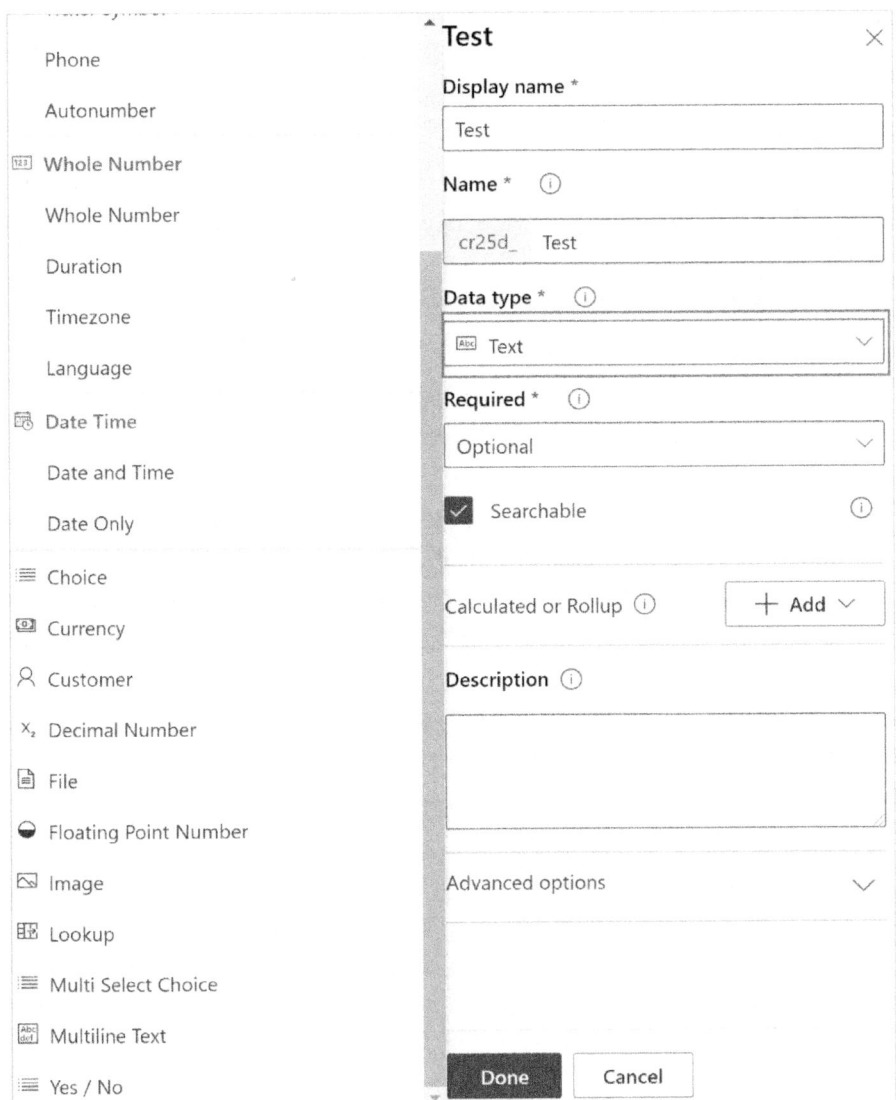

- From the **Choice** drop-down list choose the **New choice**
- A new panel will appear to allow you to make your selection; the Display name and Name will be based on the name of the column but may be modified if necessary. To begin building your list of possibilities, click Add new item. Rep this process until all of your things have been made.
- After entering the items, choose to **Save** to then create the choice.
- Then select done for the panel to close and **Save table** so that the save table to save the Microsoft data verse.

Defining calculated and rollup columns

By monitoring critical business KPIs, rollup columns assist users in gaining insights from data. A rollup column includes an aggregate value calculated across all rows connected to a certain row. This covers both normal and activity tables like emails and appointments.

Creating calculated columns

- Log in to Power Apps.
- Expand Data and then Tables.
- Open the desired table, navigate to the Columns section, and then click Add Column.
- Provide the necessary column information, such as the Display name, Name, and Data type.
- If the data type is one of those that support calculations, you may convert the column to a calculated column by going to **Add > Calculation.**
- When you pick Calculation, you are asked to save the modifications to the table. Select Save from the Pending changes dialog.
- Open the column you saved in the previous step in the Columns box.
- Select Open computation from the column properties box.
- In the calculated column definition editor, notice that the new calculated column has been created, but no formula has been set. The calculated column definition consists of two sections: **CONDITION** and **ACTION**.

- Select **Add condition** in the Condition section to specify a table, column, operator, type, and value. You can select a current table or a related table from the Table selection box. The Column dropdown box contains a list of all possible columns for the table. Depending on the operator, you may be required to specify type and value. Using the AND and OR operators, you may define several criteria. When you're through setting the condition, click the Save condition button.
- After specifying the criteria, choose to **Add action** in the Action section to provide the formula for the computed column. When you've completed specifying the action, check the box **Save condition.**

Review Question

- How do you create a virtual table?
- How do you create sets of choices?
- What is a choice function?

Summary

In this section, we delved into the world of dataverse and we hope that now, you are privy to the ins and outs of it.

CHAPTER THIRTEEN

DEVELOPING A MODEL-DRIVEN APP

Introducing the model-driven apps

Model-driven apps use the new Unified Interface client, which offers a responsive, accessible design that works in browsers and on major mobile devices. This app type combines numerous component types, including dashboards, forms, views, charts, and business processes, to provide an excellent user interface. You are already familiar with the PowerApps platform and Model-driven Apps if you are familiar with the Dynamics 365 platform.

Model-driven applications are created and managed through the PowerApps Portal in the same way that canvas apps are. A mode switch in the lower left corner allows you to move between canvas and model-driven design modes.

The model-driven mode displays a navigation pane containing model-driven app-related material. The Home tab contains access to crucial elements related to data modeling, business process creation, and app creation. After a PowerApps trial environment is set up, it comes with three example apps. Key elements of model-driven apps are highlighted in the Innovation Challenge, Fundraiser, and Asset Checkout demos.

Demonstration of a basic app

When you create or change a model-driven app, the App Designer appears, allowing you to define navigation in a site map, dashboards, business processes, forms, and views.

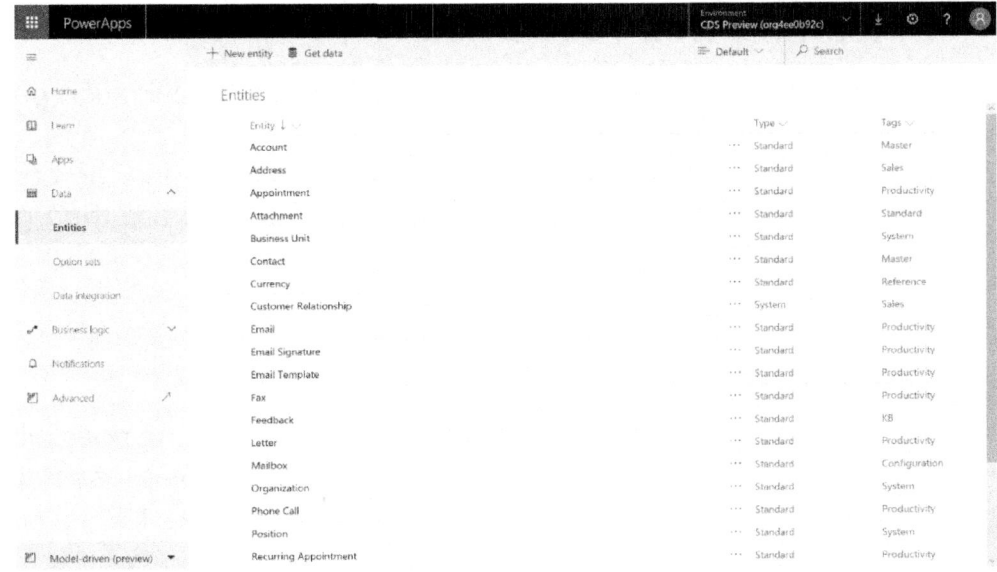

Creating an app

It is better to create model-driven apps based on solutions. Solutions are packages that contain dataverse tables, views, apps, forms, flows, and other parts. When you build it with solutions, then you can then take it around environments. And you can also preserve copies in the source control repository.

- Go to the left navigation pane, select **Solutions**, and then **New solution**.
- Name the solution in the **Display name**. The account table that will be included in your model-driven app is then added.
- The first pick add **existing**, then **Table** in your solution.
- Select the **Account** table from the Add existing table's page, then click **Next**.
- Select **Include all components**, followed by Add.
  Then you're ready to build a model-driven app now that you've created a solution and added the account table to it.
- Select **New** in your solution, then **App**, and then **Model-driven app**.
- Give the app a name

Uploading web resources

- Sign in to Power Apps, and then go to the left navigation pane and click **Solutions**
- Go to an unmanaged solution, click Add existing in the command bar, then **More**, and finally **Web** resource. You are then going to see all of the web resources.
- Choose the web resource and choose to **Add.**

Exploring the designer

You can use the sample app in other to go through the possibilities for design. The sample apps, use fake data in other to represent the real-world possibility.

The sample apps that you have is determined by the provision of the environment database. To then install the sample app, you need to first create the trial environment and a trial database. Then make sure that you choose. **Deploy sample apps and data.**

Showing lists of data

Forms offer the user interface that users use to interact with the data they need to accomplish what they want to do in the model-driven apps. It is critical that the forms you use be structured so that they can quickly access or enter the data they require.

Creating and editing records

One of the most important aspects of model-driven apps are things like creating tables, data vies, and creating and editing a form.

Before you start building forms, make sure you have access to all of the columns you need to address your business problem. You should also grasp how to organize these in terms of sections and tabs. In general, how complex your forms will mirror the number of columns in your table as well as how complex the business process is.

Validating data

You must store your data correctly when you are developing an app. You do not have to wait till the time that you want to submit the data. The first thing that you want to do is to validate the form fields once a user exits the field and goes to the next one.

There are two ways to validate data. You can do it after you submit the form or once a user leaves the current field and goes into the next one.

There are two functions for the validation and they are the ISMATCH and VALIDATE

The VALIDATE function looks for the values of a column and accesses if the complete record has been validated for a specific data source.

Here is the syntax

Validate(DataSource, Column, Value)

Validate(DataSource, OriginalRecord, Updates)

Then you can use ISMATCH to see if a string matches a pattern.

IsMatch(Text, Pattern [, Options]) for example you can use this to text if a user has inputted hello IsMatch(TextInput1.Text, "Hello")

Building dashboards

- Login to the power apps
- Open the desired solution after selecting Solutions.
- Pick New from the toolbar, then **Dashboard**, and then select one of the layouts below. 2-column overview
- 3-column overview (varied width)
- 3-column overview
- Power BI embedded
- 4-column overview

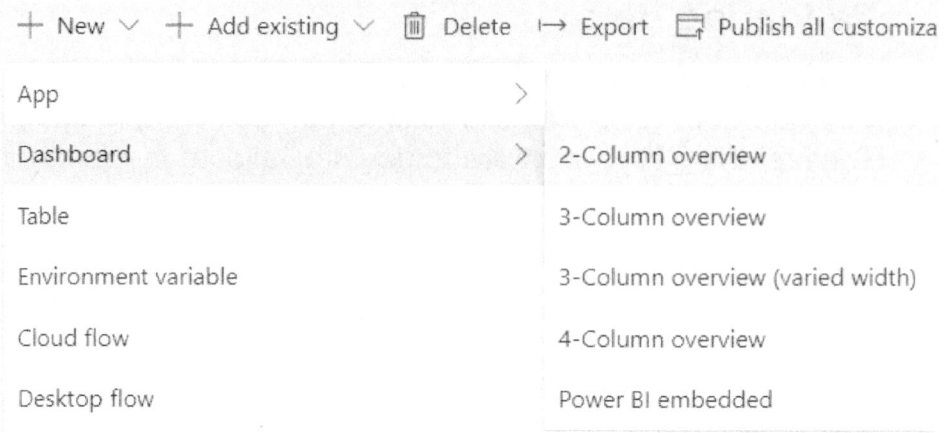

- Enter a name for the dashboard on the Dashboard: **New** page.
- Choose a component region, then the icon for the chart or a list. A dashboard can have up to six components.
- If you want to then add a chart, click the chart icon on the dashboard canvas tile where you want the chart to appear. Select settings for the View, Row Type, and Chart in the Add Component dialog. Then click the Add button to add the chart to the dashboard.
- When you're through adding dashboard components, click Save and then Close.
- Select **Publish** from the solution toolbar.

Customizing model-driven app

You can use the tools in the power apps in other to customize a model-driven app.

You can use the following to customize Power Apps.

- Solution Explorer
- Settings in the web app
- Reporting services.

EMBEDDED CANVAS APPS: OVERVIEW

Makers may bring the power of canvas applications to their model-driven forms by embedding them. Using integrated canvas applications, you can create good visual sections on forms and show data from several sources alongside Microsoft Dataverse data.

Canvas applications, like other custom controls, may be integrated into model-driven forms. The embedded canvas app provides powerful data integration features that allow it to get contextual information from a model-driven form.

Customizing apps with JavaScript

There is also a way to customize applications with JavaScript. There are three areas you can work with.

- Form Script event handlers: Form event handlers can be configured to invoke practical tasks in JavaScript web resources.
- Commands for the command bar (ribbon): To specify actions that invoke functions specified inside JavaScript web resources, you should use CustomRule> or JavaScriptFunction> components.
- Web resources with IFRAMEs: JavaScript web resources can be used within HTML web resources. IFRAMES with inter scripting enabled, or scripts within HTML web resources provided in a form may link with the described Xrm. Page or Xrm. A parent reference is used to access utility methods within the form.

Activity/ Review Question

We are going to be giving you an example of Power App validation. We are going to be using these columns on a SharePoint list.
- Employee name
- Employee ID
- Email address
- Age
- Phone

Here is then how to integrate the required field validation with the Power App.

- Choose a card
- Choose to unlock to alter attributes from the advanced options.

- Then go to the required property of the card and change it to true.
- When you submit the power apps required field validation this is how it looks.

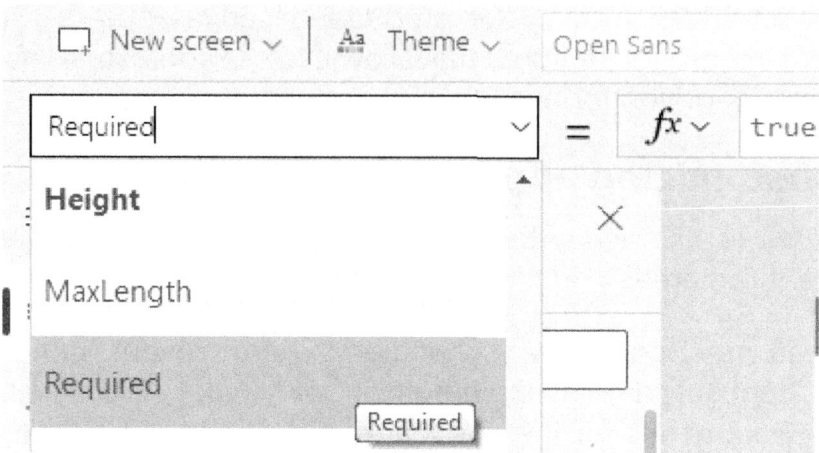

- How do you create an app?
- How do you build a dashboard?
- How do you Upload web resources?

Summary

In this section, we delved into model-driven apps and we said that we can embed canvas apps in them. Furthermore, they are responsive and accessible.

CHAPTER FOURTEEN

BUILDING A PORTAL APP

Introducing

This is one of the platforms produced by Microsoft and it allows businesses to create personalized websites for users to be able to interact with the selective Dynamics 365 data and capabilities.

Pricing

The power app pricing cuts across all platforms within the Microsoft power app.

Creating a portal

- Access Power Apps by logging in.
- Select **Blank app** from **Create your app**.

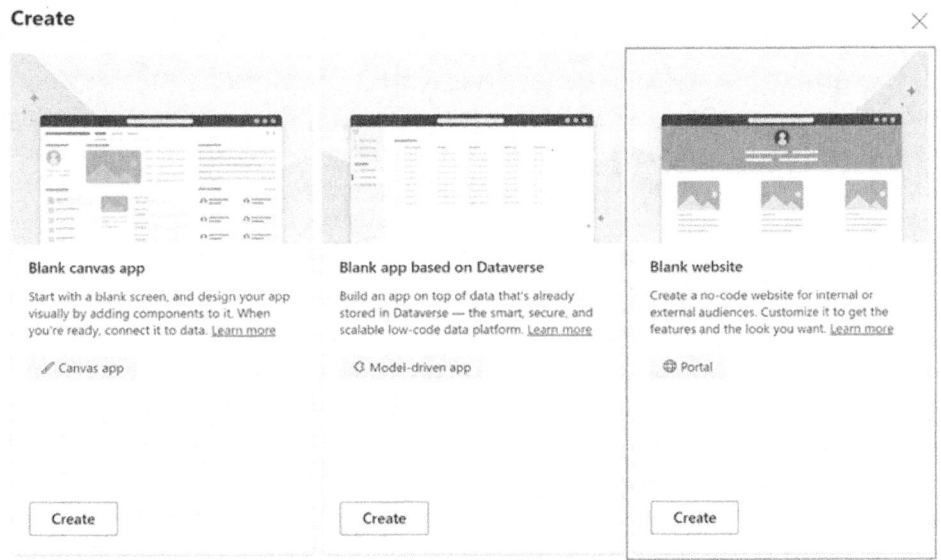

- Choose to **Create** in the **Blank website** menu.
- If the selected environment lacks portal prerequisites, a notice appears in the **Portal from a blank** window recommending that you choose another environment or build a new one.
- Make a new environment message.
- If you want to keep the present environment, input the necessary information in the window as described in the following steps. If you want to make a new environment, see Make a new environment.
- Enter a name for the **Portal**, the website address, and a language from the drop-down list in the Portal from Blank box.
- Once you are done, you can select create.

Managing Portal Trials

A gateway is always built as a test. A trial gateway, which expires after 30 days, is excellent for testing out its features for free. The gateway is suspended and shut off when it expires. The trial gateway gets erased seven days after it is discontinued. You'll be alerted by toast alerts and email at each stage of the portal's lifecycle—nearing suspension, suspended, erased, and converted from trial to production.

You may convert a trial to a production portal as an administrator. When converting a portal trial to a production portal, make sure that the environment is likewise in production mode. When you are in a trial environment, you cannot convert portals in trial to production portals.

Working with the designer

When developing and creating portals, you should pay attention to certain elements. Implementing a portal solution necessitates an understanding of the customer's individual business requirements and demands. A good portal should be simple and well-designed, as well as useful in terms of geographical location, languages, and accessibility requirements. Additionally, portal creators should guarantee that portal metadata is consistently as well as structurally supported to source control and distributed to testing and production environments.

Adding pages

The first thing that you have to do is to edit the portal so that you can open it in the Power App portal studio.

- Go to the command bar and choose a **New page** then you can then select a page from the **Layouts** or the **Fixed layout**

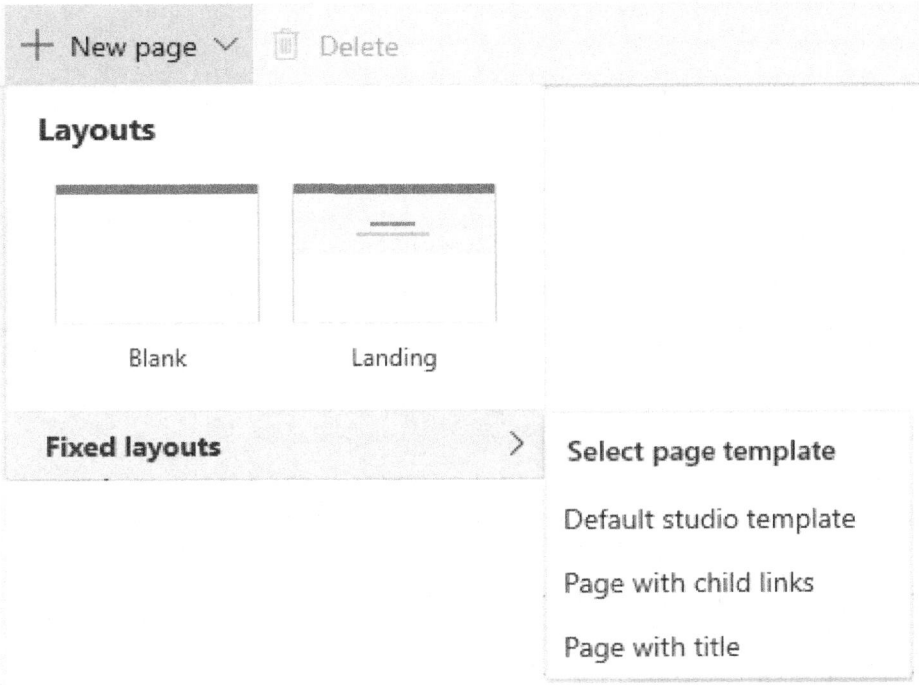

- Go to the properties pane then enter the name of the page, the partial URL, and the template.

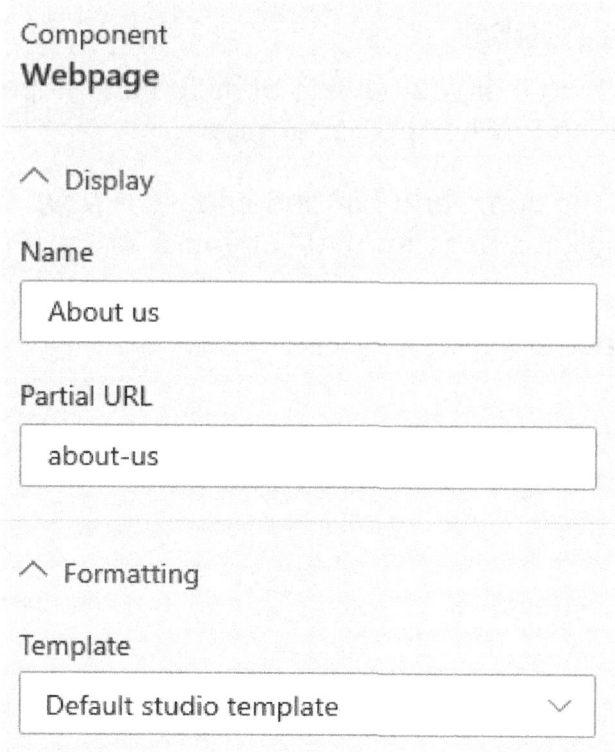

- Then the webpage that you create will then be added and also the hierarchy is going to be seen when you go to the pages and navigation pane. If you want to see the page, choose **Pages and Navigation** on the tool belt.

Designing web pages

After creating a webpage, you can also manage them. Here are the steps.

The first thing to do as usual is to edit the portal so that it can then run on the **Power app portal studio.**

- Then choose **Pages and navigation** when you enter the tool belt. You are going to find it on the left side of the screen.
- Then go to the page that you want to manage and hover above it to reveal the ellipsis.
- Then in the context menu, you can choose a required action.

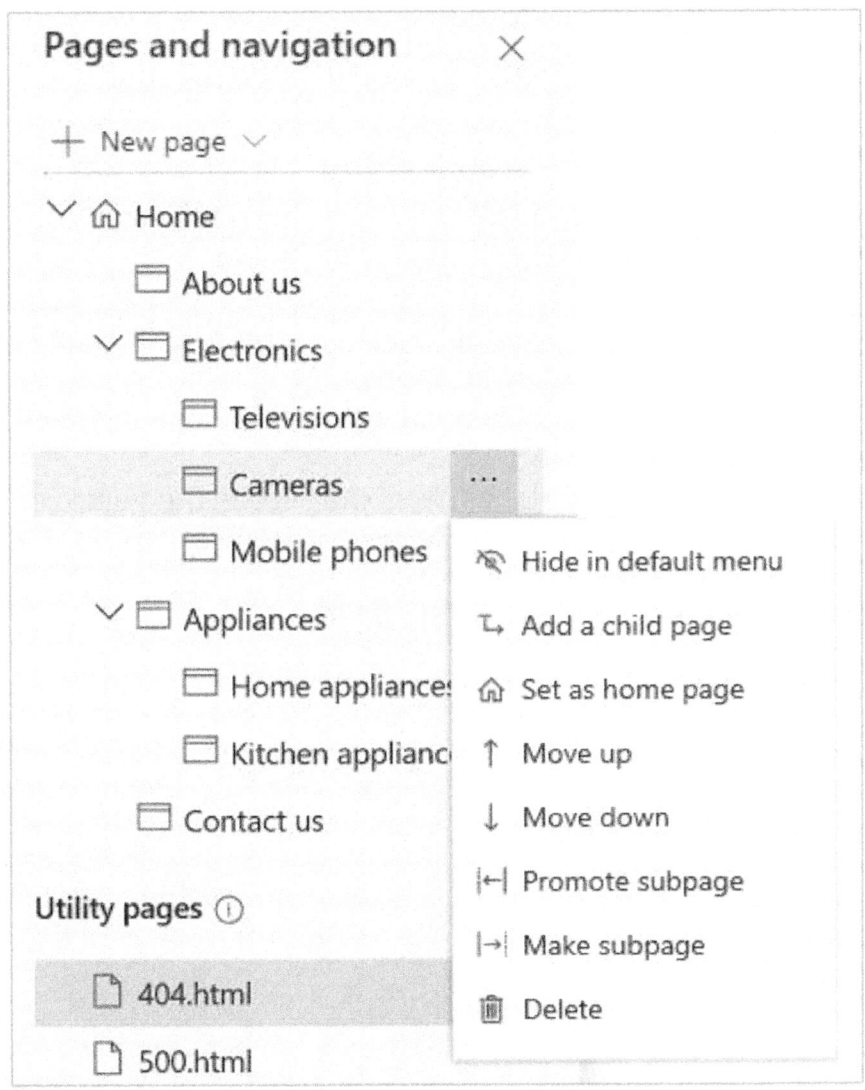

Adding text and images

Now when you have a text box component you can add text to the portal page.

1. The first thing to do is to edit the portal so that you can then open it in the power app portal studio.
2. Then pick the page where you will like the component.
3. Select an element that you can edit from the canvas.

4. Then choose **Components.**
5. When you are in the portal component, choose **Text.**
6. Then enter the text required into the text box.

Adding section

1. The first thing to do is to edit the portal so that you can then open it in the power app portal studio.
2. Then pick the page that you will like the component to be in.
3. Select an element that you can edit from the canvas.
4. Then choose **Components.**
5. Then go to the section layout and choose the section type that you want to insert.
6. Then go to the right side of the screen then enter or choose any of these. **Min height, Alignment, Background, Fill, Image**

MANAGING A PORTAL APP

The anatomy of a web page

The image below shows you the parts of a web page.

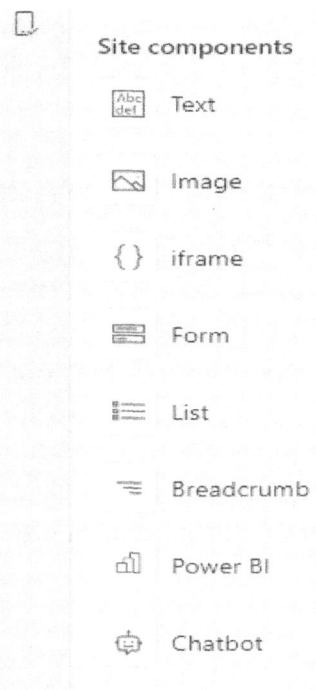

Site components

Text

Image

iframe

Form

List

Breadcrumb

Power BI

Chatbot

Understanding page templates

Just the way web pages are nodes in your portal's sitemap that reflect information that portal users may access, page templates are actual app pages that allow you to keep a consistent display and feel across your whole website. Page templates are created using ASP.NET pages, master pages, CSS, user controls, and server controls.

Web templates

A gateway comes with a set of prebuilt web layouts. As designers encounter more complicated circumstances, the liquid template language is the way to go to construct web templates that meet project specifications.

Securing a portal

The idea of presenting Dataverse on a public webpage appeals to a variety of business requirements. However, extreme caution is required to avoid disclosing private or sensitive data. This module will assist you in understanding and configuring portal security to safeguard dynamic and static information while restricting visibility to specified audiences.

Configuring authentication providers

Each authorized portal user in Power Apps portals is linked to a contact in Microsoft Dataverse. To get access beyond those granted to unauthenticated users, portal users must be allocated web roles. Specify the webpage access and website access control rules for a web role to set its permissions. Portals allow the portal users to sign in using an external account of their choosing based on ASP.NET Identity. Though not encouraged, portals also enable users to sign in using a local contact membership provider-based account.

Setting up web roles

After configuring a contact to utilize the portal, it must be assigned one or more web roles to execute any specific operations or access any protected material on the site. To visit a restricted page, for example, the contact must be assigned to a role that has read access to that page. To publish new material, the contact must be assigned to a role with content publishing privileges.

Here is how to create a web role:

- Start the Portal Management application.
- Navigate to **Portals > Web Roles**. You may also access the Web Roles page when you go to the   Share pane.
- Choose **New**.
- Fill in the blanks with the right values.
- Choose **Save**.

Controlling access to web pages

If you want to control the permission for access to web pages here is what you are going to do.

- Launch the Portal Management application.
- Navigate to **Portals > Web Access Permissions**.

- Choose **New**.
- Enter your name, the website, and the appropriate permissions under General.

Controlling access to data verse

Here are the things that you must know about how the security model in Dataverse works.

- Azure Active Directory authenticates users (Azure AD).
- The first control-gate to gaining access to Power Apps components is licensing.
- Security roles in the context of environments govern the ability to build applications and flows.
- Sharing the application with the user controls the user's access to see and utilize apps. Canvas apps are shared directly with a user or Azure AD group, but they are still subject to Dataverse security roles. Dataverse security roles are used to share model-driven programs.
- Environments serve as security boundaries, enabling distinct security requirements to be enforced in each.
- When apps utilize connectors in Flows or Canvas, the exact connections credentials and accompanying service entitlements define permissions.

Clearing the cache

Here are the steps to clear a server-side cache

- The first thing to do is sign into the portal as an administrator.
- Then go to the following URL <portal_path>/_services/about.
- Choose **Clear cache**

Then the servers side cache will be deleted and the data is going to be reloaded to the Dataverse

Portals

Details

Geo	
Org Id	
Portal Id	
Portal Type	
Tenant Id	

Tools

Clear Cache | Warning: Clearing the cache will result in a temporary slowness in your portal as it reloads data from Dynamics 365

Activity

- How do you create a power app portal?
- What does it mean to secure a portal?
- How do you configure authentication providers?

Summary

In this section, we went through power app portals, and also we got through some of the technicalities of building a power app portal and also the components of it.

CHAPTER FIFTEEN

RETRIEVING DATA FROM THE PORTAL APP

In this section, we are going to be taking you through how to retrieve data from a portal app.

Adding a new record

Here is how to add list components:

- To launch the portal in Power Apps portals Studio, edit it.
- Choose the page where you want to add the part.
- Choose an editable component from the canvas.
- From the left side of the screen, select the **Components** icon.
- Select **List** from the Portal components menu.
- Select one of the following choices inside the properties pane just on the right side of the screen: you can create a new list or you can use the existing list.

Editing a record

To edit a table, the first thing to do is to choose the table that you will like to edit then choose the properties from the command bar to then edit the properties of the table.

Viewing a record

To view tables in power apps the first thing to do is to sign into the power apps and enter **Data** then **Tables.** Then you are going to see a list of the table displayed.

Listing data

Without requiring a developer to expose the grid inside the portal, you may add a webpage that renders a list of records that use the data-driven configuration known as a list. You may expose records for portal display by utilizing lists.

If there are more records than the chosen number of pages, the grid will be paginated and enable sorting. If Web Page for Details View has been provided, all records will have a link to the page, and its ID as well as the ID Query String Parameter Name will be included in the query string. Additionally, the list supports several perspectives. When multiple views are provided, you are then going to see a drop-down list you can choose from.

The list comes with a relationship to the webpage and also different properties that you can control the initialization of the list of records inside the portal. The relationship that exists between the webpage then makes for a dynamic way to retrieve list definitions for specific page nodes inside the website. To then see the existing table views or to then create a brand new table view, you can enter **Portals** and choose a **List.**

Creating web forms

In Power Apps Portals, Web Forms let you create multi-page wizard-style forms. The simplest online forms follow a single wizard route where each step may only possibly be followed by one subsequent step. However, based on the information given in earlier phases, you might wish to have various wizard pathways for more complicated circumstances.

The specific situation where you can use web forms is when building registration for the portal. In one instance, customers may input their membership number to request an invitation code. Then you build a web form, and the first question requested a membership number from us. Whether the user supplied a legitimate membership number or not, we wanted the consequent step can behave differently.

Creating a portal web form

The advanced form has links to websites and a step that regulates how the form is initialized inside the portal. The form specification for a certain page node inside the website may be dynamically retrieved thanks to the relationships to the webpage.

The additional settings on the advanced form record itself manage the overall preferences for the multi-step procedure, such as whether or not you want to show a progress bar.

Launch the Portal Management app then select **Portals > Advanced Forms** to build new advanced forms or inspect those that already exist.

Defining web form steps

The Advanced Form Step offers the user interface flow logic for the form, including stages and conditional splitting. It also offered information about additional behaviors and the form rendering.

Each of the advanced forms can be seen in the portal and they have a few more steps. These steps also have some properties that they have in common. They have pointers that take you to the consequent step. And the terminal steps do not come with next time. Making them the final step for the advanced form.

Configure the form fields

The configuration of advanced form subgrids is the same as that of basic form subgrids: To include configuration metadata, you must first build a record for the Advanced form step that has a subgrid.

It's simple to add subgrids to a form you administer just on the portal. Simply use the built-in form designer to add the subgrid to the form you're managing. When the option to display just related entries was selected, the grid will utilize the view that's been provided in the Microsoft Dataverse form designer, show a search box if it is enabled, and even take account of table permissions for portals. Displaying a read-only list of records is as easy as it gets.

To then add sun grid metadata into the forms, you have to enter the **basic form metadata** either through the top drop-down list or through the subgrid that is on the main form for the record you are working with.

If you want to add a new record choose **Add new basic from metadata.**

Then to edit the existing record, choose one of the records on the grid. When you choose **Subgrid** as a **type** value, then you will see another attribute, which is the **subgrid name.**

When you choose **Subgrid** from the form editor, then you are going to see the properties window. It has a name field that you can use to assign inside the **subgrid name** field from the basic form metadata record.

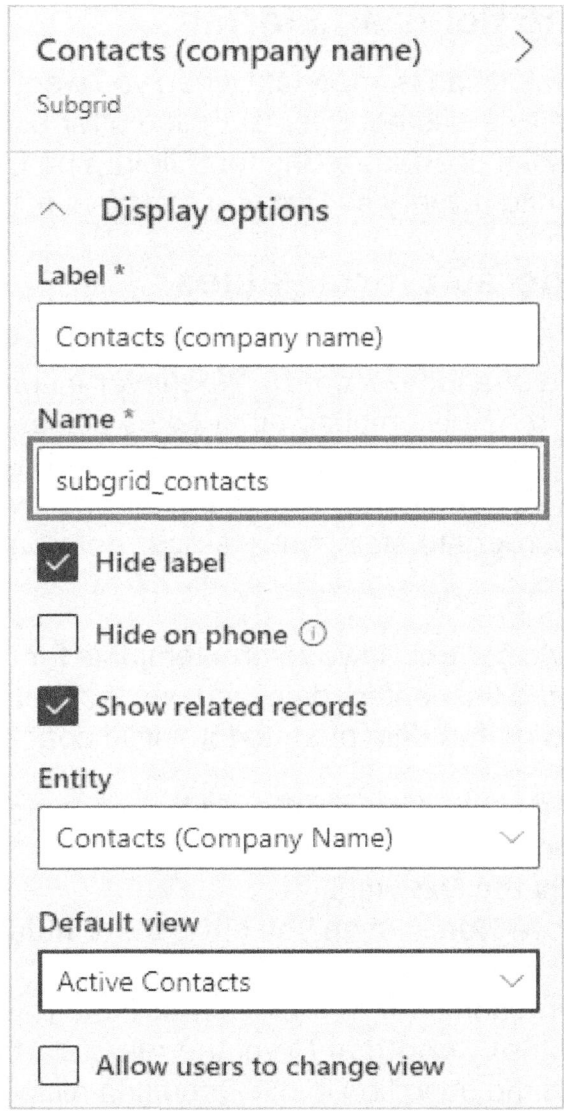

The subgrid configuration parameters are displayed when a valid subgrid name is provided. Only the Basic Settings are shown by default. To see more settings, choose **Advanced** Settings.

Most options are presented flattened by default to conserve space.

Validating fields and forms

The client validation is important when you want to alert the user when some field value has not been supplied after users select the **Submit** button or make changes to the form field. You can then add a custom JavaScript and JQuery so that you can have a custom field validation.

Setting default form values

A rule can be used to determine a control's default value depending on the value of another control. Whenever a condition inside the form is satisfied, a rule is an action that takes place. As an illustration, you may create a form template using two controls—one for the state and one for the ZIP Code. The state control is automatically prepopulated with the appropriate state when a user enters a ZIP Code in the ZIP Code control.

You need two controls in your form template for this technique to work: one where the user enters data, and one that gets filled with the default value based on the data put into the initial control.

1. First double click on the control on which the default value is based.
2. Select the **Data** tab.
3. Choose **Rules** when you enter the **Validation and rules.**
4. Click **Add** in the Rules dialog box.
5. Enter a name for the rule in the Name box.
6. Click **Set Condition** to set the rule's start and end times.
7. Insert the condition in the Condition dialog box, then select **OK**.
8. Select **Add Actions** by clicking the **Rule** dialog box.
9. Set a field's value by clicking it in the **Action** list.
10. In the Select a Field or Group dialog, select the control with the default value you wish to set after clicking adjacent to a Field box.
11. Type a value into the Value box, hit OK, as well as the value will be used as the default value.
12. Click Insert Formula, type an XPath expression to construct the default value inside the Insert Formula dialog box, then select OK.

13. Press CTRL+SHIFT+B or select Preview in the Standard toolbar to preview your changes.

Searching data

In portals, dataverse search provides quick and thorough search results organized by relevance. Model-driven apps as well as other Microsoft Power Platform services developed on Microsoft Dataverse use the same search function, which is called Dataverse search. Add the site option Search/EnableDataverseSearch and change that to true to allow Dataverse search. If this option is disabled or not present at all, Lucene.NET search will be activated in its place.

Then you can enable the data verse search

1. The first step is to activate the Dataverse search.
2. Add the search site settings after that.
3. Next, you must either build or validate the portal search view.
4. Create table permission after that.
5. Add record information to the webpage.
6. After that, place a location marker on the record details page.
7. Check the Dataverse search features.

Customizing content

To first create the custom portal management app, the first thing to do is

1. Sign in to the Power Apps.
2. Then pick **Create** inside the left navigation pane.
3. Then choose a **Model-driven app from blank.**

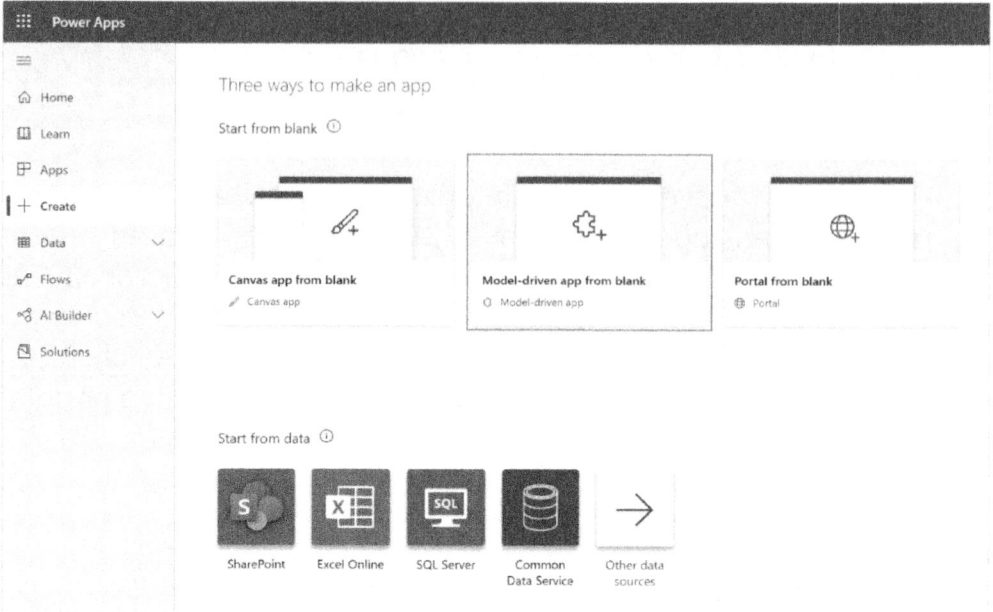

4. Then pick **Create.**
5. The Create button launches the Create a New App form in the app designer: app creator.
6. For the app's name, type it in. As an illustration, Portal Management (custom)

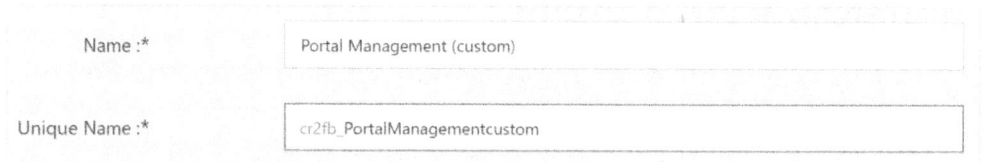

| Name :* | Portal Management (custom) |
| Unique Name :* | cr2fb_PortalManagementcustom |

The app's Unique Name gets updated automatically.

7. If necessary, include a description.
8. Uncheck Use Default Image for Icon and use adx nav portals 32.png as the image file:

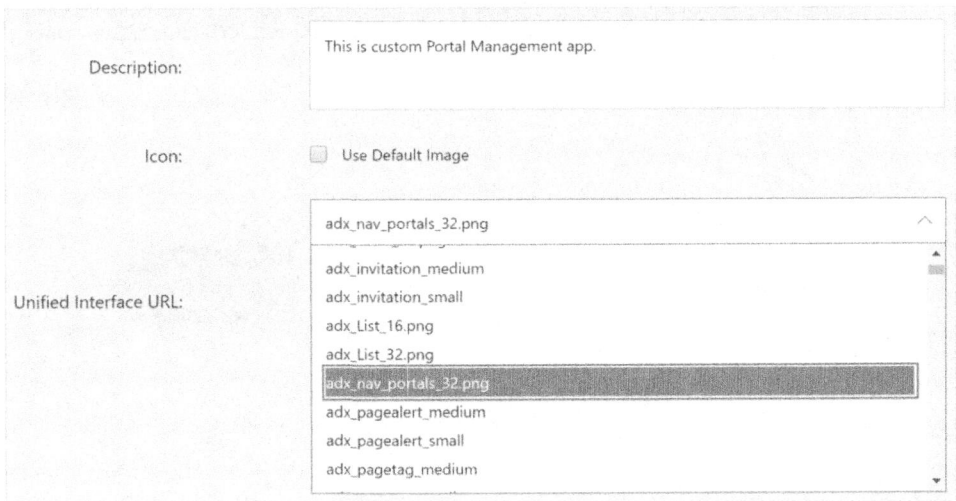

9. Check to **Use existing solution to create the app.**

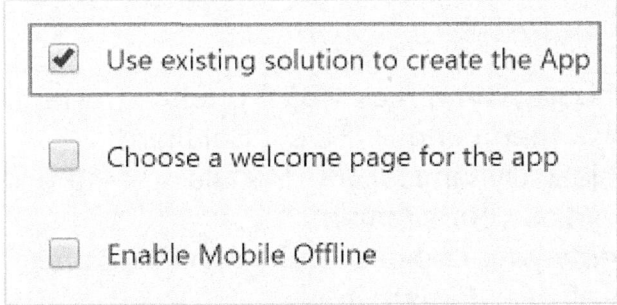

10. Verify every setting, then click **Next**.

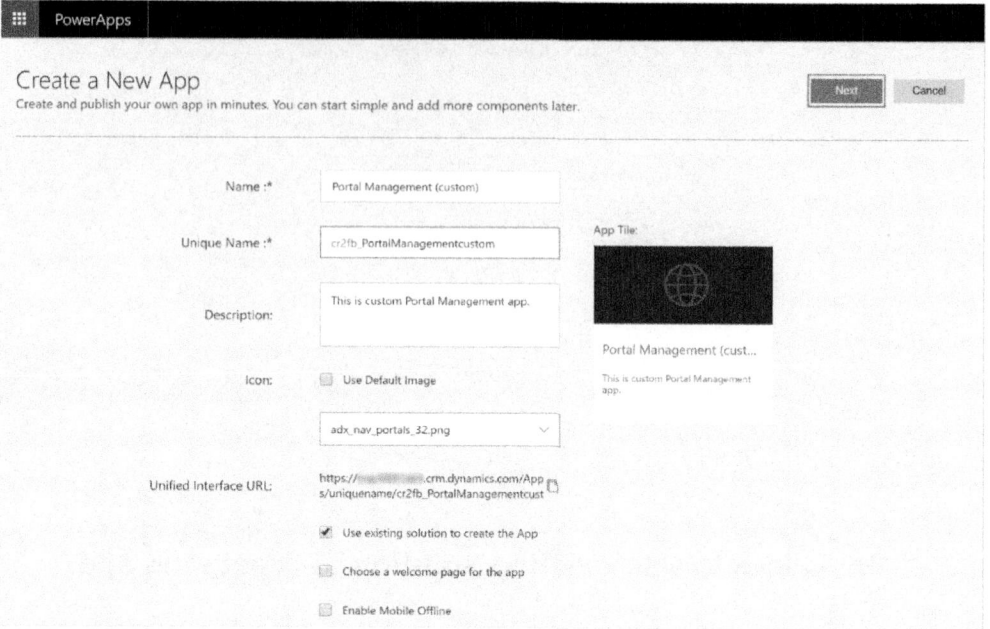

11. Choose **Dynamics 365** Portals - Portal base from the drop-down menu under "Select Solution":

12. Select Dynamics 365 Portals from the drop-down menu to serve as your sitemap:

13. Verify your choices, and then click **Done**.

14. Verify, the **Finish**.

15. Once the app then opens in the **App designer,** you can choose to **Publish.**

16. Close the App Designer tab in the browser.

17. Power Apps open.

18. From the left menu, choose **Apps**.

19. The newly developed custom app for Portal Management is shown here:

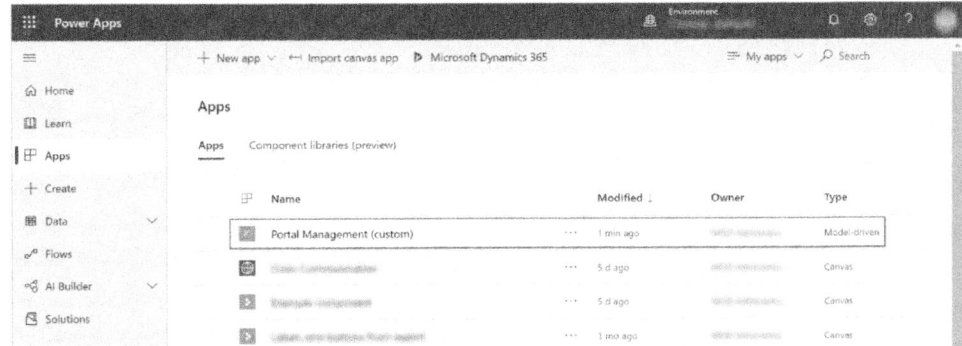

20. Then you can finally hover above the new app and choose to open the new **Portal Management.**

Liquid language

Open-source Liquid is a template language that is built into Microsoft Power Apps portals. It serves as a link between the HTML or text output given to the browser and Dataverse. The liquid may be used to build several unique layouts and add dynamic content to pages. Additionally, Liquid only grants access to the actions and data that the portals have specifically authorized.

Retrieving the current user

You can use the user function in the power app to get the information of the current user. The syntax for this is User() this will give all of the information about the user.

Uploading JavaScript files

We are going to use the image below as a resource for uploading a JavaScript file.

Sample Script
Web File

General   Administration   **Notes**   Related

Timeline

🔍 Search timeline

✏️ Enter a note...

DD 📝 Note modified by Debajit Dutta

📎 samplescript

So to then refer to it as my web template, then you can use this script reference.

```
<script type="text/javascript" src="~/samplescript.js" ></script>
```

Review Question

- How do you create a portal?
- How do you configure a form field?
- How do you upload Java script files?

Summary

In this section, we have gone through the simple steps of creating portal apps and went into the word of Dataverse, web forms, etc. we hope that you can then create one.

PART FIVE: ENHANCING APPS

CHAPTER SIXTEEN

WORKING WITH IMAGES AND MEDIA

In this chapter, we are going to be working with images while using the power apps.

Choosing where to store the images

There are three options to store images that you have.

- You can store the images as attachments to the items.
- Store them in a share point library.
- And you can write them on a multi-line text field.

Setting up a data source

- To open the Data window, choose **Connect to Data** in the center pane.
- Choose **View > Data sources** to open the same pane if the app already existed and there was a control on the screen.
- Choose **Add data source**.
- If the connection you're looking for is in the list of connections after expanding **Connectors**, choose it to add it to the app. If not, move on to the next step. Instead, select a table from the list of tables to connect to one in Microsoft Dataverse.

- Find or choose a connector, such as SharePoint, to start a new connection.

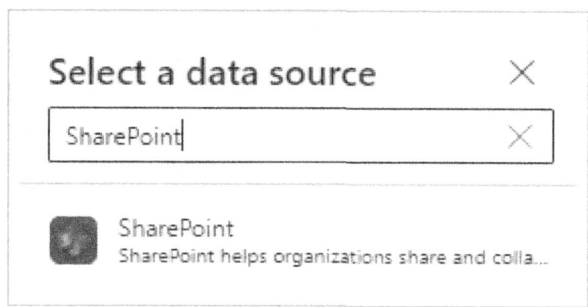

- To build the connection and add it to your app, select **Create**.

Setting up an Excel spreadsheet

- The first thing to do is to create the data on the Excel table and format it.
- Then save the file to a cloud location.
- Then choose **Excel** as a data source. You can do this in two ways.
- The first method is to start with Excel.
  By using data from an Excel file to construct a canvas app, you can immediately include Excel and produce a three-screen application. When you're done, you'll have an application and see that your data source has been added with a OneDrive connector in the Data Source pane.

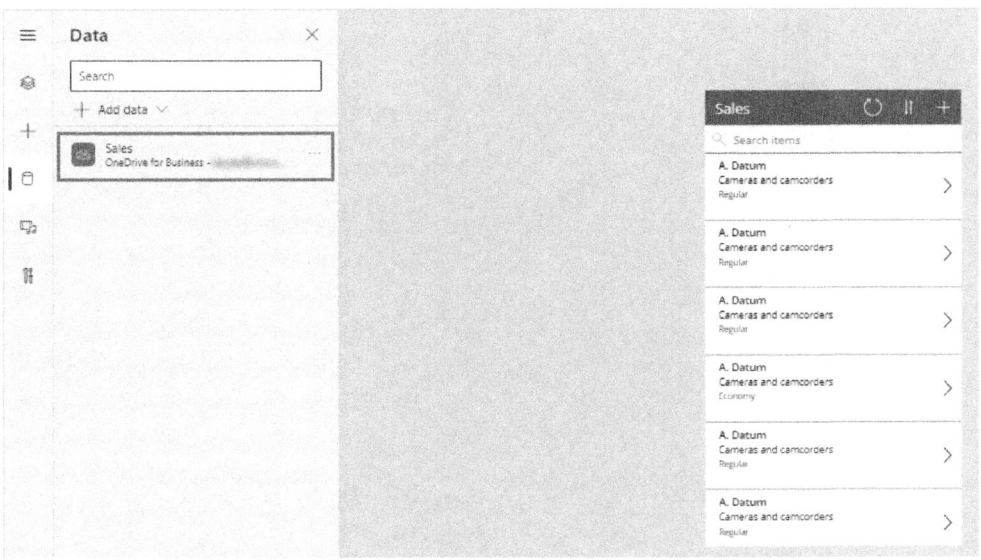

Then, you can start from excel with the new connector. Build an app from new in Excel first if you wish to start using data from the more recent connection and Excel data. Drop OneDrive or a different cloud data source that contains your Excel file after that, and then reconnect to Excel Online (Business) by using a new connection. The Power Apps will access the revised data source and function without further modification because the table names and files are identical.

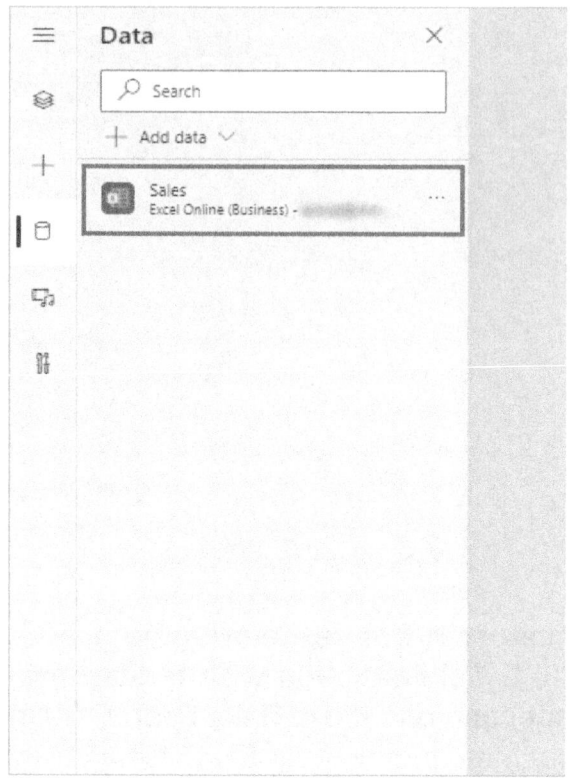

- The other method is by adding a new data source. To add a new Excel data source, you can either construct a brand-new app from scratch or make changes to an already-existing one.
  Users of OneDrive for Business, and Microsoft 365 Groups may interact with Excel files in the documents library by using the Excel Online (Business) Connector.
- The previous Excel connection had several restrictions, along with the reality that only one person could operate on the Excel file at once and that documents on a SharePoint site couldn't be accessed (preview).
  The upgraded Excel Online (Business) Connector can connect with all common document libraries, including OneDrive for Business, and Microsoft 365 Groups. It is also quicker and more reliable, supports multiple users, and is user-friendly.
  Locate the Excel Online (Business) connector from the list of connectors to add Excel as a data source.

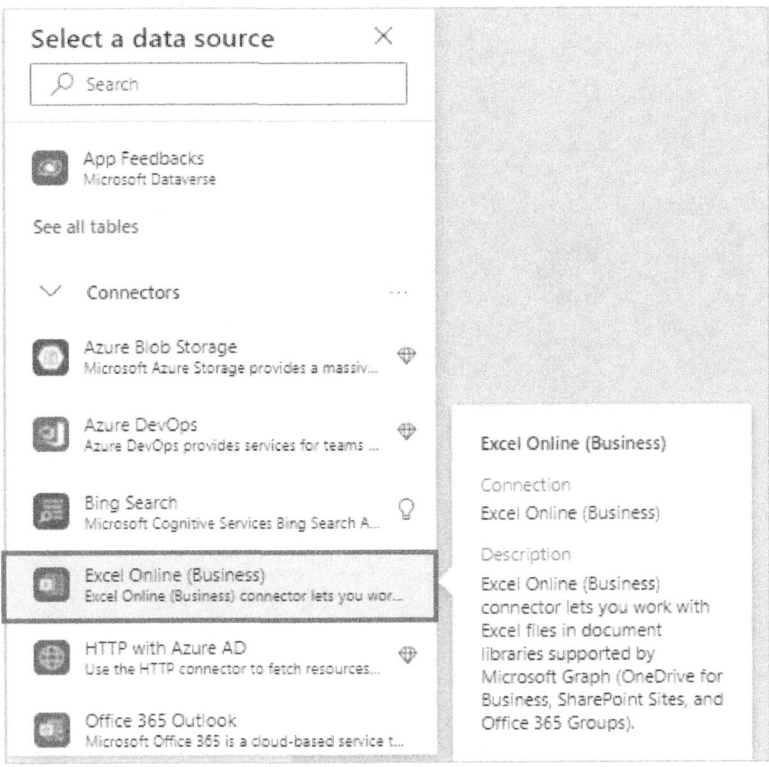

You have additional options when it comes to where to look for your Excel file using the Excel Online (Business) connection. Only one of them is OneDrive. Go over to OneDrive and choose your Excel file to locate a file there.

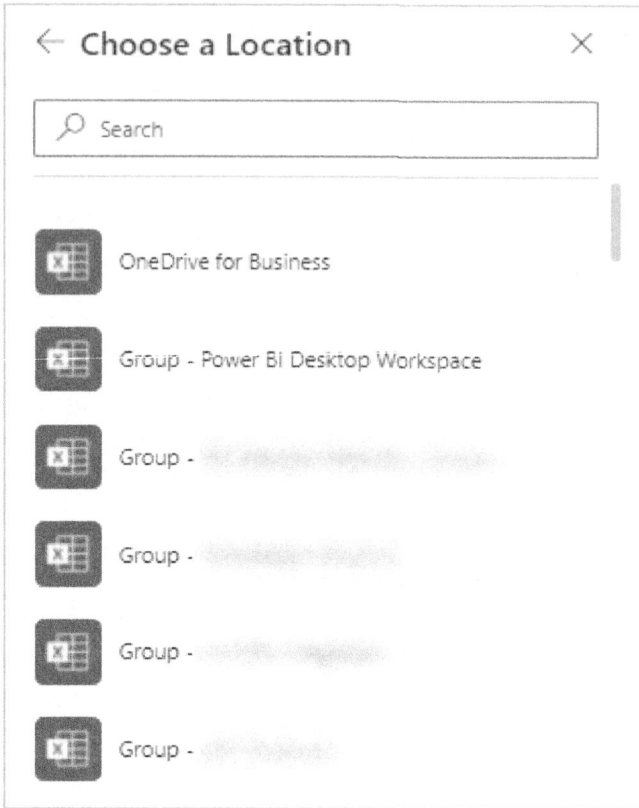

After choosing the file and the table inside, then you have added an excel data source to the application. Then you can go ahead to verify that you have used a new connector that has an excel icon and not a OneDrive Icon for the older connectors.

Setting up a Dataverse table to store images

Here is how to create a table in the Microsoft Dataverse.

- Start using the Office 365 login credentials to log in to Power Apps. Open the **Dataverse** first from the left menu and select **Tables** just on the Power Apps Home page.
- The new table pane will open whenever you choose **+New table** from the top command bar, allowing you to add the table's details such as Description, Display name, etc.

- There are two parts or tabs labeled Attributes and Primary column in the screenshot below.

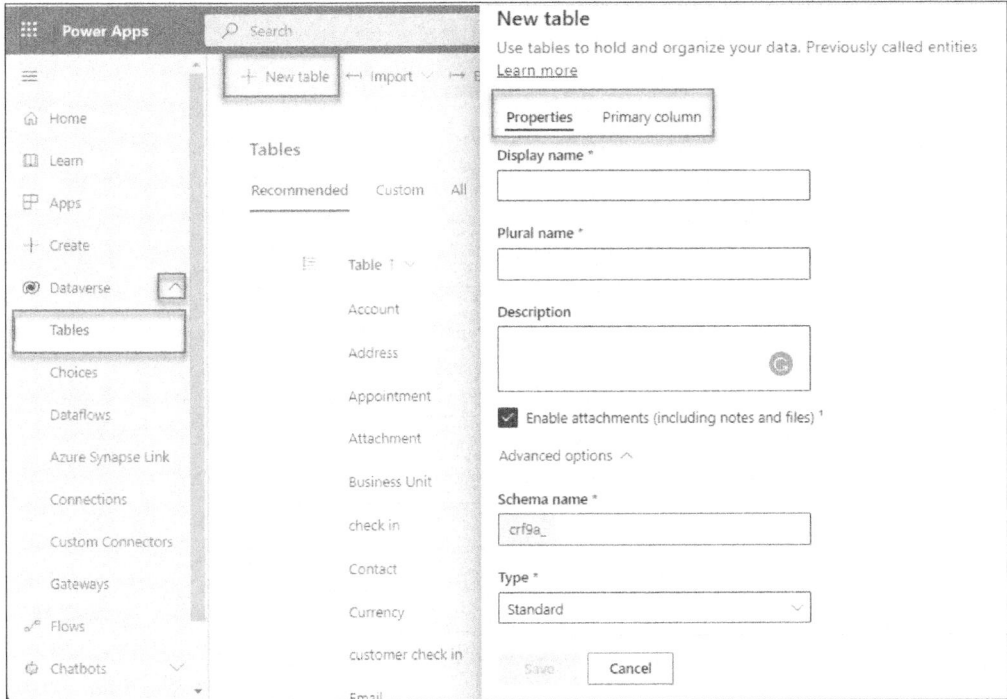

- Then select the properties tab and enter the display name, the plural name, the description, and whether to enable an attachment.
- Then to add a table image, choose the **Table image** by expanding the **Advanced option**

Setting up SharePoint

Here is how to use the SharePoint list image column

1. Your SharePoint list should have a column for SharePoint images. A portion of a SharePoint list is located beneath the "Item Photo" column.

Asset Manager ☆

Item Code ∨	Item Photo ∨	Manufacturer ∨	Model ∨	Asset type ∨	Color ∨	Serial number ∨
LT1956		Contoso, Ltd.	Surface Go 2	Laptop	Silver	0QSK91HJ900798
LT8320		Microsoft	Surface Go	Laptop	Silver	T348V430YF670
SP2735		Fabrikam, Inc.	Fabrikam D200	Smartphone	Dark Blue	23XC5R2TY7219O
SP2735		Fabrikam, Inc.	Surface Pro X	Laptop	Black	3523381OWS24336
FD1000		Trey Research	Ergonomic Keyboard	Accessory	Black	FILSD8428450101
AC1200		Trey Research	Surface Headphones 2	Accessory	Black	8892901N048SA
AC7320		Microsoft	Surface Headphones	Accessory	Silver	PR34DF672XBY0
FC1000		Contoso, Ltd.	Ergonomic Mouse	Accessory	Black	3DE5200125433

2. Use the picture column as a component of a gallery or data card in your Power App.

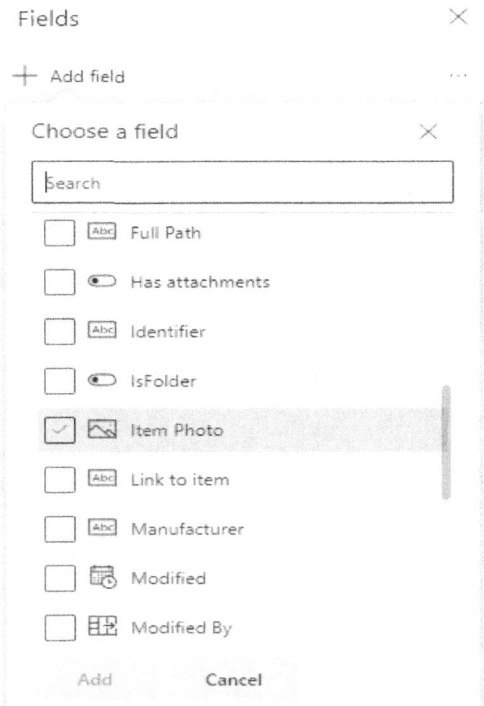

3. If necessary, change the image's size inside the gallery or data card. A full-sized image could be too big to show correctly to meet your performance objectives. To choose Small, Medium, Large, or Full, change the pictured formula. The formula below has been enhanced to show the image's small version. A slimmer version of the picture with a Small classification is appropriate for quickly scrolling through the entries in a gallery.

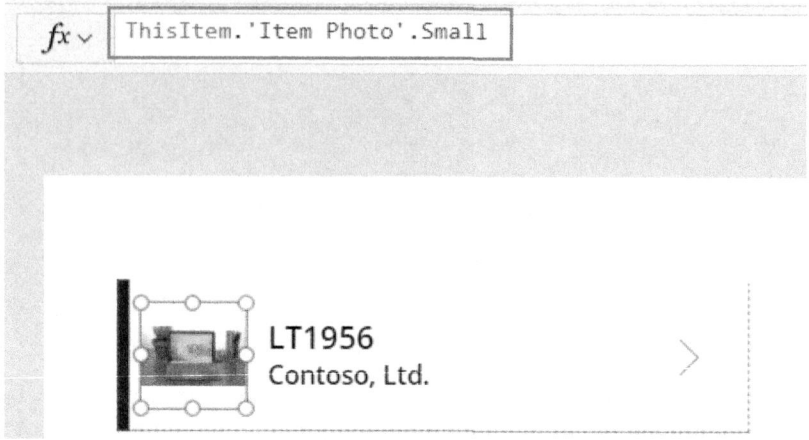

4. We then adjust the formula to show the large size.

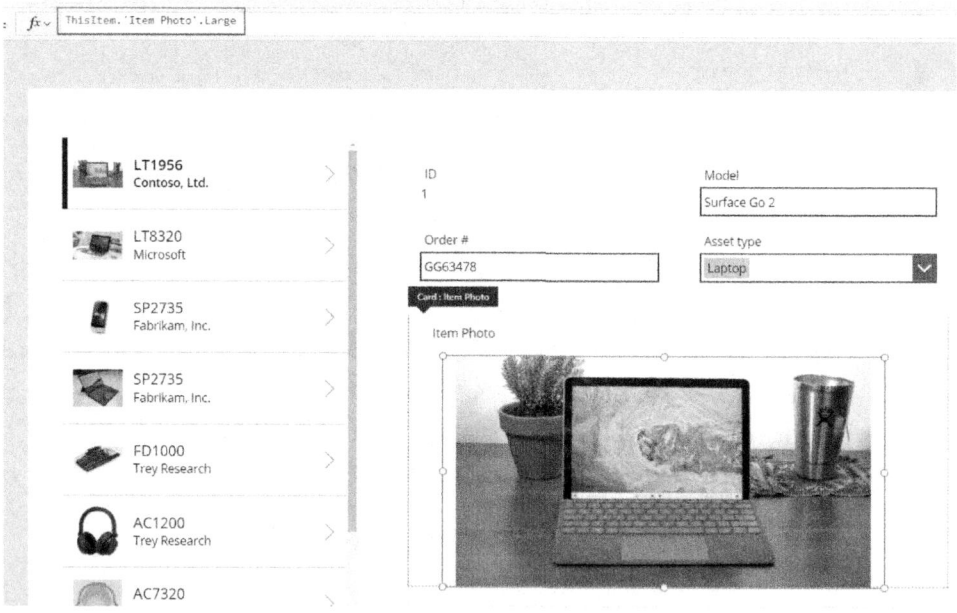

Creating an image app

There is a new feature called the **Image to app**. They help you to create apps from visual designs and then connect them to data with a few steps in the guided interface. This way it is easier for even amateurs to jumpstart an app development process.

Here are the steps:

- First sign into the power app.
- Then choose **+create** when you go to the left pane.

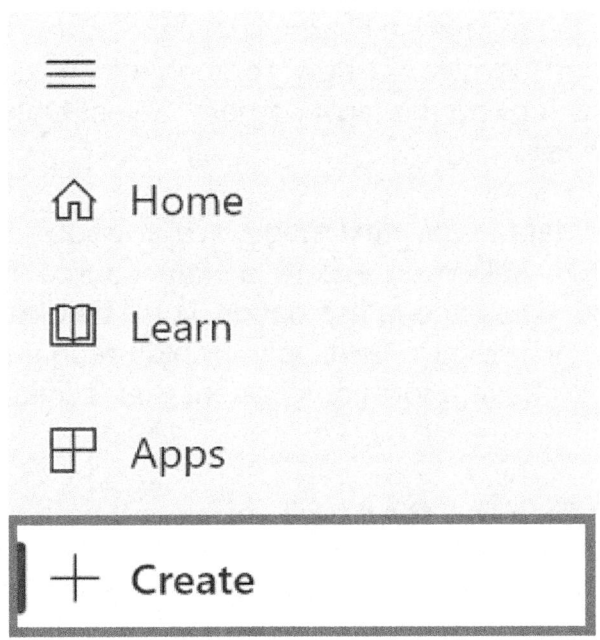

- Then choose **Image.**
- Review the suggested picture and tip samples. Ensure your image follows these guidelines for the best service. When finished, proceed to the next step.
- Type in the app.
- Upload a photo of your own. You may also employ one of the sample photos that are offered if you have no image ready. The format (Tablet or Phone) would be instantly chosen for you depending on the image's dimensions. We advise you to stick with the recommended format for the best results. The proposed format will guarantee that your image and the finished app are as similar as possible. Choose **Next.**

A tag would be automatically added to your picture based on the elements that were discovered. For instance, the "Enter your first name" box in the sample picture below was recognized as a Text input control. By choosing and dragging to choose the area that includes the component, you may create a new tag. Next, decide the category of component you wish to tie the new tag too.

Select the tag to change it, add a new one, or remove the old one. The tag can then be given a new component, or its dimensions can be changed by moving the tag's corners. Select **Delete** tag if you want to **Delete** the tag.

Setting up data is the next stage. We advise creating a new table in Dataverse to link your app to a data source for the optimal user experience. By selecting this option, you'll be directed to add columns depending on the form fields in your picture in the following step, and your app will have a form component that is linked to your Dataverse database.

Choose to **Skip this for now** if you do not wish to add a new table to Dataverse. Your app will be built in its current state, which implies that the elements you identified in the previous stage will be constructed immediately if you pick this option and **Create**. They are not going to be inside a form component and the app will not be connected to the data.

Using the camera control

To use a device's camera to take images, use the Camera control. The app must have the user's permission to access the camera on the device, which must have a camera.

To take a photo with the camera, tap or choose the camera control.

The Photo property provides access to the most recent image that was taken. The photos with this characteristic can be:

- Using the Image control to see. To view the image that was captured, use the Image control. See the examples for further details.
- Temporarily insert into a collection or variable. To save photos in a variable or collection, just use the Set or Collect functions. Due to a device's limited memory, use caution while utilizing numerous

photographs in a collection at once. To transport photos to the device's local storage or for offline circumstances, use the SaveData and LoadData methods.

- Taken from a database. If you want to save photos in a database, use the Patch function.
- Sent as a text string using **base64** encoding. Images may be base64 encoded using the JSON method.

Switching between cameras

You can specify the ID of the camera with the camera property. 0 can be for the front camera and 1 can be for the back camera. But you can hardcode the ID so that you can have a list of all of the devices.

Setting brightness, contrast, and zoom levels

You can use image control to set all of these.

Working with the add picture control

Here is how to insert the image control into the power apps

- Go to the Insert tab, select Media, and then select Image just on the Power Apps screen as seen below. The screen will then show the picture control.
- The image control's Image property will always be Sample Image by default. Any picture can be uploaded using this Image attribute.

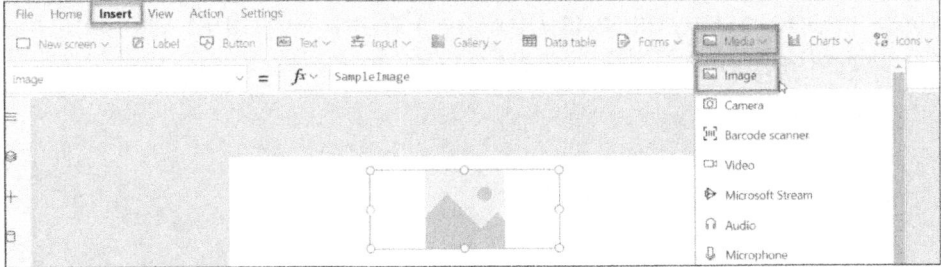

Converting images to text

- First, log in to the power app.
- Then choose **AI Builder** and select **Build.**
- Then choose **Text Recognition.**

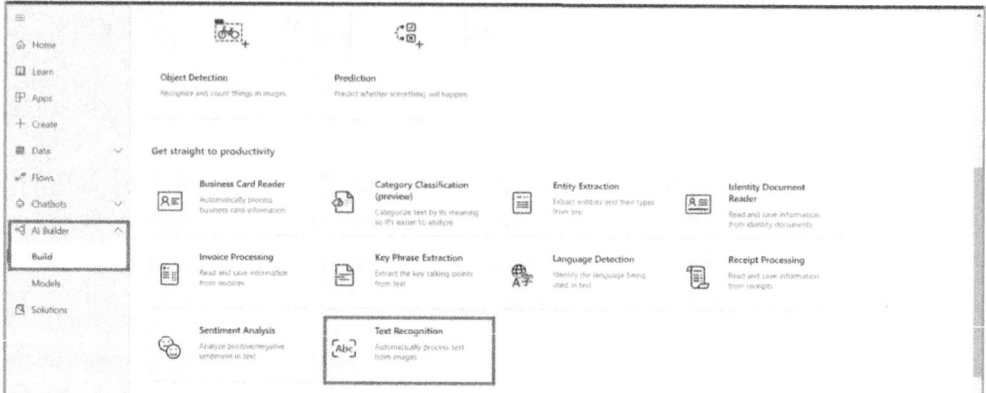

- Use any of the models on the power automate flow or on the power app
- Then choose **Test** and then find the file that you want to run through the flow. Here are the images that we used. You can test it out with the same one.

VIEWING DATA

Building a photo gallery

- The first thing you do is make a document library from the SharePoint site.
- Then build a power automate gotten from the Power Apps then we pass the document library item id and then get the base64 of an image as a response to the Power App that we will show in the gallery.

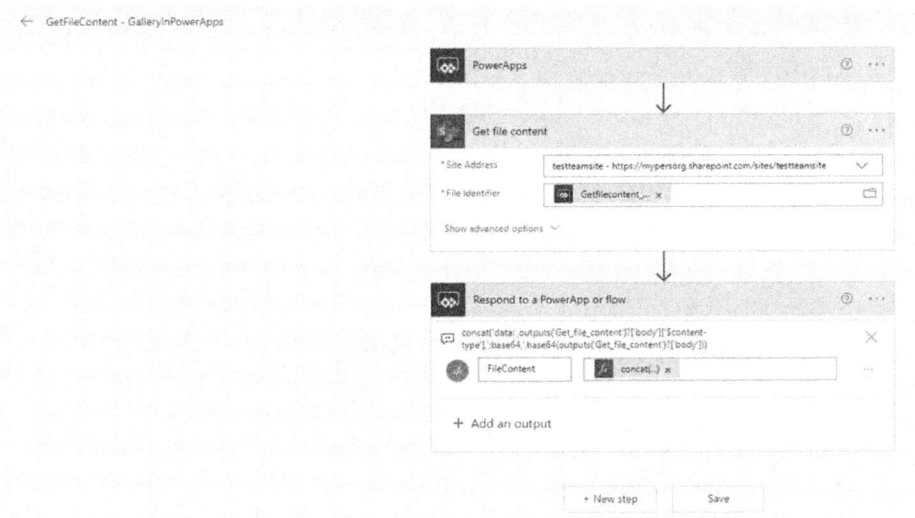

- Then create a new Power App.
- Then add a document library as the data source.
- Then add the Power automated inside the Power Apps from the **Action > Power Automate** option.

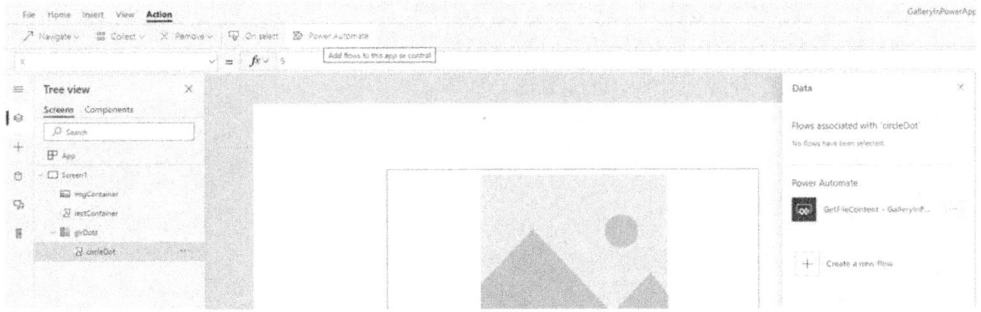

- Then add the controls and set the properties.
- Then save the app and publish it.

Uploading and viewing images

Here is how to upload an image to the SharePoint list with the Power Apps

- Build a sample file in the SharePoint list using the required columns.
- Once you have created the SharePoint list, then create a new app.
- Then connect to SharePoint.
- Once connected, there is going to be a different list. There you can choose the list that you want to create the form.
- Once you create the form, you are going to get a required column in the SharePoint list.
- Then create a variable for the image.
- Then select **Add an idea.**
- You are then going to see the image stored using a link format in the list. after you click on the button inside the Power App, then you are going to see the image in gallery form

CANVAS APP FEATURES

Here is some image-centered canvas app feature.

Using the pen control

Here is how to add the pen control:

- Login to the Power Apps
- Then create a canvas app
- Go to the power apps blank screen and go to **Insert** then **Input** then **Pen Input.**

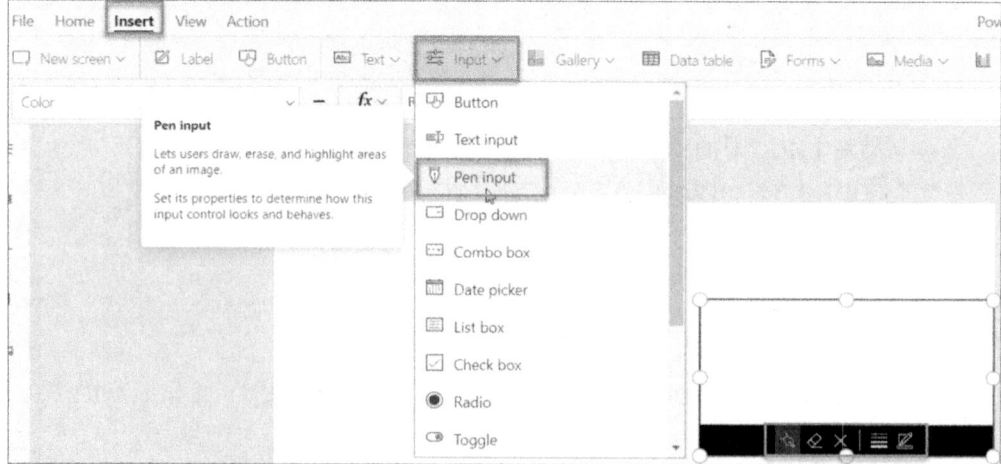

Scanning barcodes

The control launches a native scanner on Android devices or iOS smartphones. When one of these codes is visible, the scanner instantly recognizes it as a barcode, QR code, or data matrix. The control doesn't allow for web browser scanning.

Review Question

- How do you set up a data source with Image?
- How do you switch between cameras?
- How do you store an Image in SharePoint?

Summary

In this chapter, we discussed images in power apps. We talked about setting the images up in different conditions, and storing and uploading them too.

CHAPTER SEVENTEEN

STORING AND RETRIEVING FILES

Overview

In this chapter, we are going to be taking you through the ways to store and retrieve data in power apps. There are two methods for utilizing existing data in Power Apps applications. One is via directly connecting to a source data utilizing a connection. The alternative is to copy a picture of the data using a data flow.

Using a connector: this is a tool in Power Apps that enables you to connect to other sources and systems and immediately get or save data to them. Examples of these sources and systems include SharePoint, SQL Server, and Office 365.

Using a dataflow: A Power Apps feature called a dataflow allows you to extract, manipulate, then load data from one system into Azure Data Lake or Dataverse storage. It retrieves data in a scheduled batch, as opposed to a connector. Power Query Online allows you to edit, purge, and transform information before saving it to the destination storage, as opposed to just receiving it from the data source.

Storing files in SharePoint

There is one quick and easy way to store files into the contracted app and that is with the submit A. Salespeople use it to upload contracts to the SharePoint document library. Immediately after that contact is signed, you can just attach the file and insert some metadata like the customer name, the date, and the type to organize the contract and just submit the file.

Direct document uploads from Power Apps to a SharePoint library are not possible. To accomplish that instead, we must design a Power

Automate flow. Choose to **Create** a new flow when you select the Power Automate action from the menu bar.

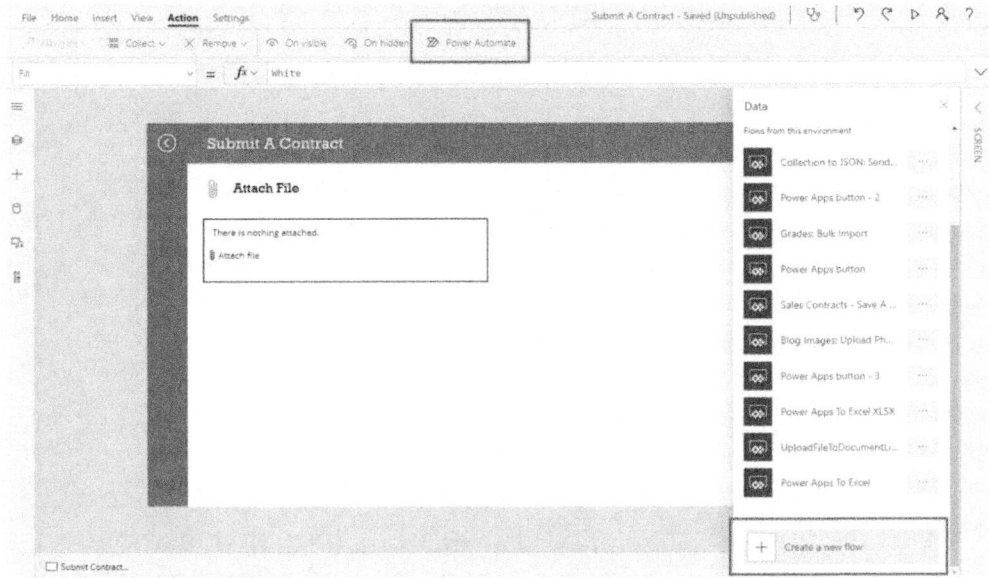

Then select the Power App button template.

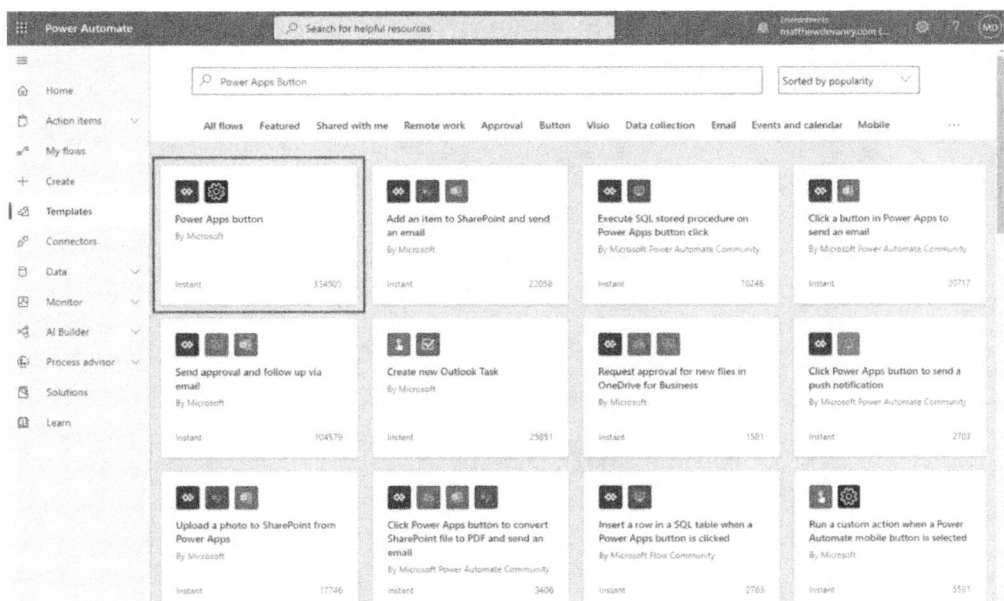

Then give the flow a name and select **Save.**

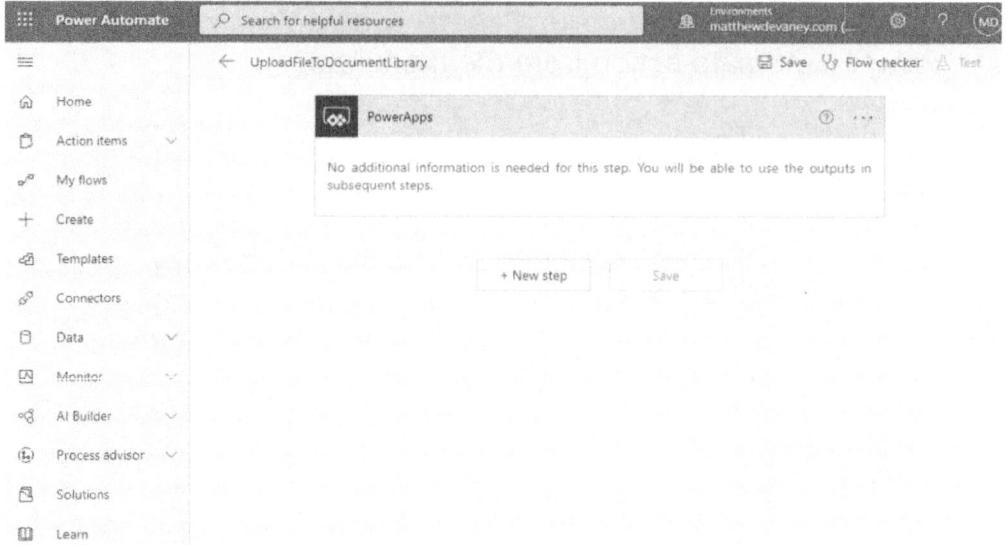

It is preferable to use the PowerApps (V2) trigger since it works with files as input. However, the PowerApps trigger does not do the same. Then delete the power app trigger then add **PowerApps(V2)**.

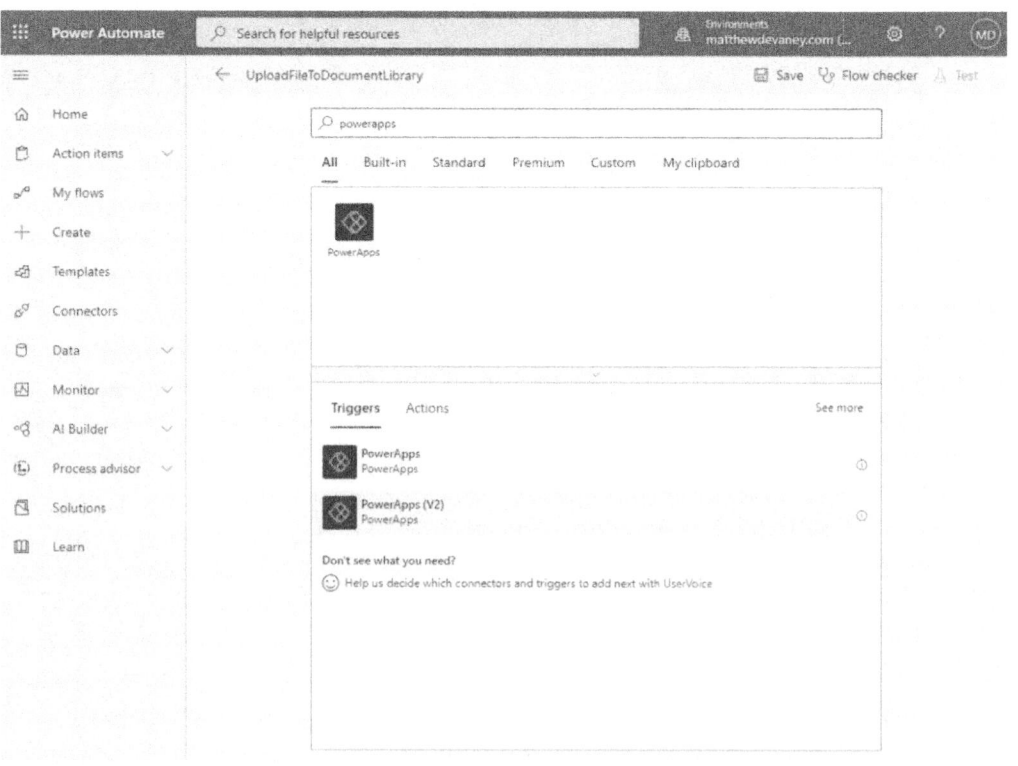

Then choose the input type and name it. Then make it a **required** input.

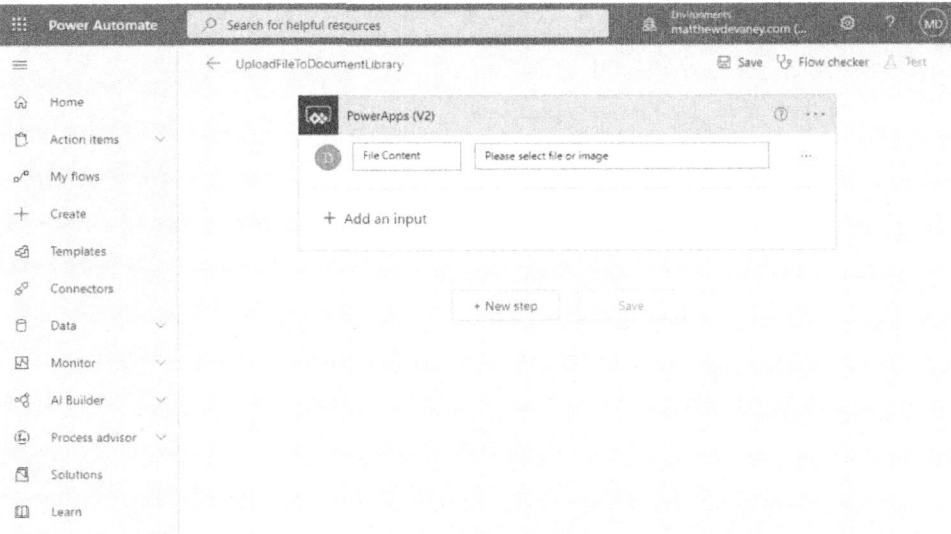

Then place a SharePoint action inside the flow. Select a file. Make use of the SharePoint site address and the document library folder path as the input. Make sure that the file content field references the file that is in the flow trigger.

The file name will then need an expression. Go to the flow expression editor and copy and paste the code below. trigger body()['file']['name']

Restricting file types

You can use a custom list form built from the Power App to restrict the SharePoint list attachments.

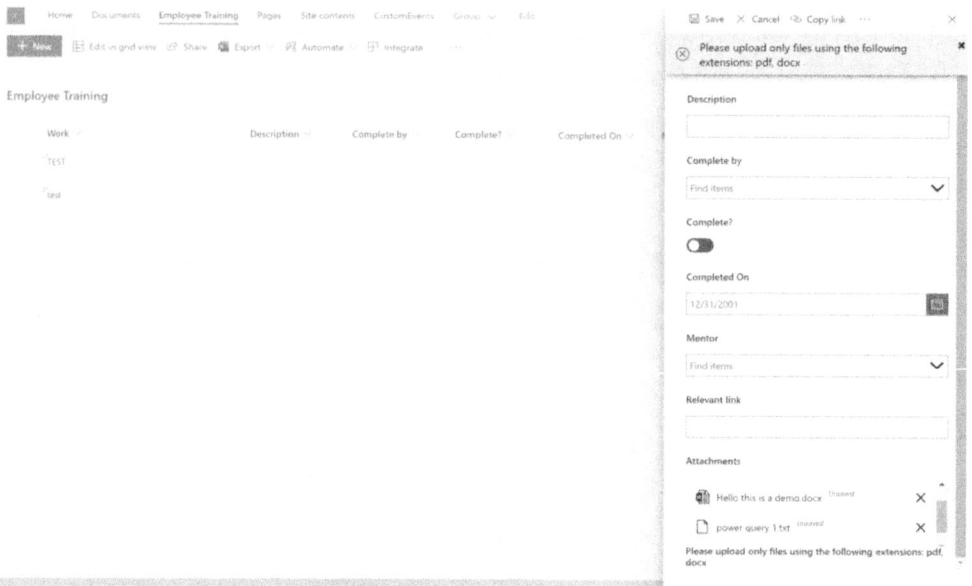

Here is what you are going to do:

First, create a custom form using the PowerApp. Go to the list that you will like to customize and choose the option to customize the form using the PowerApps. Then you need to add some extra fields to the form. Furthermore, you can reorder the field too.

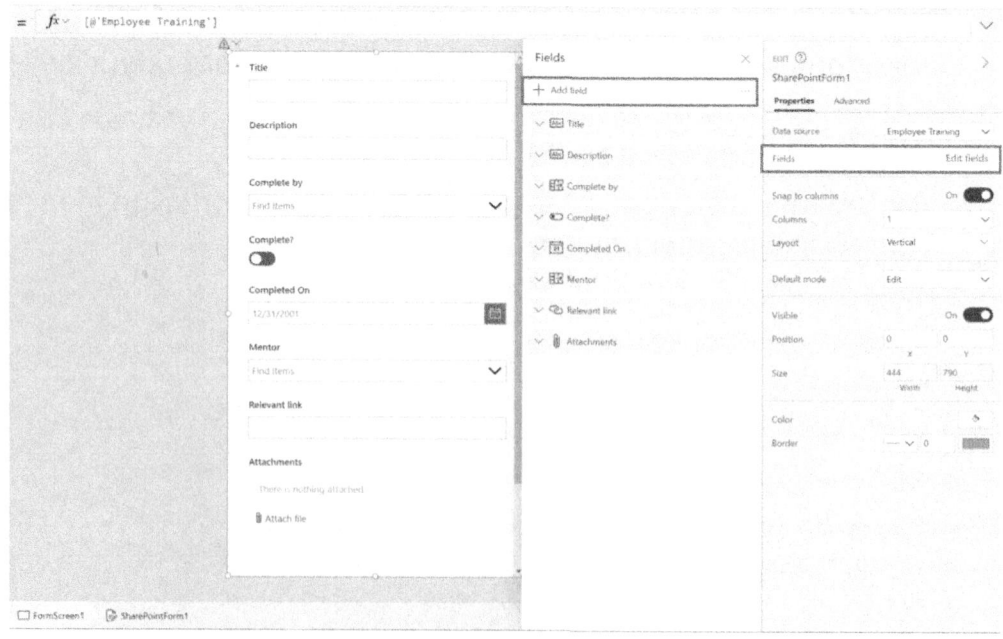

Then you want to edit the attachment card/control.

So that the formula is clearer, you need to rename the controls in the attachment from the standard pattern.

DataCardValue** to attControl

ErrorMessage** to lblErrorAttachment

Furthermore, you need to update the control height attcontrol to just 100 pixel.

Then unlock the attachment card so that you can update the formulas inside the controls

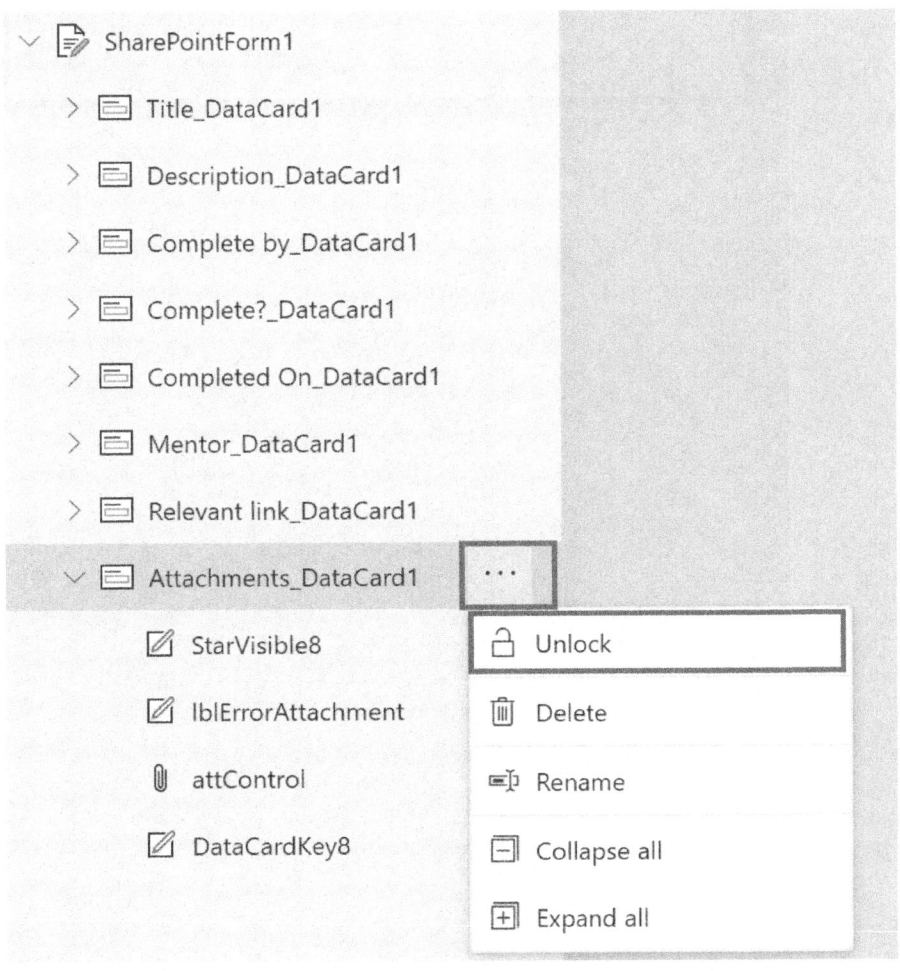

Choose the control lblErrorAttachment then update its TEXT formula to thisCoalesce(

```
    Parent.Error,

    With(

        {

    //Simply add extra allowed file extensions here in this array

            allowedFileExtensions: [

                "pdf",

                "Docx"

            ]

        },
```

```
                    ]
      },
            If(
                IsBlank(
                    LookUp(
                        attControl.Attachments,
//split file name, last item in the result array is the file extension
                        !(Last(Split(
                            Name,
                            "."
                        )).Result in allowedFileExtensions)
                    )
                ),
                "",
                "Please upload only files using the following extensions: "&
                With({strList:Concat(allowedFileExtensions,Value&", ")},Left(strList,Len(strList)-2))
            )
        )
    )
)
```

If at minimum one attachment file has extensions that aren't on the authorized list, this will change the error message that appears on the attachment card to either show the standard error code or the custom message. Only pdf and docx files are permitted in the aforementioned example, but you may modify the formula and modify the allowedFileExtensions array value that matches the precise extensions list required.

However, by itself, this formula does not stop the item from being submitted; instead, we must additionally change the OnSave event formula again for SharePoint Connection.

Then edit the OnSave event formula

Every time the 'Save' button is pressed on the SharePoint list form, the OnSave event's formula is activated. By default, it merely sends the custom form, but we may add further logic to stop the submission of forms with invalid attachments.

Edit the OnSave formula for the SharePointIntegration component by choosing it.

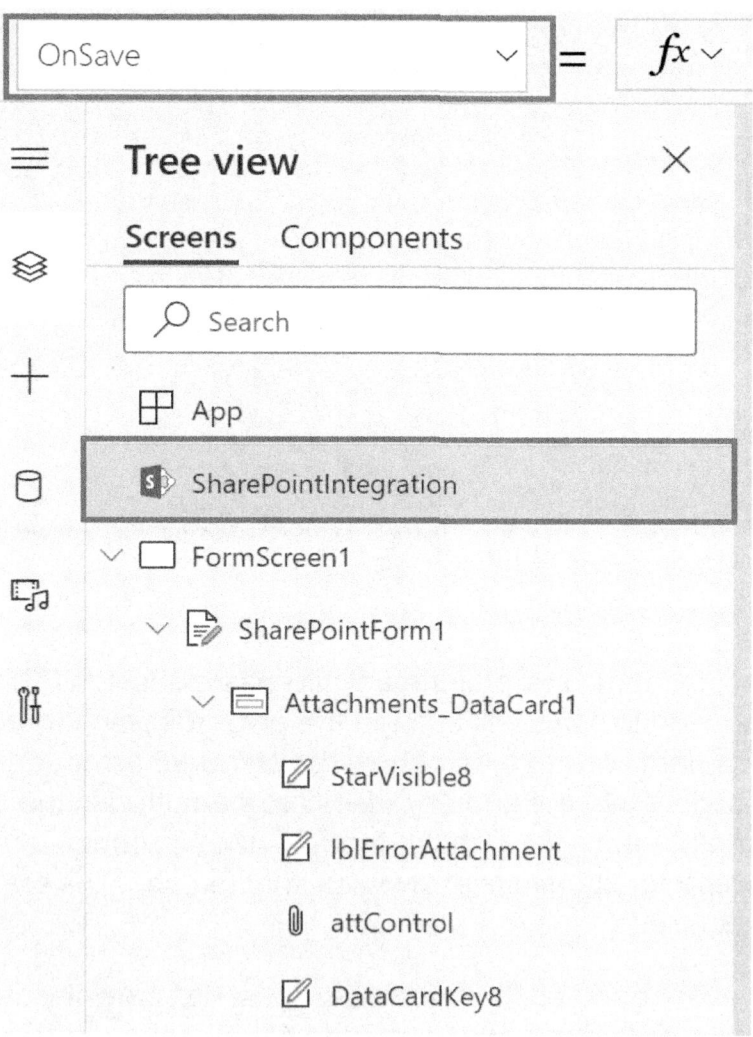

This formula then will tell you if there is an error inside the attachment card, and if there is any, it is going to notify you. But, if not then the form will be submitted normally. If (

   !IsBlank(lblErrorAttachment.Text),

   Notify(

      lblErrorAttachment.Text,

      NotificationType.Error

   ),

   SubmitForm(SharePointForm1)

)

Connecting to document libraries

Here are the steps to connect to document libraries

- Establish a document library. (You may utilize the current Documents library.)
- Make a choice-type column and give it a name. Status Document Library Content Type Enabled.
- Add two columns with just one line of text each, named hiddenIsFolder and hiddenFolderPath.
- Set the column hiddenIsFolder's default value to No
- Set hiddenFolderPath default settings according to the video.

Folders' hiddenFolderPath values can be manually set.

- Step 2: Import an application zip file into Power Apps.
- Step 3

Format the app.

Add a new SharePoint data source connection referring to your Document Library and delete the SharePoint data source from the App.

Set the relative path to your document library in the app's OnStart method. Setting the current path as "Shared Documents"

Storing files in Dataverse

Here are the steps to upload files into the Dataverse.

- Choose the table where you wish to add the file or picture content from the drop-down list for the Table name or type in a custom value.
- For the row toward which you wish to upload the file or picture content, input the identification in Row ID.
- Choose the column to which you wish to upload the picture from the Column name, or input a custom value.
- The content you wish to submit should be entered.
- In this illustration, the files that need to be uploaded are the email attachments that were previously intercepted. When you click Add dynamic content just on Upload a file or an image card, you may choose Attachments Material from the selection of dynamic content that appears.

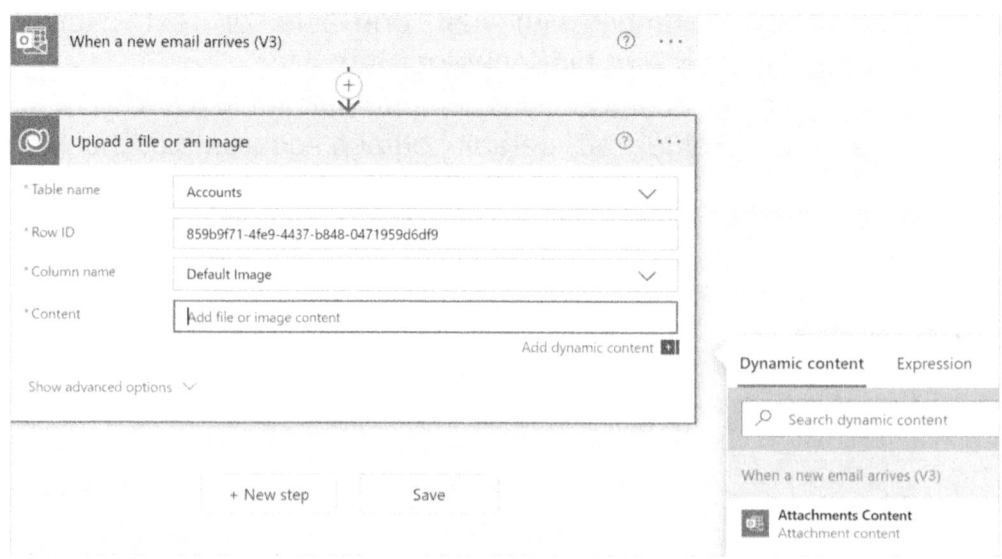

Storing files in SQL Server

If you want to use the SQL Server to store your data here is what you are going to have to do.

Setting up a SQL Server table

Using Management Studio or another SQL Server tool, add a new column that is an image type to a new or existing table.

Make sure to provide one of the columns with a primary key so that PowerApps may add and update entries to this new table.

New PowerApps App creation.

Increase Your App's SQL Connection (View, Data Sources).

Choose the table that has the picture column there.

Then there are two options to then upload the data to the SQL. Either by inserting a form or writing a patch statement.

For the Power App form based, here is what to do.

- First, add new for to the canvas.
- Then change the default mode to new.
- Choose the table.
- Choose the field that you want to add to the form.

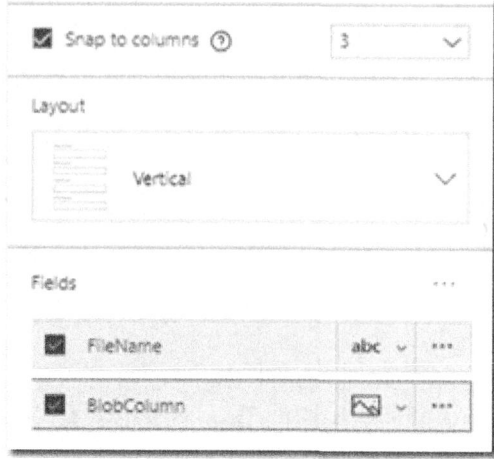

- Then on the form, you are going to see the type of media and also the text box.
- Then place a button on the canvas.
- Enter the OnSelect property off button and type submitform(form1).
- This then submits the form to the SQL server. If you want to reset the form, insert; resetform(form1) inside the OnSelect of the button property.
  The other way is by writing a patch statement.
- Add a control, such as the Add Picture Control, to record a file (Insert, Media, Add Picture).

- Other choices include:
  Pen-input
  Cameras
- Add Image
- Add a text input field so that you can type the file name into it.
- Add a link to the canvas so you can take the user-entered file or data and save it to SQL Server.
- Add the following to the button's OnSelect attribute.
  Patch('[dbo].[TestBlobUpload]',
      Defaults('[dbo].[TestBlobUpload]'),
      {
          FileName:TextInput1.Text,
          BlobColumn:UploadedImage1.Image

```
        }
    )
```
- Then add the gallery so that the file is displayed in the table.

Adding and updating a record

You can use the update and the Updatelf functions to update records. If you want to replace a complete record inside a data source, use the Update function. The Patch and **Updatelf** functions, on the other hand, change one or more values inside a record while keeping the other values intact.

The complete record must match a collection. Multiple records may match because collections allow for duplicate records. A record can be modified across all copies by using the All argument; otherwise, just one version of the data is changed.

The value of a column must be confirmed if somehow the data source automatically creates its value.

For the **Updatelf** to change one or more values in one or more entries that satisfy one or more conditions, use the Updatelf function. Any formula that yields a true or false result can serve as the condition, and it can explicitly refer to specific columns in the data source. Each record's condition is evaluated by the function, which updates any records that have the result as true.

Use a change record that includes new property values to specify the update. Property formulae can refer to properties of the record that is being edited if you supply this change record inside curly braces. This behavior may be used to change records depending on a formula.

Downloading file attachment

A file from the web is downloaded to the local device using the Download feature.

The user is requested to choose a location to store the file in native players for Windows, Android, and iOS.

The download relies on the browser's settings when used online to control what happens to the file. A new browser tab is established to view any photos, videos, PDFs, or other file types that the browser natively supports. The ability to save material to the local file system is supported by several browsers.

Download only provides the location of the file's local storage as a string of text on Windows.

Deleting a file

You can use the remove function or the remove function to delete files from a data source. For the remove, if each condition may contain any formula which yields a true or false outcome and may specifically refer to a column of the source data. Every condition is separately assessed for every record, and if they are all assessed to be true, the record is erased.

Storing files in Azure Blob storage

The Azure Blob Storage is accessible to Owner Apps. Using the Azure Blob Storage adapter for Power Apps, you may upload documents like Word, Excel, or multimedia items like photos, music, and video.

The blob storage account name and key are used to establish a connection when you create a canvas app that links to Azure Blob Storage. After you distribute the app, users may upload files to Azure Blob Storage using the connection set up there without revealing the blob storage names and keys to the users.

Setting up an Azure Blob storage

You have to first set up the azure bob storage before it can connect to the storage. Here is what to do

- Activate Power Apps.
- Expand Data in the left-hand window.
- Choosing **Connections**.
- Choose to **Create** a new connection.
- Opt for Azure Blob Storage.

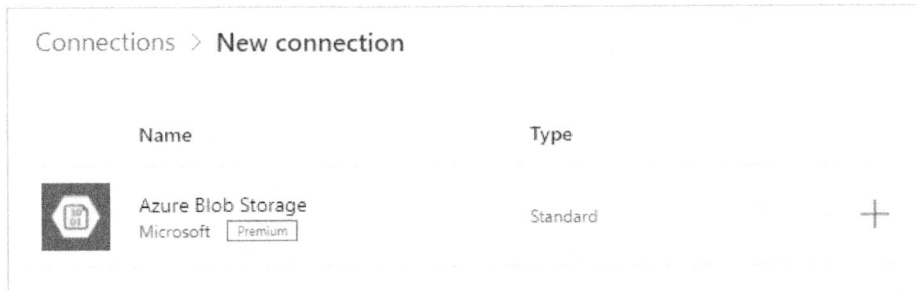

- Then copy and paste the name of the account and the access key
- Then choose to **Create.**

Managing an Azure Blob storage

Here is how to view containers and files in power apps

- Click **Gallery > Blank** vertical under Insert.
- Choose Title from the layout drop-down menu in the property pane on the right side of the screen.
- Then choose the arrow pointing right inside the gallery then **Delete** it.

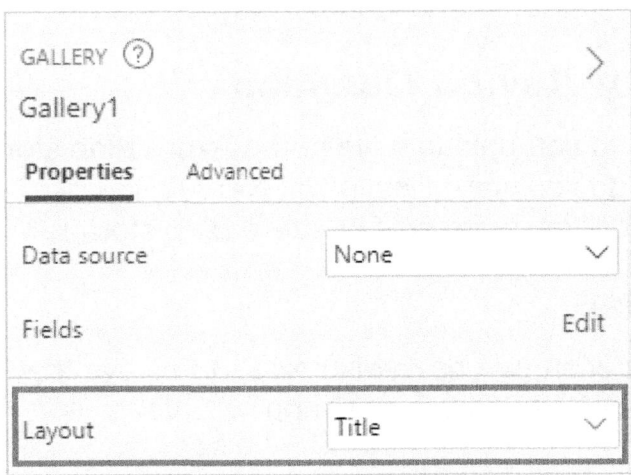

- Then go to the right side of the screen and choose the property pane and choose drop-down for the data source then choose the **Azure Blob Storage.**
- To add another blank vertical gallery, choose **Insert > Gallery > Blank** vertical.

- The gallery that displays the list of containers should be placed beneath the gallery you previously built.
- Select Title, Subtitle, and Body from the layout drop-down in the property window on the right side of the screen.
- Inside the gallery, choose the first Arrow icon, then remove it.
- Select Azure Blob Storage from the data source drop-down menu in the property pane on the right side of the screen.
- Set the gallery's Items property to: AzureBlobStorage.ListFolderV2(Gallery1.Selected.Id).value
- Choose **Edit** from the right side of the screen
- Then switch the field chosen for the gallery title as a display name and the subtitle as last modified and the body as the path.
- Select the Text label under Insert.
- Affix the label to the app's screen's top.
- "Select a container" should be set as the label's Text attribute.
- To change the label text color, size, and background color, just use the properties pane just on the right side of the screen.
- Select the Text label under Insert.
- Place the label above the file list and gallery.
- Put "Files list" in the label's Text attribute.

Activity/ Review Question

- How do you upload a file to the Azure Blob storage?
- How do you store files in Dataverse?
- How do you store files in Azure Blob storage?

Summary

In this section, we have discussed the ways that you can store files and access them with power apps.

CHAPTER EIGHTEEN

INTEGRATING MAPS AND LOCATION SERVICES

In this chapter, we are going to be taking you through integrating maps and location services into your power apps

Introduction to location services and GPS

With the use of GPS or cellular data, PowerApps has the great ability to interact with location services offered by a mobile device. Utilizing latitude and longitude, in addition to the orientation the device is facing, we may locate the device using this service.

Longitudes and latitudes

The position of two fictitious lines around the planet is used to establish the GPS location. The equator, which denotes 0° latitude and separates the northern and southern hemispheres, is the first. Up to a maximum value of 90, the latitude value rises as you move more north and drops as you move farther south. As a result, the South Pole is 90° latitude South of the North Pole.

The prime meridian, or the second imaginary line, is located at longitude 0°. The Western and Eastern hemispheres of the Earth are divided by this line. As you travel away from the prime median, the longitude values rise and fall until they reach a maximum of +/- 180°, which corresponds to a second line called the international dateline.

Retrieving location details

Let's utilize PowerApps to locate ourselves using latitude and longitude now that we have a better understanding of how they operate.

With PowerApps, you can obtain existing locations by using a fairly straightforward formula. The GPS's accuracy, however, can vary greatly, and it will be less precise if indeed the user just turned on their GPS because there won't have been enough time for the GPS to latch onto enough satellites to offer an accurate reading.

The values of the objects used by PowerApps, known as signals, change at any moment without the user having to engage with the program directly. These signals will cause any formula that depends on them to be updated when the values change. This is why you want to think about freezing and capturing the GPS position.

To then retrieve the latitude and longitude, we will first record the basic location and put it on the label. To record the location, we will change the buttons On the Select attribute. To make it easier to view what has been recorded, you need to put it into a collection. However, it's not necessary to follow these steps when developing your app.

However, from this, you are going to see the latitude, the longitude, and the attitude of the device and then we can place them inside a label or in an alternative control so that the user can see it.

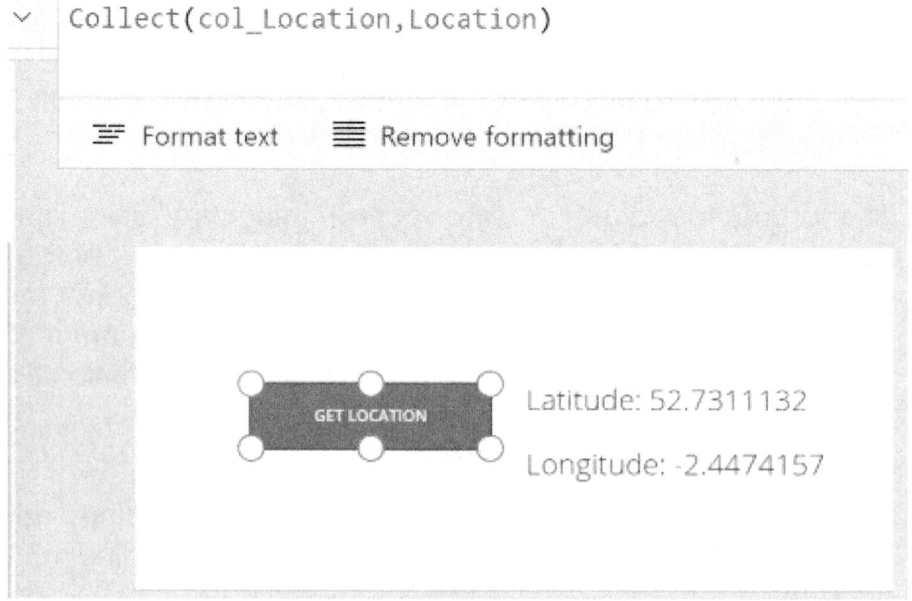

Verify that the operating system has permitted the usage of location services if you do not see the data being supplied here after you launch this in PowerApps.

Allowing the user to activate and stop location monitoring within the app is good practice. You should be careful with how you utilize location because apps that use location services and GPS by nature consume more power than those that do not. Use Enable to activate GPS (Location). To disable it, use Disable (Location).

Mobile phones can track a user's direction in addition to their present position.

Introducing signals

The values of the objects used by PowerApps, known as signals, can alter at any moment without the user having to engage with the program directly. Those signals will cause any formula that depends upon them to be updated when the values change. This is why you want to think about freezing and capturing the GPS position.

Switching the signal on/off

Some signals might fluctuate frequently, necessitating constant app recalculation. A device's battery might become discharged if there are many modifications made over time. These features allow you to manually switch on or off a signal.

A signal is automatically switched off when not in use.

You can then make use of the **Enable** and the **Disable** function to then turn signals on and off.

Other signals

Regardless of how the user may be using the app, signals represent values that really can change at any moment. Signal-based formulas update themselves automatically as these variables change.

Signals often provide back a list of data. This data may be used and saved as a record, or you can just use the. Operator to retrieve certain characteristics.

Here are some of the other signals:

Acceleration

The device's acceleration in three dimensions about the screen is returned through the acceleration signal.

App

This includes signal indication which screen is displaying.

Compass

This signal gives you the compass heading on top of the screen. And this is based on the magnetic north.

Connection

With this signal, you are going to get information about the network connection.

Displaying maps

So you can build the app by adding a map view to a view form that shows the geographic location of where the asset can be added to the register.

Using google maps

You may express location data in a meaningful way by using maps to provide context data to your users. Google Maps is one of the most widely used mapping tools that we may employ, and our PowerApp can make use of both of them. These mapping systems offer free services that may be utilized for business endeavors, which contributes to their acceptance.

Bing maps

So we can use the Bing maps API to display the geographic location of where the asset was added to the register.

Here are the steps:

- Choose the view assets display first

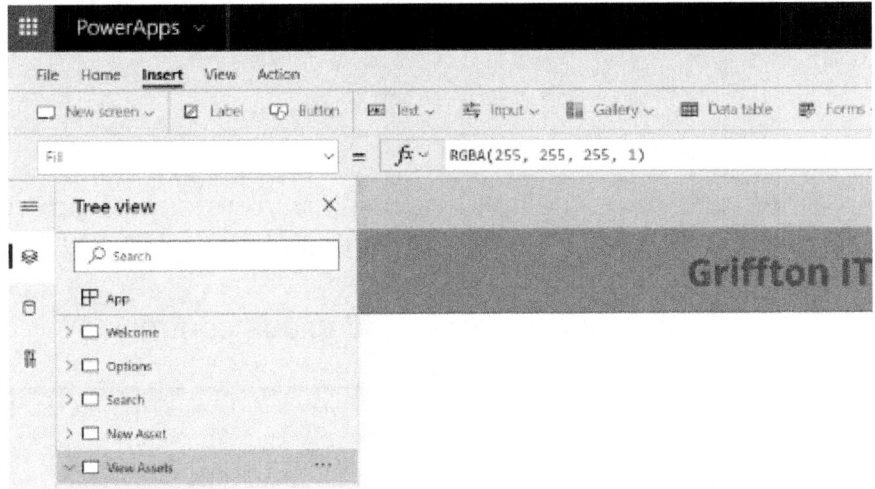

- Then add a display form to the screen then choose **Assets** as the data source.
- If you are making use of the edit fields, then add all of the fields but not the location.
- Place the number of the column as 1.

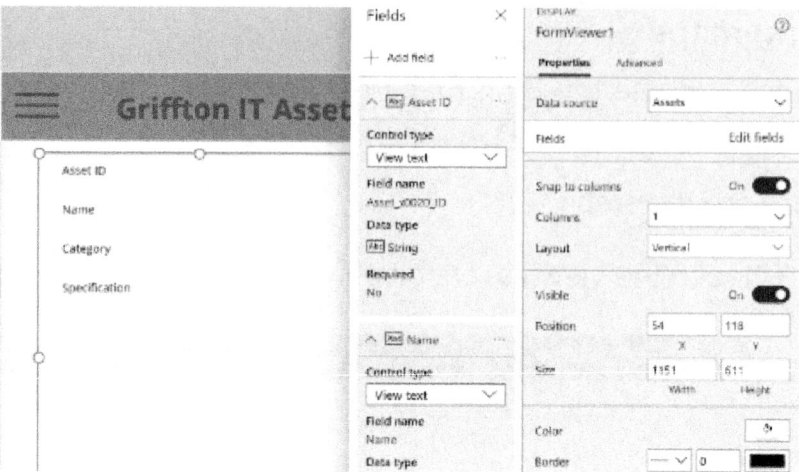

- Since you have the field now, then you need to add the custom card with the map. Then choose the ellipsis then add a custom card into the form.
- Select the custom card then add image control.

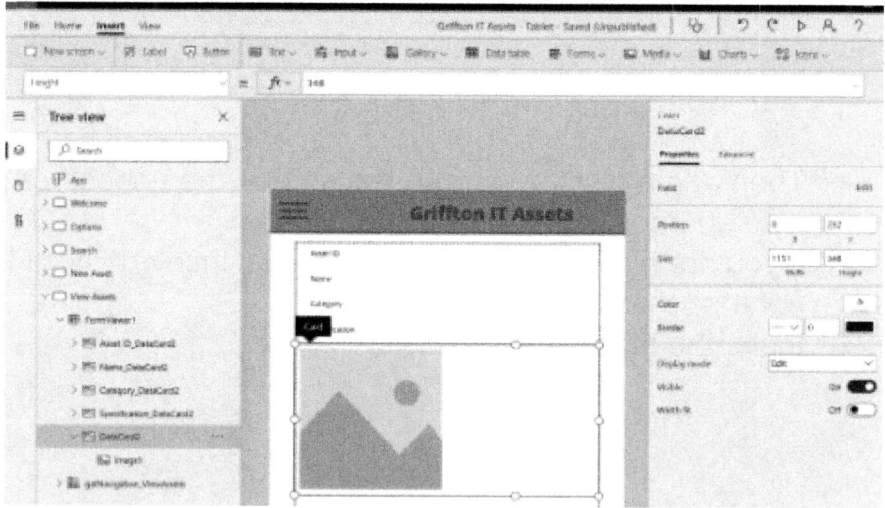

- Then configure the image into the Bing API Url "https://dev.virtualearth.net/REST/v1/Imagery/Map/AerialWithLabels?pp="& ThisItem.Location &";;"& ThisItem.'Asset ID' &"&key={Your API Key}".
- This then takes the location field and then uses it to add a pin to the map. It also put the asset ID inside the pin.

Using Azure maps services interactive maps

Azure Maps is a group of geospatial services and SDKs called uses up-to-date mapping data to provide online and mobile apps in a geographic context. Azure Maps gives you:

- REST APIs are used to render several types of raster and vector maps, as well as satellite images.
- There are several different routing possibilities, including point-to-point, multipoint, multipoint optimization, electric vehicle, isochrones, traffic influenced, commercial vehicle, and matrix routing.
- Map rendering and creation services using confidential interior map data.
- Applications that need real-time traffic information can use the traffic flow view and incidents view.
- Geolocation and time zone services.
- Services to find addresses, locations, and points of interest globally.
- Elevation services with a geo-fencing service based on a Digital Elevation Model and storage for mapping data that is stored in Azure.

Review Question

- How do you add signals to the Power App?
- How do you integrate google maps with Power Apps?
- How do you use the Azure maps service?

Summary

The most popular kind of data visualization that we examined in this chapter was mapping. Instead of just presenting latitude and longitude information on a screen, mapping enables you to put data in a context that is more easily understood by your consumers. Since both Bing Maps and Google Maps give free APIs for you to utilize within your apps, we concentrated on how to present mapping data using these APIs.

PowerApps send out signals that enable us to keep track of the device's GPS position and orientation. The most important thing to keep in mind about signals is that their values are dynamic. Therefore, you need collect signal values if you want to use them.

CHAPTER NINETEEN

CHARTING DATA

In this section, we are going to be taking you through how to represent data in a chart.

Introduction canvas apps

You can make use of the line charts, pie charts, and column charts to show the data inside canvas apps. When you are working with a chart, the data imported has to be structured using the following criteria.

- The series has to be in the first row.
- The labels have to be inside the leftmost column.

Transforming data

The first thing to do is to import the sample data.

- Go to the **Insert** tab and choose **Controls** then choose **Import.**

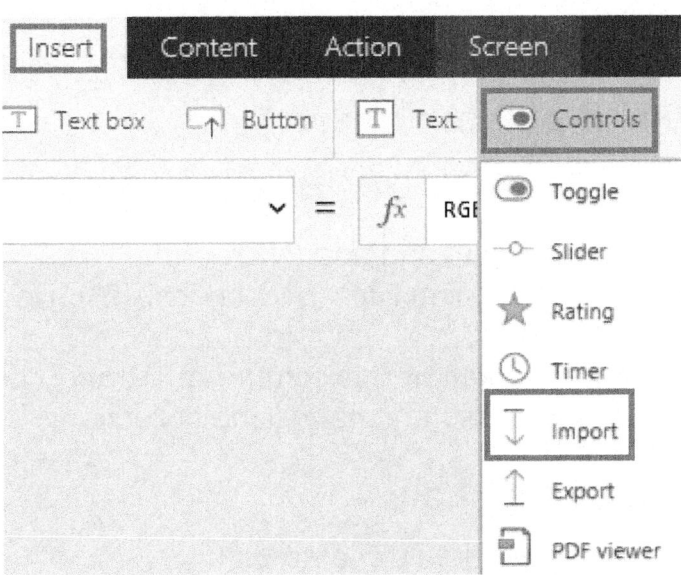

- Set the following action as the control's OnSelect property: Collect (ProductRevenue, Import1.Data)
- Open the Preview mode by pressing F5, then choose the **Import Data** option.
- Choose ChartData.zip from the open context box, click **Open**, and afterward hit Esc in the Open dialog box.
- You may choose **Collections** from the File menu.
- The imported chart data is listed beside the ProductRevenue collection:

Collections

ProductRevenue

ProductRevenue

Product	Revenue2012	Revenue2013	Revenue2014
Europa	21000	26000	28000
Ganymede	15000	17000	21000
Callisto	14000	19000	23000

Building a column chart

Then here is how to add bar charts so that you can see the data:

- Go to the home tab and add a screen.
- Then enter the **Insert** tab and choose **Charts** then choose the **Column chart.**
- Choose the center of the column chart and configure the items property of the column chart to the collection.

Building a pie chart

To add a pie chart here is what to do:

- Choose the **Insert** tab and choose **Charts,** then choose the **Pie Chart**
- Then take the pie chart to the button **Import data**
- Go to the pie chart control and choose the center of the pie chart.
- Then configure the **Items** property of the pie chart inside this expression

Building a line chart

- Go to the home tab and add a screen.
- Then enter the **Insert** tab and choose **Charts** then choose the **Line Chart.**
- Choose the center of the line chart and configure the items property of the line chart to the collection.

Model-driven apps

In this section, we are going to be telling you how to create a model-driven app chart system too.

Displaying charts

The first thing to do is sign into the power apps.

Then go to the left navigation pane and choose the Dataverse, then choose tables. This also requires a chart. Then choose charts:

- Choose a **New chart.**

- You are then going to see a new window to create a chart.

- Then you need to choose the chart type and how the data should be seen inside the chart.
- Then enter the chart name.
- Then go to the **Select column** dropdown and enter the following:
- Inside the **Legend, Entries** choose a column like the **number of employees.**
- And inside the **Horizontal axis** choose columns like the **Account name.**
- Then add descriptions that identify the chart purpose, like this column chart below shows the number of employees by their account name

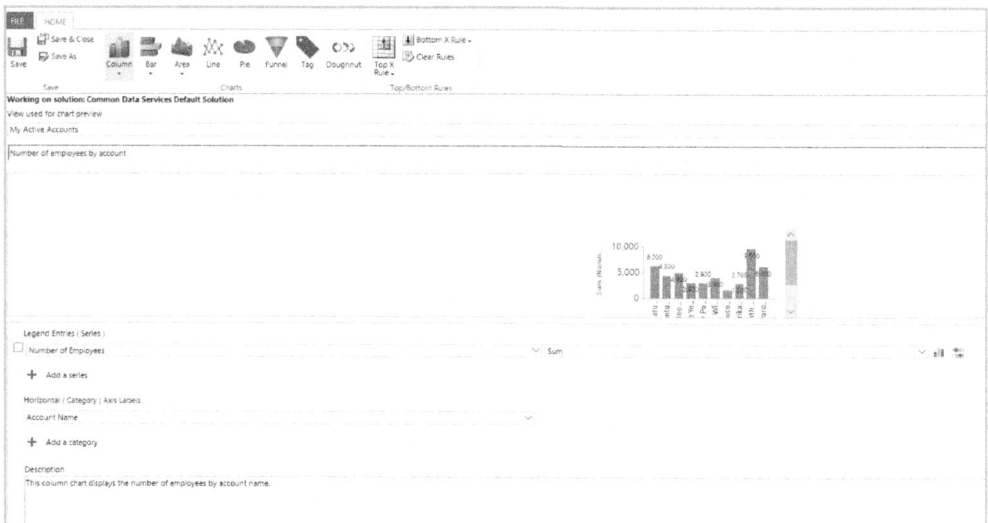

- Then choose to **Save** and close.
- Since you have created the chart, you can display table data inside the model-driven apps. Here are the steps.
- Open the application straight from the Apps section or use a solution to launch a model-driven app that includes your table.
- Choose the ellipsis next to the app and select play. You are then going to see a new browser tab with the model-driven application.
- Choose a table, like Accounts, from the left navigation window.
- You may choose Show Chart from the command bar.
- Then the chart is going to open

- Once you choose the dropdown chart list, any of the system charts inside the app will then be available to choose from. The chart is going to appear next to the data view.

Displaying dashboards

Chart groups related to Microsoft Dataverse tables make up dashboards.

User dashboards and systems dashboards are indeed two different categories of dashboards. Inside the app sections where they have access, an application developer can establish a dashboard that is solely accessible to them.

All app developers can see system dashboards when they have been published by an admin or customizer. A user has the option to override the system dashboard and make their dashboard the standard.

Here is how to create a new dashboard

- First, sign into the power apps.
- Choose **Solutions** and open the solution that is required.
- Go to the toolbar and choose **New** then choose **Dashboard**. Then choose any of the layouts displayed.

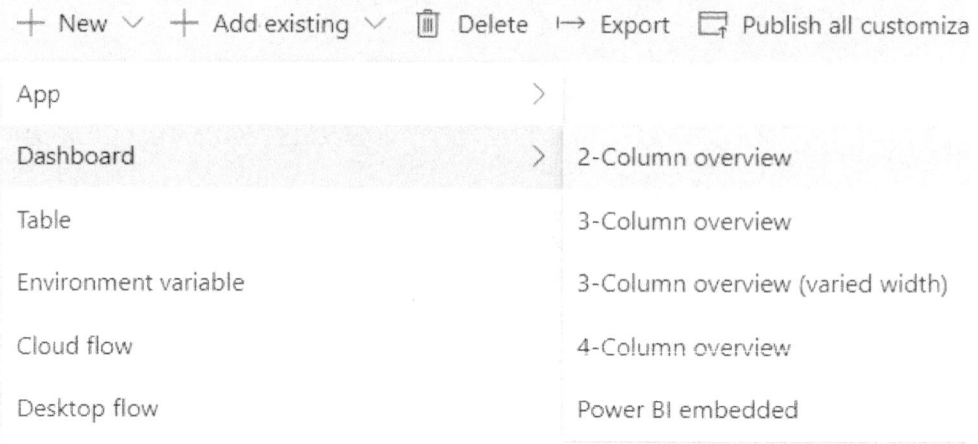

- Give the dashboard a name on the Dashboard: New page.
- Choose the icon for just a chart or a list after choosing one of the component regions.
- A dashboard may have up to six components.
- For instance, to add a chart, click the chart icon on the dashboard canvas tile where the chart is to be shown. Select settings for Row Type, View, and Chart in the Add Component dialog after that. Choose to Add to include the chart on the dashboard after that.
- Once you are done adding the component to the dashboard, then you can choose to **Save** and close
- Then go to the solution toolbar and choose to **Publish.**

Customizing XML

Among the files contained inside an exported unmanaged solution is the customizations.xml file. The modifications and setups for your system are all contained in the file or only some parts of them.

The solutions file is published as an a.zip file that has been compressed. Before editing the customization file, the contents of the unmanaged solutions file must first be extracted. Before it can be re-imported, the unmanaged solution's files must be all put into a compressed.zip file.

To carry out special customization operations, the customizations.xml file that is generated as a part of an uncontrolled solution can be changed. After making changes to a file, you can compress it along with any other files exported from the managed solution. By having to import that altered unmanaged solution, you make the changes.

If you use a tool made to enable schema validation, editing a complicated XML file like the customizations.xml file is simpler and less error-prone. While changing this file with a basic text editor like Notepad is doable, it is not advised unless you have extensive experience doing so.

Activity/ Review Question

- Edit a model-driven app dashboard that already exists.
- How do you display a dashboard?
- How do you display charts in Power App?

Summary

In this section, we have gone through model-driven apps and how to present data in charts with them. Visualization is important sometimes with data management. We hope that we have sent that message across here.

CHAPTER TWENTY

ADDS ARTIFICIAL INTELLIGENCE

INTRODUCING ARTIFICIAL INTELLIGENCE

Microsoft's artificial intelligence platform is called AI Builder. It uses a "low-code" concept as a component of the Power Platform and enables you to include artificial intelligence in your projects without the need for coding specialists.

What can we do with all AI Builder

A feature of the Microsoft Power Platform called AI Builder offers AI models that are intended to streamline your company's operations. With the aid of AI Builder, your company may apply intelligence to streamline procedures and extract knowledge from data using Power Applications and Power Automate. With AI Builder, you can leverage the power of AI without having any coding or data science expertise. You may either pick a preconfigured model that is prepared to use for many typical business scenarios or you can develop a bespoke model that is suited to your needs.

When you integrate the power apps and power automate into the AI things are easier. If you want to add intelligence to the power apps, here is what to do

- **First select a class of AI model**: Choose a model type based on your company's needs. Pick from an expanding range of AI solutions.
- **Data connection**: Choose your company's particular data from the list of alternatives.
- Custom models can be adjusted based on the type of model to improve how well your AI functions.
- **Train your AI model**; the procedure is automated. Based on your business data and customizing, it trains your AI model on how to

solve your business problem (for instance, how to detect your items on a picture). Your AI model can produce insights after training, such as the outcome of a prediction or the listing and number of items found in an image.

Prebuilt models vs Custom models

Prebuilt models from AI Builder make it easier to incorporate intelligence into apps and workflows without having to collect data, construct, train, and upload your models. For instance, you may add a component to Power Apps that use a prebuilt model to identify contact details from business cards. If you need to determine if client feedback was favorable or unfavorable, you may utilize a prebuilt model in Power Automate.

As soon as you choose a pre-built model from among the tiles in Try out the AI features for each type of data, select how you want to utilize the model (in a flow or app), and AI Builder will walk you through the construction process. The phrase Custom does not appear in the upper-right corner of a prebuilt model tile. When you click it, the following screen's top right corner displays the prebuilt model. The screen for the model of the business card reader is displayed in the example below.

Licensing

Your license for Power Apps, Power Automate, or Dynamics 365 now includes access to AI Builder. This means that once you have a Power Apps, or Dynamics, Power Automate 365 license that enables you to construct a Microsoft Power Platform environment, you may begin your AI Builder trial.

The first thing that you need to do is to buy the AI builder capacity add-on for the power apps, or power automates license. Then the administrator has to then choose the capacity of the power apps environment where the AI builder is going to be used from.

A billing administrator in the Microsoft 365 admin center can purchase the AI Builder capacity add-on, or you can use your normal channel.

Based on your anticipated use, the AI Builder calculator may help you determine the necessary add-on capacity.

Power Apps per app plan, Power Apps per user plan, and Power Automate per user plan with attended RPA are some Microsoft products that have some AI Builder capabilities. In the Capacity add-ons section of the Power Platform admin center, your environment admin may check entitlement. If this quantity is insufficient, you can add one or more AI Builder capacity add-ons to make up the difference.

Credits are unallocated and accessible as a pool on the tenant after they have been granted access to AI Builder capability; they may be utilized in any environment. By assigning all credits to certain contexts, the administrator can impose restrictions on usage.

Here is how to activate the AI builder license

- Log in to Power Automate or Power Apps.
- Select **Explore** in AI Builder.
- (If prompted) Select a currency and language, then create a database.
- Select **Create my database**.

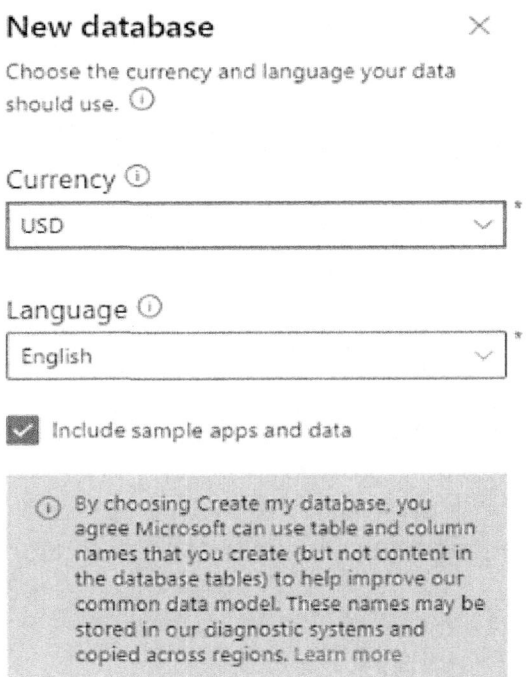

- Then refresh **Explore.**
- Then go to the top of the screen and choose **Start free trial.**

Processing images

To process images, you can use the Object detection parts in power apps. The component that performs the object detection scan takes a picture or loads an image file. The user of a mobile device has the option of shooting their photo or picking one from the device's user interface. The component automatically scans a specified picture to locate items.

Reading business cards

You can make Use of the AI Builder business card reader component to find and collect information from business cards. You have the option of taking photos right in the component or loading already-taken pictures. These characteristics are used to extract and identify data.

Recognizing text

Make a canvas project and add the AI Builder component for text recognition to the screen. The text recognition prebuilt model is used by this component to process photos or images that are loaded locally to find and extract text. If the component finds text in the image, it prints the text and marks each incidence in the image with a rectangle to identify it.

Detecting objects

You can use the Microsoft power AI builder to detect an object. Here is how:

- First sign into the power apps.
- Then select the AI builder on the left pane then select **Build**

- Then choose Object detection.
- Then name the AI model and create.
- Based on the image you will like to train, choose the model domain and select **Create**.

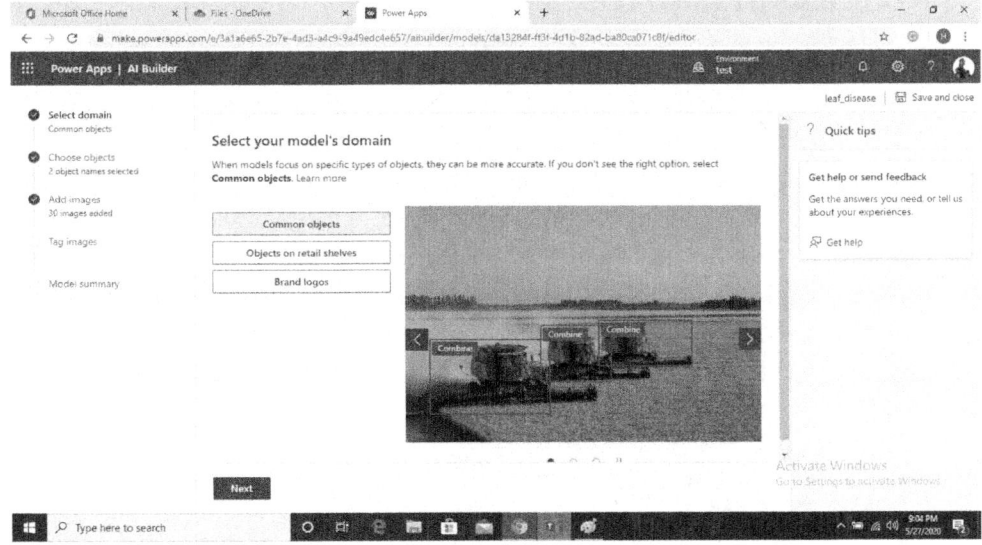

- Then you need to choose the object that you will like to detect.
- Then add the image to the train.
- Tag the images with the object type.

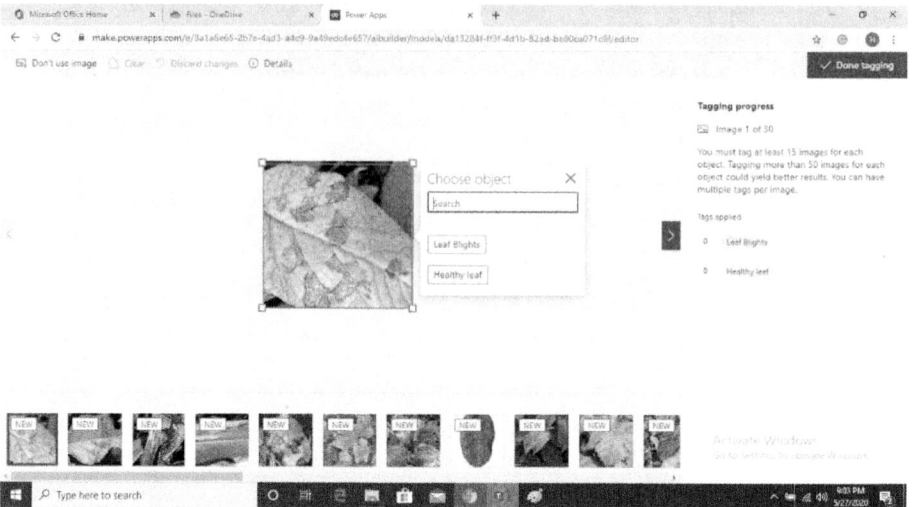

- Then you can display the **Model summary.** This shows the number of images per object.
- Then once the training is done, you need to test the model before working with it in the power apps.

Processing forms

When you process documents, you may read and store data from common papers like tax forms or invoices. By utilizing Power Automate and Power Apps to evaluate, extract, organize, and store the data automatically during this process, you may save a lot of time.

Develop your model and specify the data that will be taken from your forms. To get started, you simply need five form papers. Get precise results quickly that are suited to your particular content. You don't require a lot of manual labor or data science knowledge while using AI Builder.

Processing text

When you process files, you may read and store data from common papers like tax forms or invoices. By utilizing Power Automate and Power Apps to evaluate, extract, organize, and store the data automatically during this process, you may save a lot of time.

Develop your model and specify the data that will be taken from your forms. To get started, you simply need five form papers. Get precise results quickly that are suited to your particular content. You don't necessitate a great deal of manual labor or data science knowledge while using AI Builder.

- Log in to Power Automate or Power Apps.
- Navigate to **AI Builder > Explore** in the left pane.
- Choose **Extract** specific data from documents.
- Choose "**Get Started**."

You will be guided through the process by a step-by-step wizard, which will ask you to make a list of all the data you wish to take out of your document. Make that you have at least five examples using the same structure if you plan to build your model from documents that you already have. If not, you can build the model using test data.

Choose **Train**.

Make a quick test of the model by choosing it.

Choose the type of document from which you wish to automate data extraction in the Choose document type phase. There are two possibilities:

Documents that are organized and semi-structured. Structured and semi-structured files have fields, tables, checkboxes, and other elements that may be found in comparable locations for a particular layout. Invoices, purchase orders, delivery orders, tax paperwork, and other types of documents are examples of structured and semi-structured documents.

Free-form and ad hoc papers (preview). Unstructured papers lack a predetermined framework and typically include a variable number of paragraphs. Contracts, statements of labor, letters, and other similar papers are examples of unstructured documents. Currently, this document type is under preview. Your comments on this new preview feature are appreciated.

Analyzing text with formulas

With the help of the open-source, low-code Power Fx formula language, you can now integrate AI models into any Power Apps control. For instance, you may translate any user-contributed content into a different language by identifying the language it is written in. You already know Power Fx if you've used canvas applications.

Here is how to enable the power FX feature.

Categorizing text

- Sign in to the power apps
- Then create the canvas apps choosing to **Create then blank.**
- Go to the blank canvas app and choose to **Create.**
- Enter a name in the App name area and click **Create**.
- Select **Skip** if you come across the Power Apps Studio Welcome screen.
- Select **Settings** from the toolbar at the top
- Select **Preview** under Upcoming features.
- Scroll to the bottom and click On to enable the option for using AI models as data sources.

Extracting entities

The prebuilt entity extraction model can identify specific text data that is relevant to your company. The model extracts important textual components and groups them into predetermined categories. This can assist in converting unstructured data into machine-readable structured data. Processing can then be used to extract facts, retrieve data, and provide answers.

Then you need to work with the entity extraction. Here is how.

- First sign into the power apps
- Then go to the left pane and choose AI Builder and select **Explore**
- When you go to **Get straight to productivity,** choose **Entity extraction**

- When you enter the **Entity extraction window,** choose to **Try it out**
- Then you need to choose a default text sample in another analysis or to add the text inside the **or add your own here** box so that you can see how the model analyzes the text.

Using a prediction model

- To create a prediction model that makes of the online shopper intention table inside the Microsoft Dataverse, here is what you need to do.
- Sign in to the power apps and choose **AI builder** and select **Explore.**
- Then choose the **Prediction** and name the model and choose to **Create.**
- Then choose the historical outcome. Think of where the table with the information is, look for the specific detail in that table you want to predict, then find any missing details.
- Go to the **Table** drop-down menu and choose a table with the data and the outcome that you will like to predict.
- Then go to the columns drop-down menu and choose the column with the outcome.
- If you have chosen an option with multiple outcomes then you need to decide whether to map it as yes or no.
- To then predict multiple outcomes, make use of the Brazilian e-commerce dataset inside the sample and choose BC order inside the table drop-down menu and also inside the **delivery timelines** inside the column dropdown.
- Then choose the data column that will train the model.
- Then filter the data.

Review question

- How do you integrate AI builder?
- How do you analyze text with formula?
- How can one categorize text?
- Analyze a text using the formulas
- How does one extract entities?

Summary

In this section, we talked about the power of AI in your power apps and how to integrate them to make your work better.

PART SIX

CHAPTER TWEENTY ONE

BUILDING REUSABLE CANVAS COMPONENTS

In this chapter, we are going to be taking you through the ways to build reusable canvas components.

What can we do with canvas components

The majority of your app's UI requirements can be satisfied by using the robust components of Canvas apps. They should be your top priority because, in most circumstances, the cost of building and maintaining them might be less than that of the Power Apps component framework.

There are two options to create a reusable component. They are the canvas apps component. And this is a low code option in other to create a control that is used inside the power apps studio.

Then there is the power apps component framework. This is used by professional developers another build a reusable control inside the HTML, Typescript, and CSS.

Here is an image with examples of the canvas app component.

Component libraries, which are containers that enable it simple to reuse components across several apps, can be used to package Canvas apps' parts. It is simple to search for and find components, publish changes, and alert app developers when component updates are available thanks to component libraries.

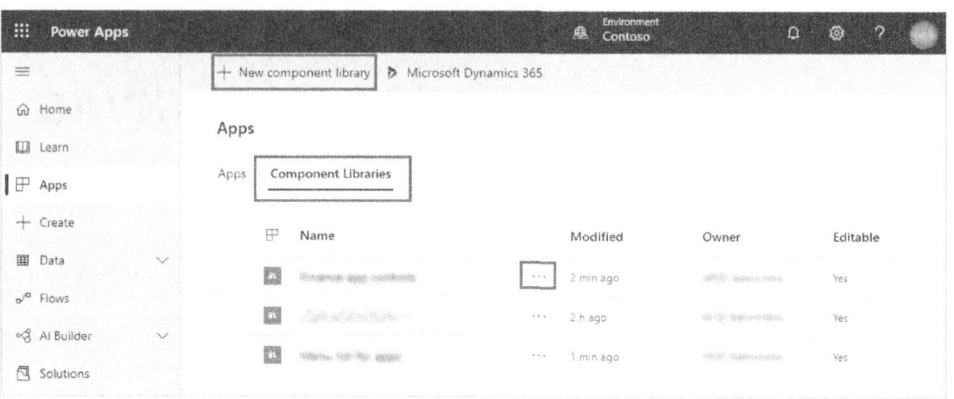

The Power Apps component framework provides access to a wide range of framework APIs for more complex scenarios, exposing features like component, contextual data, lifecycle management, and metadata. The sole alternative in situations when access to device functionalities is required, such as the camera or microphone, is to create a code component utilizing the Power Apps component framework. Model-driven apps, canvas apps, and Power Apps portals can all use code components made with the Power Apps component framework.

Designing a component

As described in this article, you can create a component from within an application or by adding a new component to an existing component library. For the requirement to use components throughout various app screens, a component library has to be employed. The current components can also be copied into an existing or brand-new component library.

If you want to build a component inside an app you need to enter the **Tree view,** choose the **Components** tab, and then choose a **New component.**

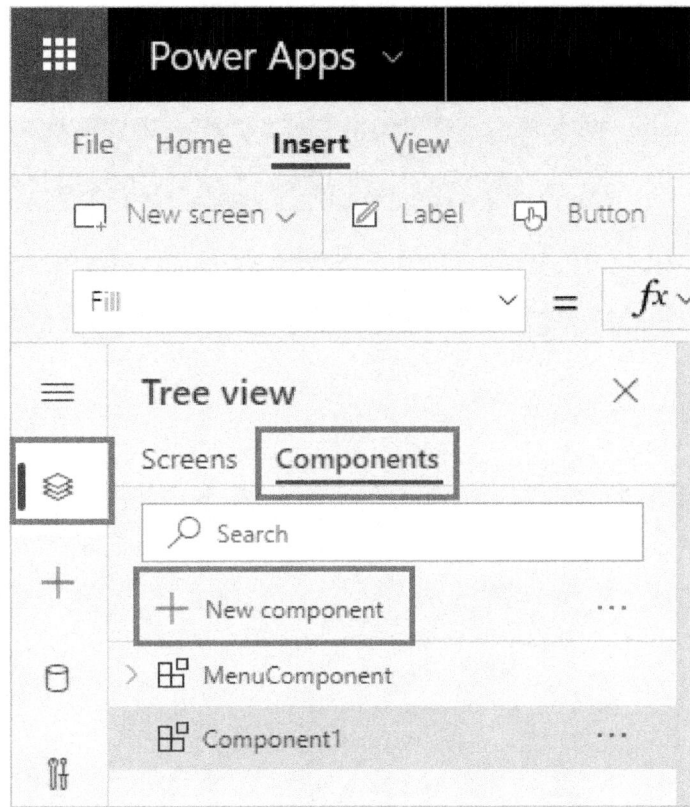

Selecting a **New component** displays a blank canvas. As an element of the component specification on the canvas, controls can be added. You can update instances of a component in those other app screens if you make changes to it in the canvas. When you publish component changes, apps that utilize previously built components can also get component updates.

After choosing a screen, you can choose a component first from the left pane's list of already-existing components. Similar to inserting a control, selecting a component causes you to place an example of that component on the screen.

You are going to see the components that are available inside the applications that are listed in the custom part inside a list of components in the **Tree view.** When you import a component from the component library, you will see them inside the **Library component** section.

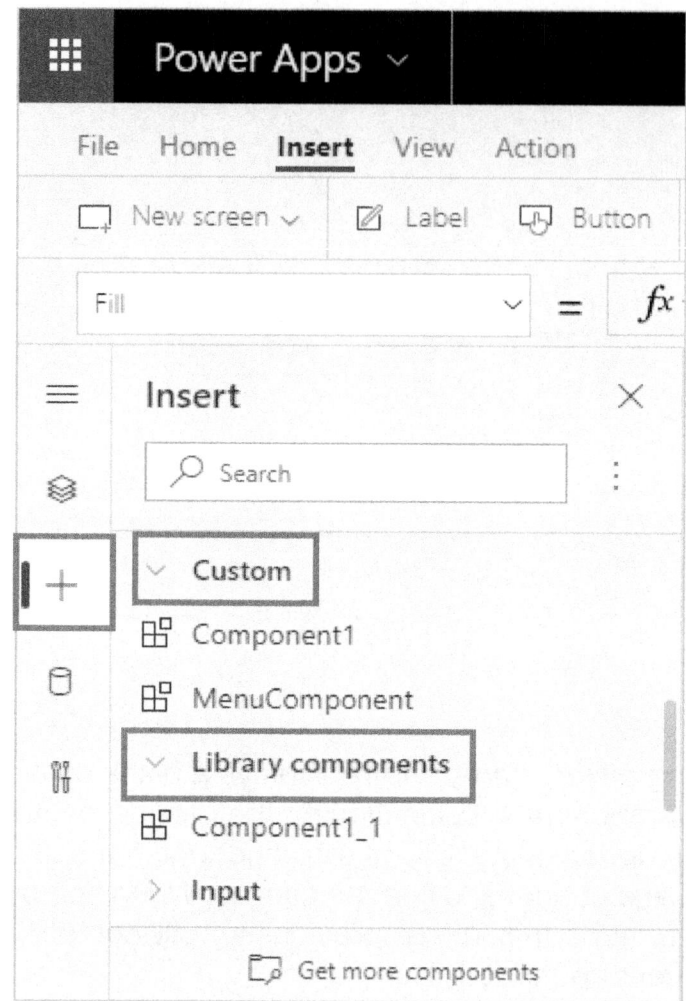

Where to define components

The interface between such a component as well as its host app is explicitly defined by the input and output properties. To make it simpler to recycle the component between apps, it is by default enclosed, necessitating the usage of properties to transfer data into and out of the component. Scope limitations allow permit component-definition modifications, especially when used with component libraries, and they keep the data contract of a component straightforward and consistent.

A component might, however, occasionally desire to connect a source of data or a variable including its host. Particularly when the component is only meant to be used with one specific app. In certain circumstances, setting on the Access app scope switch in the component's property will allow you to directly access app-level data:

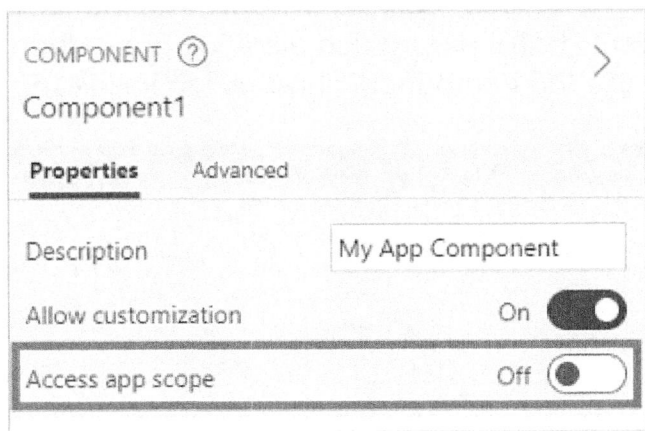

After you turn on the Access app scope, then you are going to see the global variable, the collections, the controls and components on the site like the text input control, and finally the tabular data source like the data verse table.

None of the aforementioned options are available to the component when this setting is Off. The generated variables and collections are scoped to the component instances and not distributed with the app, although the Set and Collect functions are still available.

Whether or not this setting is enabled, non-tabular data sources like Azure Blob Storage or a custom connector are accessible. Instead of being app resources, think about these data sources as referencing an environment resource. These environment data sources are included whenever a component is added to an app from such a component library.

Since there is no one app scope to refer to, components in a component library will never have a connection to the app scope. This setting is therefore ineffective because it isn't accessible in this situation. The switch can be turned on and the component updated to use the app scope after being imported into an app and if customization was permitted by the component maker.

Creating a component library

You can create a component of the canvassing app with the component library or you can also edit one either using the solutions area or also the component libraries tab inside the apps area.

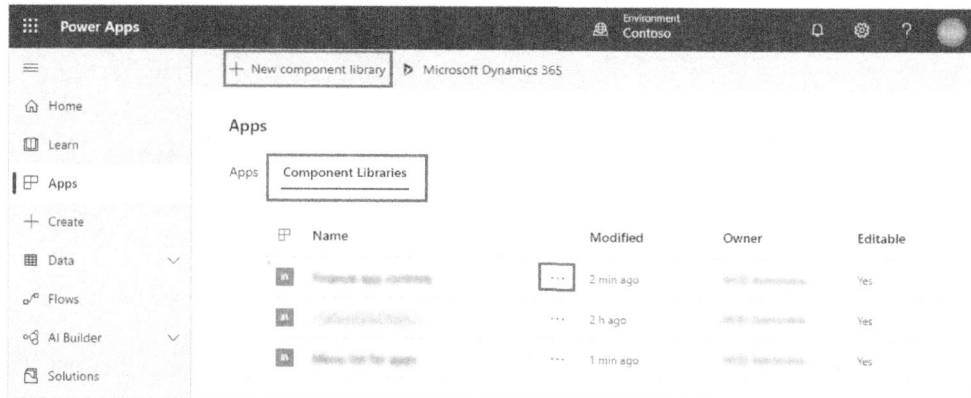

Adding controls to a component

Due to the lack of a single app scope, components in component libraries will never have a connection to the app scope. This setting is therefore ineffective in this situation because it isn't available. The switch can be turned on and the component adjusted to use the app scope if customization was permitted by component makers and was imported into an app.

Defining properties

If you construct one or even more custom properties, a component can accept input values and emit data. You must comprehend formulas and legally binding agreements to understand these complex issues.

A component gets data that will be used by the component using input properties. If an instance of the component is selected, input properties are displayed in the Properties tab on the right side of the window. Similar to how you can create standard attributes in other controls, you can configure input properties using expressions or formulas. The Default property of a Text input control is one example of an input property found in other controls.

Data or component status can be emitted using the output property. An example of an output property is indeed the Chosen property on the Gallery control. You may choose which other controls can make references to the component status when you add an output property.

Setting property values

Here is how to create a new component.

- The first thing to do is to build a blank canvas app.
- Then go to **Tree view** and choose **components** then choose **New components** so that you are going to create a new component.

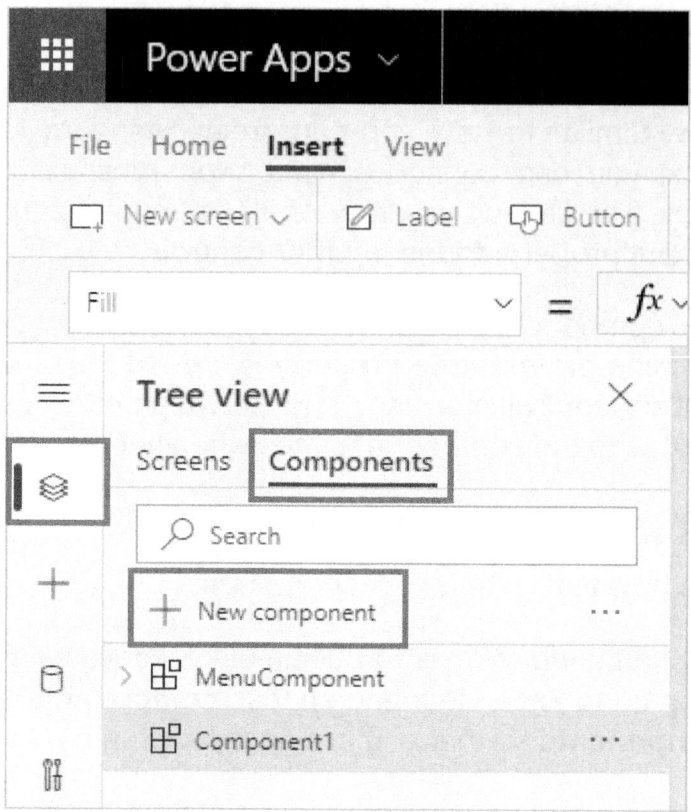

- Choose the new component made on the left pane and choose **Ellipsis...**then choose **Rename.** Then name the **MenuComponent.**
- Go to the right-hand side of the window then configure the width of the component to 150 than the height to 250 then choose **New custom property.** Then you can configure the height and the width to the value the way that you want it to be.

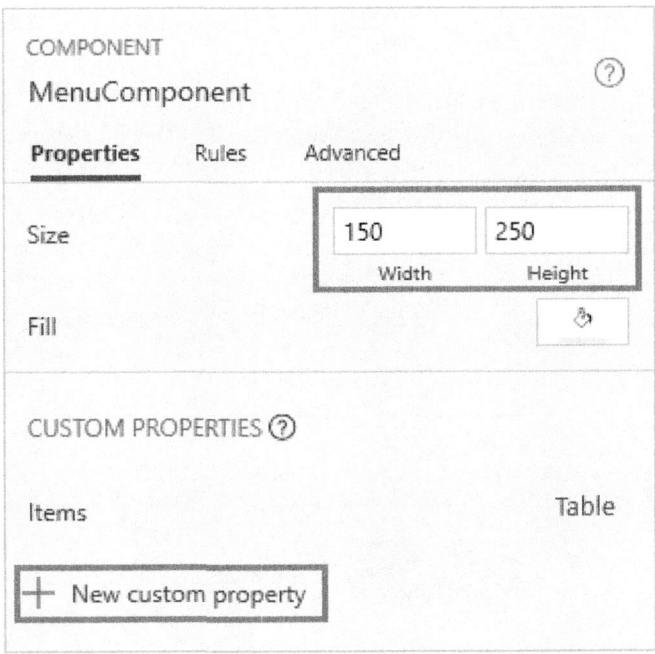

- Then inside the **Display name**, the property name, and the description boxes, enter **Items.** In the property, the name makes sure that you do not add space this is because you are going to refer to the component by the name when you are writing the formula. Take for example **componentname.propertyname**
- Inside the **Data type** list choose a **Table** and choose to **Create**

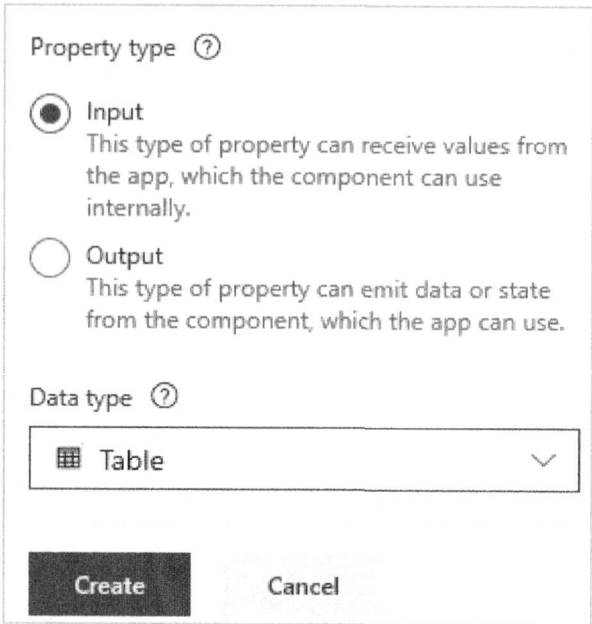

Property type ⑦

⦿ Input
This type of property can receive values from
the app, which the component can use
internally.

○ Output
This type of property can emit data or state
from the component, which the app can use.

Data type ⑦

▦ Table   ⌄

[Create]   Cancel

- Based on the data type you chose, the Items property will then
be set to a default value. It can be set to a value based on your
requirements. You might want to modify the value of the Items
property if you provided a data type of Table or Record so that it
corresponds to the data format you intend to feed into the
component. You'll convert it to a collection of strings in this
situation. If you choose the property's name just on the Properties
tab on the right side of the window, you can change the value of
the property in the formula bar.

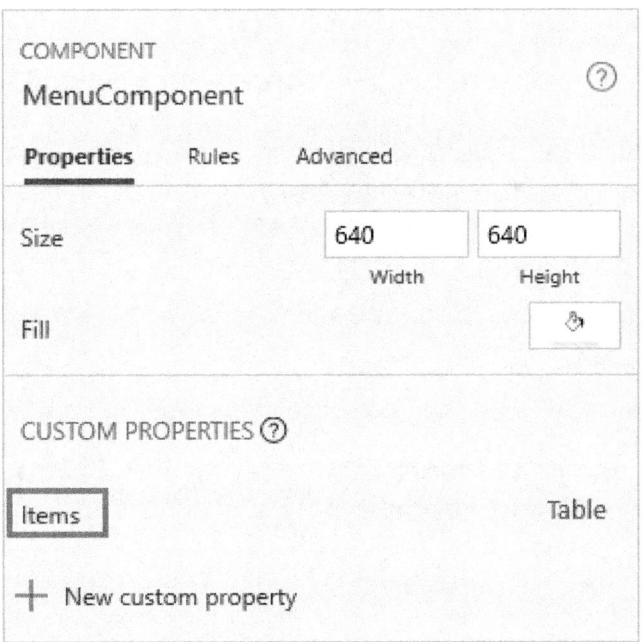

- Then set the component's **Items** property to the formula.

- Go to the component then add blank vertical **Gallery** control then choose **a Layout** inside the property pane as the title.
- Ensure that inside the property list there is an **Item** property. Then make sure that you set the value of the property as the following expression MenuComponent.Items. This means that the **Item** property inside the **Gallery** control reads depending on the item input property inside the component.

Adding components to apps

Adding a component inside a screen here is what to do

- Enter the left side of the screen and choose from the list of screens then choose the default screen

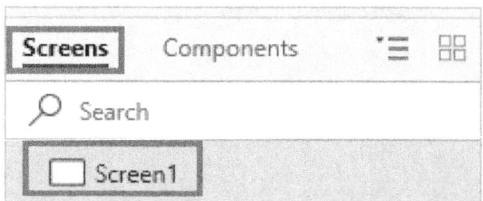

- Then enter the **Insert** tab and enter the **Components menu** then choose **MenuComponent**

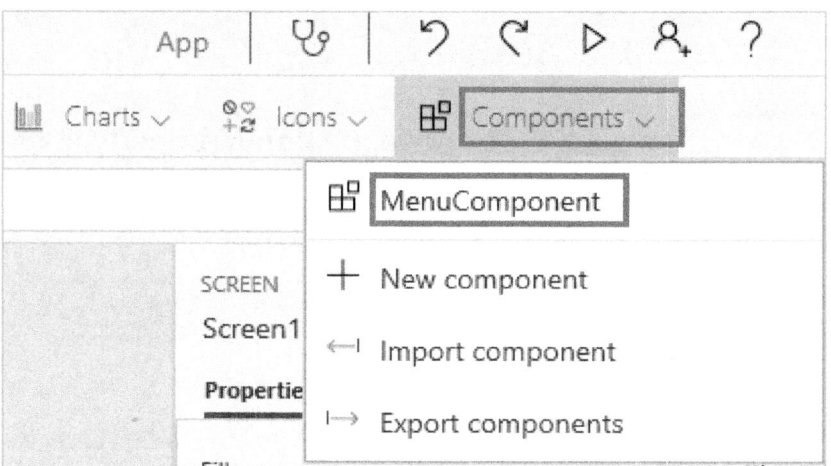

- Configure the item property for the menucomponent_1 to the following formula Table({Item:"Home"}, {Item:"Admin"}, {Item:"About"}, {Item:"Help"}) and you are going to get the following image

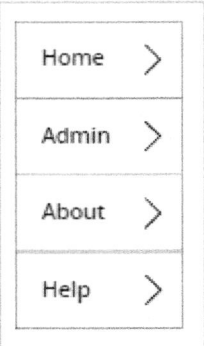

Updating a component

Here is how to update a component that is inside the app. There is a prompt that appears when you open an app that has a component inside. To make it show, close and reopen **My new app.** Then if you want to update the component, select the **Review** button.

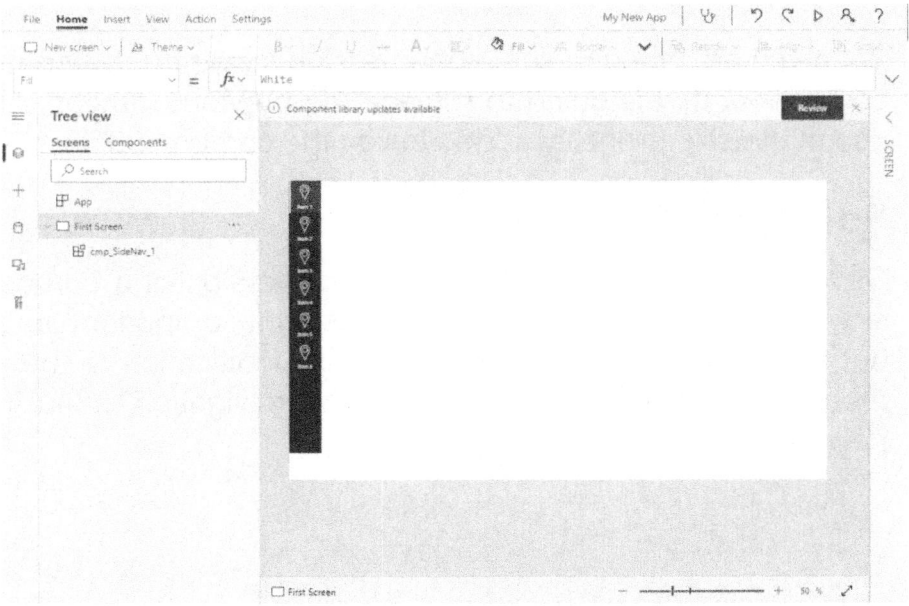

The list of component libraries that are used by the app appears with the modified date. Choose the component library that has been changed and select **Update.**

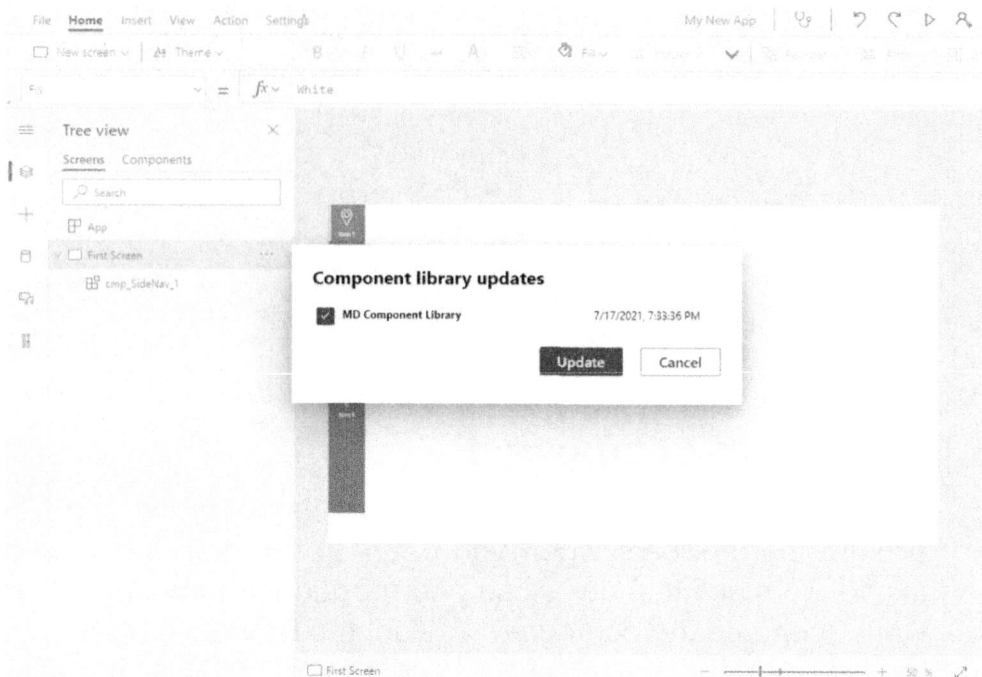

Then you are going to see a new version inside the **Navigation menu** component that is going to replace the previous version. Then make use of the size property added inside the component library.

Editing a component

Developers can instantly import a new version of a component with any apps that are currently using it using a component library. To try out this feature, we can make a minor modification to the navigation menu. As illustrated below, choose the navigation menu then add a new Size custom attribute.

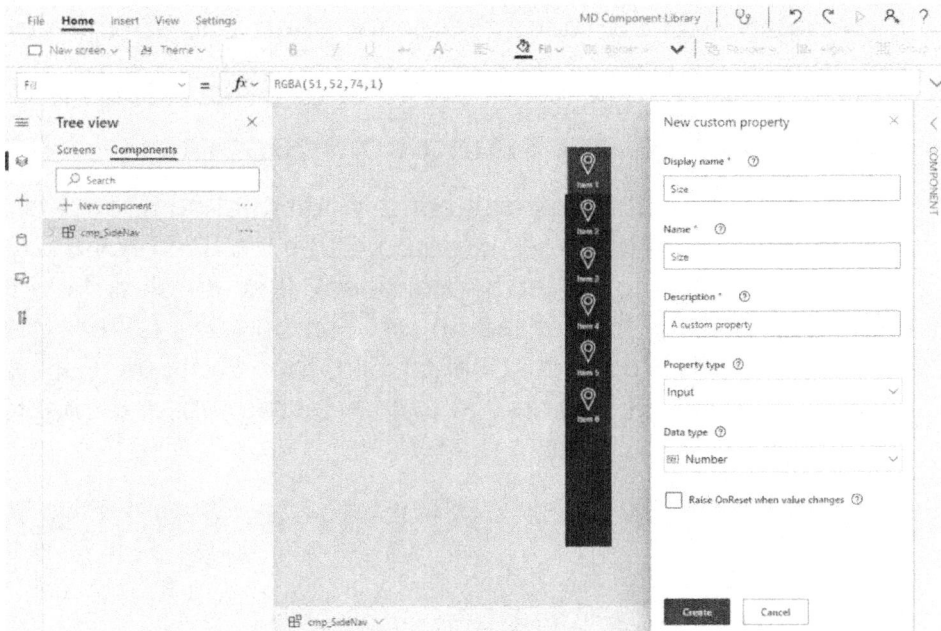

The reason why there is size a Size's function is to regulate the font size of all menu content. Change the Size property of the label lbl SideNav Value to cmp SideNav.Size. By entering a new value inside the component's size property, you can verify the changes.

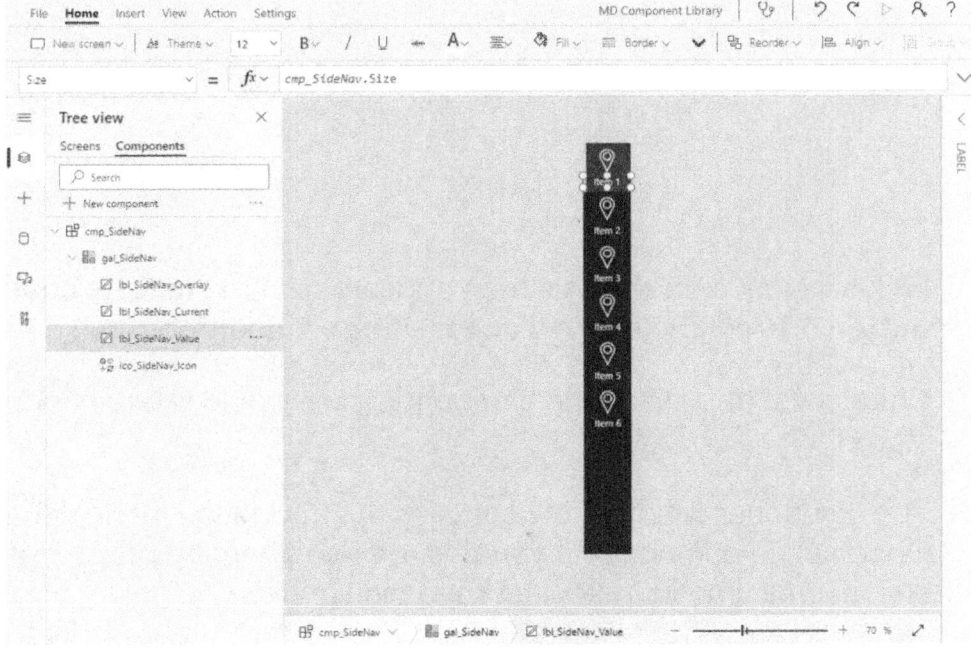

Immediately you are done, save and then publish the component library.

Exporting and importing components

The next stage is to construct some additional components after the component library has been created. But if we had previously created some of the parts for other applications? It is not clear how to import them. Fortunately, the retired import components feature can still be activated. On the top menu, select File, then Settings. Following that, choose Upcoming Features, go to the Retired tab, and enable **Export and Import** Components.

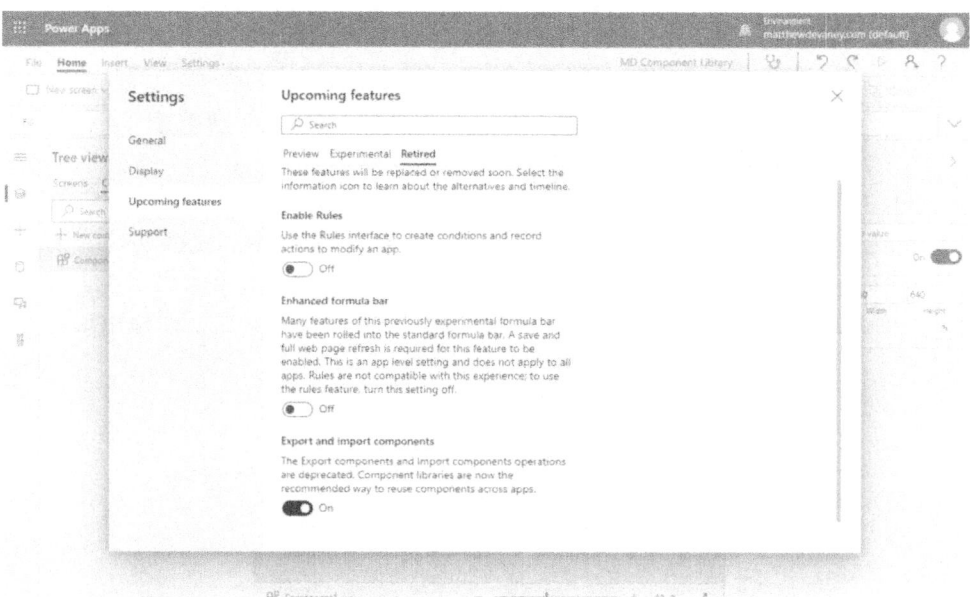

In this instance, the ellipsis then appears next to the **New component button.** Select the dot and choose **Import components.**

Choose the app inside the components we would like to import is also stored.

The component library now contains the navigation menu component. Once all the components you desire have been imported, repeat this step as much as you like, just save the library.

Importing and Exporting Components Libraries

Now, any app can import components from the library. Visit make.powerapps.com and start a new project called My New App from scratch. Click Get More Components after selecting the Insert symbol from the left menu.

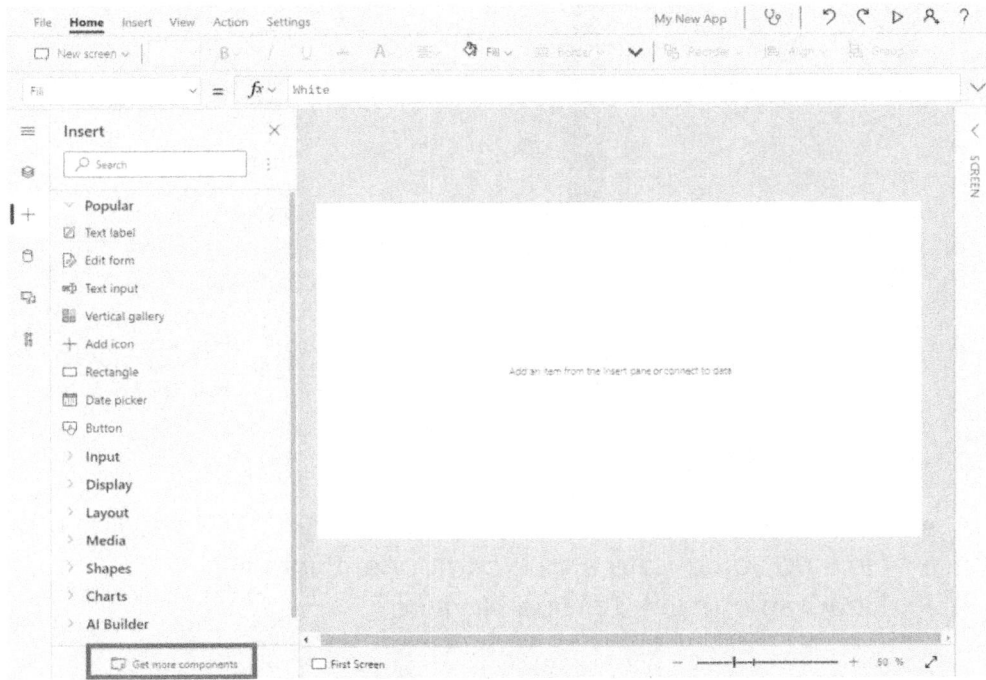

Then you are going to see the import component screen. Select the navigation menu component and select **Import**.

Then you are going to see the component on the first screen. Then if you want to use the navigation menu when you are on another screen you can see it inside the library component section in the **Insert** menu.

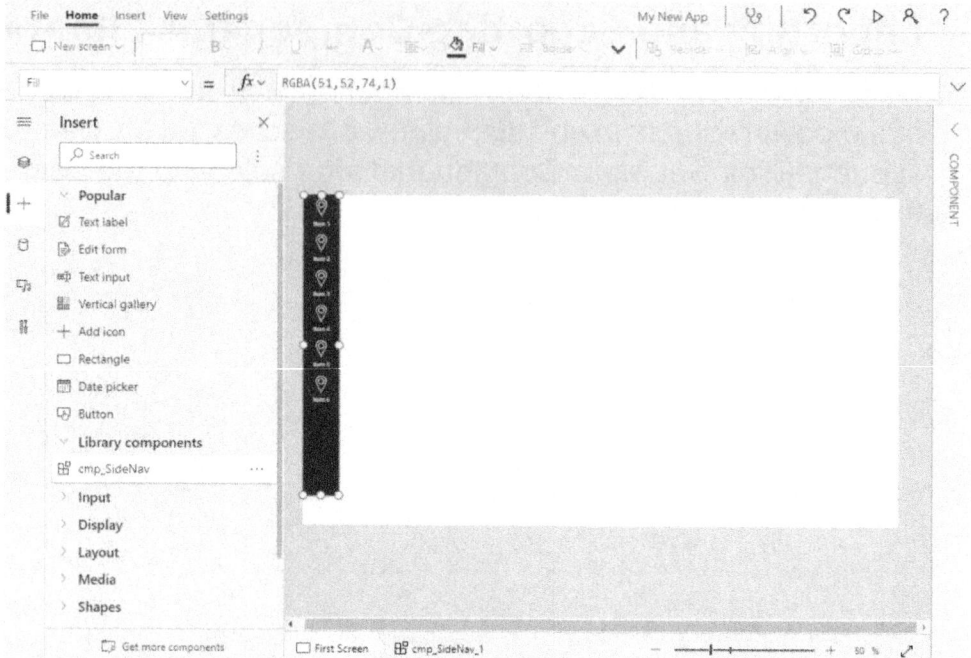

Activity/Review Question

- Add a new component inside the library
- How do you create a new component library?
- How can one set a property value?

Summary

In this section, we treated what can be done with the components of the canvas app and what they are. Then we went into creating and modifying the components.

CHAPTER TWENTY TWO

BUILDING REUSABLE CODE COMPONENTS

In this section, we are going to be building a reusable code component.

The most effective approach to enhance Power Apps is to create custom controls using the PCF framework (Power Apps Component Framework). Single or tabular datasets can be shown and edited using PCF controls. PCF controls work with both canvas and model-driven programs, in contrast to canvas components.

We use web-based programming languages including HTML, CSS, Typescript, and Node to create PCF controls. Creating a PCF control is not an easy process, despite the access to a large variety of functions and capabilities that this offers. The wonderful thing is that websites exist where we may get control created by other developers. This provides a simple method for us to add PCF-based controls to our programs.

Some basic knowledge of web programming is needed for this part. We'll thus go through the steps to create a straightforward control that verifies user input to keep things simple. The most crucial components of a PCF control are covered by this control, including the ability to set input and output attributes, alter the control's look using CSS, and invoke custom JavaScript.

What can we do?

A PCF control is composed of HTML (Hypertext Markup Language) and related logic, to put it simply. Model-driven and canvas apps are capable of storing and displaying PCF control contents during runtime. Designing a PCF control has several advantages. Since PCF controls are built using HTML and web-based technologies, it is straightforward to transfer whatever knowledge we have acquired while developing websites to PCF controls. We can create controls that have access to the camera, location information, and microphone using these web-based capabilities. A code component that connects to external internet services may be written by advanced developers, as well as code that uses web frameworks like React.

PCF controls may be divided into two groups: area components and data components. One value is displayed by a field component. For instance, a field control may be created to take the role of a textbox or labels on a screen. A dataset component is bound to a data list. A custom calendar control that shows several appointments might serve as an illustration of this.

All fields and dataset components are supported by model-driven applications. Canvas applications, on the other hand, are more constrained and only support field components.

Examining some of the accessible samples is the best method to comprehend the potential of code components.

Microsoft Samples

If you go to the Microsoft website, you are going to see the source code for the sample components. In this table, we have the compatible app types for the samples.

Name	Compatibility	Description
Angular flip	Model-driven, canvas	The flip component has a label and a button, and it may be bound to a Dataverse "Yes/No" field. The button can be clicked by the user to switch between the two choices. In terms of technology, it offers a demonstration of how to include the JavaScript frameworks AngularJS and Angular UI.
Control state	Model-driven, canvas	This feature illustrates how to keep user preferences consistent over several rendering of control in a single operation.
Data set grid	Model-driven, canvas	This example uses a tile-based layout to display a list of records. It demonstrates how to create an element that is bound to a list of records.

Name	Compatibility	Description
		This sample comes in Model-driven and canvas variants, with canvas having fewer capabilities owing to dataset API restrictions.
Formatting	Model-driven, canvas	We can format currency, integers, and date/time information using a PCF formatting API. The application of this API is shown in this sample.
Iframe	Model-driven, canvas	This example shows how to create a component that accepts longitude and latitude values as inputs and how to use a Bing map that is placed in an iframe to display the location.
Image upload	Model is driven only	In a model-driven app, the image upload component allows a user to choose and upload a picture.

Name	Compatibility	Description
Increment	Model-driven, canvas	A text field and an "increment" button are both present inside the increment component. This button may be clicked by the user to increase the value by 1. This sample shows how to create error handling and tie a numeric value to control.
Linear input	Model-driven, canvas	Users can enter numerical values via a slider control in the linear input component.
Localization	Model-driven, canvas	The localization component builds on the nonlinear input component by demonstrating how to utilize RESX (web resource) files to support many languages.
Map	Model-driven, canvas	The map component uses an iframe to show Google Maps. For

Name	Compatibility	Description
		Google Maps to display a user-specified location on the map, it sends the value of an input attribute to Google Maps.
Navigation	Model is driven only	The navigational capabilities made accessible by the PCF navigation API are shown via the navigation component. It shows how to present alert dialogs, store open dialogs, and direct the user to another website.
React Facepile	Model-driven, Canvas	Pictures from profiles are shown using the React Facepile component. It shows how to connect with Office Fabric and React (a JavaScript UI framework).
Table	Model is driven only	In a two-column table, the table component presents the results of API requests. It shows

Name	Compatibility	Description
		how to navigate to the current user as well as other preferences, like language and formatting choices.
Table grid	Model-driven only	The table grid component shows how you can bind grids with the ability to page through and sort columns.
Web API	Model-driven apps	The Web API component shows how to create, get, and update records out from the Dataverse Account table using Web API calls.

There are several excellent examples. Because we can customize the iframe controls to create components that can combine web pages as well as other online information into our canvas programs, it is incredibly flexible.

The format and table samples offer an understanding of how the PCF API's assistance functions operate. For instance, we may utilize API methods to style currency-based figures following user choices. We can also access user information from model-driven apps, including the current login and preferences for language and time.

There are ways to keep the state during a user session with PCF controls. For instance, if we design control with a lengthy scrollable list of data, we may keep track of where the user ends up when they leave the list to read a particular item. We can set the list up to pick up where it left off when the user comes back to it.

Some demos demonstrate how to interact with popular frameworks like Angular, React, and Office Fabric UI components for more experienced developers. These comprise the React Facepile and angular flip samples.

To be clear, the Office Fabric UI is a platform for creating pages that resemble Microsoft Office.

Other Samples

Then there is the PCF gallery

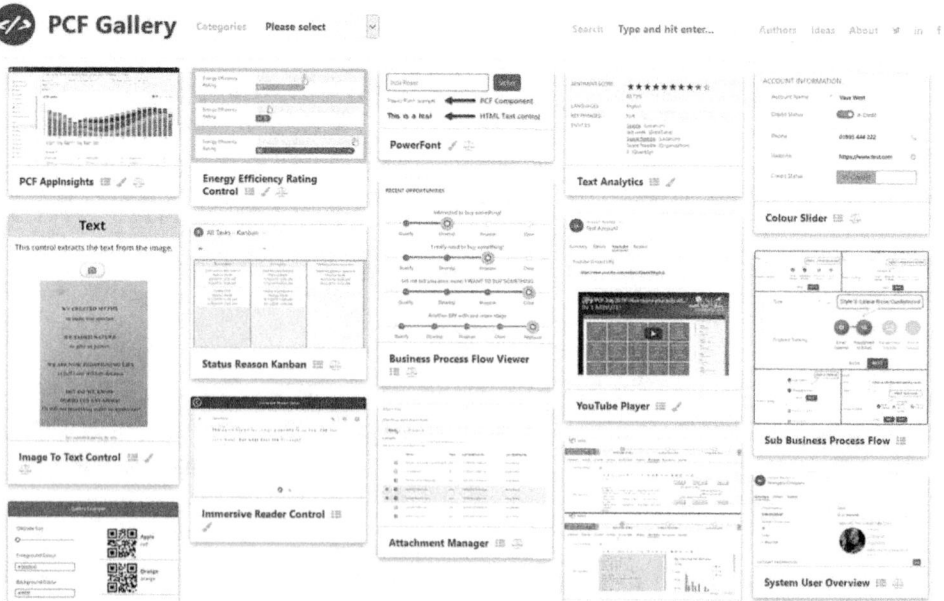

You can download other controls like the Bar code, and the validation charts.

QUICK GUIDE: AN OVERVIEW

Here we will now be taking you through the steps of building PCF control. The steps to follow consist of the following commands run with the command prompt.

Prerequisite

There are a few prerequisites that need to be prepared. And they include the NPM, the .NET framework developer pack, the visual studio code, and the power apps command line interface.

The CLI is a crucial element. PCF controls cannot be developed on devices running previous operating systems since this needs Windows 10. A Dataverse database and System Administrator or System Customizer access is required in the target environment for us to deploy a PCF control.

TypeScript is the name of the language we employ to create code components. This language was created by Microsoft and is open source. To get around the restrictions of utilizing JavaScript to create large-scale corporate programs, TypeScript was created. A superscript of JavaScript is TypeScript.

Installing NPM

An NPM is also known as the Node.js package manager. This JavaScript runtime called Node.js operates outside of a web browser. Making it possible to create JavaScript apps that can run on a server is one of Node.js core features.

We need to obtain several software packages for a PCF project utilizing the Node Package Manager (NPM). Installing the entire version of Node.js is the easiest approach to set up NPM. This is available for download from the following site:

https://nodejs.org/en/

This program will give you the option to then install the 'npm package manager'. Beyond this screen that we have here, the installer is then going to give you the notification to install other modules and they include also a package manager that is called a chocolatey. These components are optional and not required.

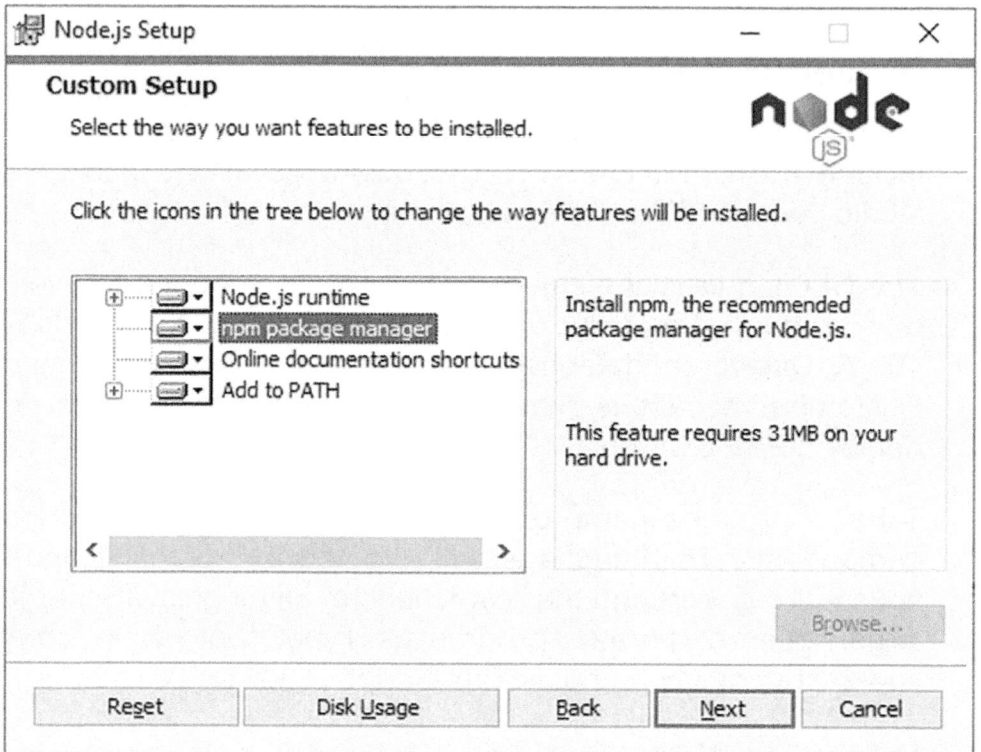

Installing the .NET Framework Developer pack

Then you need to install the microsoft.NET 4.6.2 developer pack. Then you can download it from the following site https://dotnet.microsoft.com/download/dotnet-framework/net462

The microsft.net 4.6.2 developer pack gives you the environment for the developer power shell and also the MS Build utility. You are going to need them to package and also to deploy the components

Installing the command line interface (CLI)

This is the main tool to create the code components. Enter the following site to download the CLI https://docs.microsoft.com/en-us/powerapps/developer/component-framework/get-powerapps-cli

We may design, build, and package the code components using a set of command line tools that are included in the installation package.

Through a command prompt, we may access the CLI's tools. By entering "command prompt" into the Windows Taskbar search box, we may launch a command prompt window.

Ours most often used command is Pac. As seen in the image below, we may type Pac further into the command prompt to view the use guidelines. The switches and settings depicted in this diagram should be known to you.

```
C:\WINDOWS\system32\cmd.exe                                         —    □    ×
C:\PCF>pac
Microsoft PowerApps CLI
Version: 1.3.6+gd2cc403

Usage: pac [auth] [help] [org] [pcf] [plugin] [solution] [telemetry]

   auth                    Manage how you authenticate to various services
   help                    Show help for the Microsoft PowerApps CLI
   org                     Work with your CDS Organization
   pcf                     Commands for working with PowerApps component framework projects
   plugin                  Commands for working with CDS plugin class library
   solution                Commands for working with CDS solution projects
   telemetry               Manage telemetry settings

Launcher usage: pac [install] [use]

   install <version# | latest> Install 'latest' or a specified version of the Microsoft PowerApps CLI
   use <version# | latest>    Use 'latest' or a specified version of the Microsoft PowerApps CLI
```

Installing Visual Studio Code

You are also going to need a code editor that can edit the typescript and the XML files. In other to build the example that we have in this chapter you can use notepad. However, practically you are going to need a dedicated code editor like the visual studio code.

Compared to other professional and commercial IDEs (integrated development environments), like the full version of Visual Studio, Visual Studio Code is lightweight and quick.

IntelliSense, colorful syntax highlighting, as well as the ability to personalize the editor with extensions—many of which are free—are just a few advantages of Visual Studio Code.

Creating a project

After completing the steps necessary to configure a development machine, you will now go through how to create a PCF control.

We'll create a text input control that uses a subscriber regular expression to validate user input as an example.

The control will make available two input properties: Default and Regex. The text input control's default value will be determined by the Default attribute. We may provide a regular expression that specifies a valid input by using the Regex attribute. The control will turn red if indeed the value entered by the user does not fit the regular expression pattern.

The output property IsValid will also be made available by the control. This provides a Boolean result to show whether the input is correct. We'll develop the control shown in the image below.

Despite being a straightforward control, this example will demonstrate all the crucial stages involved in creating a PCF control. This covers both how to get values out of the host screen using input attributes and how to get data back in by using output properties. Additionally, we'll discover how to customize a control's JavaScript and CSS.

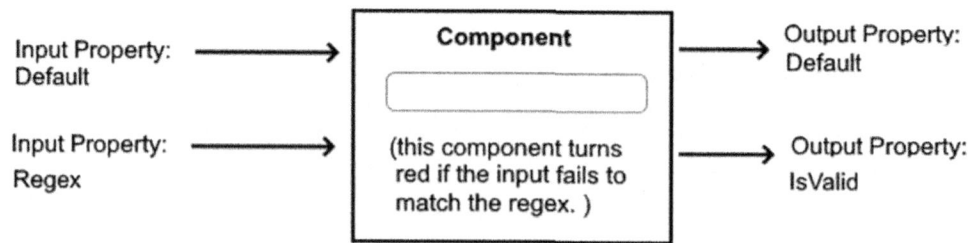

A project must be created first. An organization of code files and references to required code libraries is called a project.

Creating a PDF project

We'll save our project in our example under C:PCFValidatingControl. To set up this directory in Windows Explorer is the first thing to do.

Open a command prompt window and go to the project directory in the next step. To change the working directory, we may use the cd command as follows:

Cd C:\PCF\ValidatingControl

Then Execute the next PCI command: pac pcf init --namespace --name ValidatingInput --template field.

These are the arguments that the PCF command follows:

- The namespace. Which identifies the objects in the project.
- The name this is the name of the project.
- The template. There are two acceptable values and they are the **Field** and the **Dataset.** If you want to control binding to one value, then select the field template. Then if you want to then build the control binding to the table of data then select the dataset template.

Examining our project layout

Take a look at the file that we have added to the working folder using the pac pcf init command.

Name	Type	Size
ValidatingInput	File folder	
.gitignore	GITIGNORE File	1 KB
package	JSON File	1 KB
pcfconfig	JSON File	1 KB
tsconfig	JSON File	1 KB
ValidatingControl.pcfproj	PCFPROJ File	3 KB

This PC › Local Disk (C:) › PCF › ValidatingControl › ValidatingInput

Name	Type	Size
generated	File folder	
ControlManifest.Input	XML Document	2 KB
index	TS File	3 KB

Here the root folder has the set of files, and they also have a subfolder similar to the name of the control. In that subfolder, you are going to see the working files. Two of which are notable.

Adding project references

PCF projects are dependent on several different code packages. We return to the command prompt, go to the root directory (C:PCFValidatingControl), and enter the following line to install these packages:

Npm install

The Node Package Manager is instructed by this operation to get the required files from the internet repositories and save the results into a subdirectory named node modules.

Developing a control

Now that our project is set up, we can begin to construct our PCF control. The three steps that make up this procedure are as follows, which we'll go over in more detail:

Configure the manifest file's settings:

- The control is created using TypeScript.
- Apply CSS to the control's styling.

Defining the control manifest

Our control information is defined in the manifest file. This comprises information about a control's name, description, and version number. The manifest file is the most crucial location for defining a control's input and output attributes as well as resources like CSS files.

Three attributes will be present in our example control. An output property named IsValid, an entry property named Regex, and a Default property that determines the textbox's starting value.

Then if you want to build one of the manifest files, enter the **controlmanifest.input.xml** inside the visual studio code or the text editor.

Several comments provide thorough documentation for the manifest file. We may define information such as the control name, description, and type using the attributes of the Control element.

By placing Property elements underneath the Control element, we can then define properties. We can include references to supplementary files, such as CSS and RESX files, in the Resources section (we use RESX files to help localize the content of our control).

The file's last section contains sections that may be uncommented to grant access to app functionalities like audio and video capture.

Then if you want to then build the example control, you are going to have to modify the manifest file. Here we have a simplified version that leaves out the commented section.

```xml
<?xml version="1.0" encoding="utf-8" ?>
<manifest>
  <control namespace="timleung" constructor="ValidatingInput" version="0.0.1"
      display-name-key="ValidatingInput"
      description-key="ValidatingInput description"
      control-type="standard">
  <property name="Default" display-name-key="Default"
      description-key="The default value of the control"
      of-type="SingleLine.Text"
      usage="bound" required="true" />
  <property name="Regex" display-name-key="Regular Expression"
      description-key="The Regex that defines a valid entry"
      of-type="SingleLine.Text"
      usage="input" required="false"
      default-value=".*"/>
  <property name="IsValid" display-name-key="IsValid"
      description-key="Returns true if the input is valid"
      of-type="TwoOptions"
      usage="output" required="false" />
  <resources>
    <code path="index.ts" order="1"/>
    <css path="css/ValidatingInput.css" order="1" />
  </resources>
  </control>
</manifest>
```

We've made two significant modifications to this file. First, to specify the attributes of our control, we added three Property components. By uncommenting the CSS element in the Resources section, we have declared a CSS resource, which is the second modification.

Each property's definition calls for a brief further description. There are several qualities we may set for each property. These include:

Name- which is the term we use to reference the property in our TypeScript code. Additionally, the canvas app designer uses this name.

Then the display name Key- appears inside the app designer. When you are using a model-driven app you are going to see it when you assign controls to a field inside the form designer

Description key— you will see this inside the app designer, etc

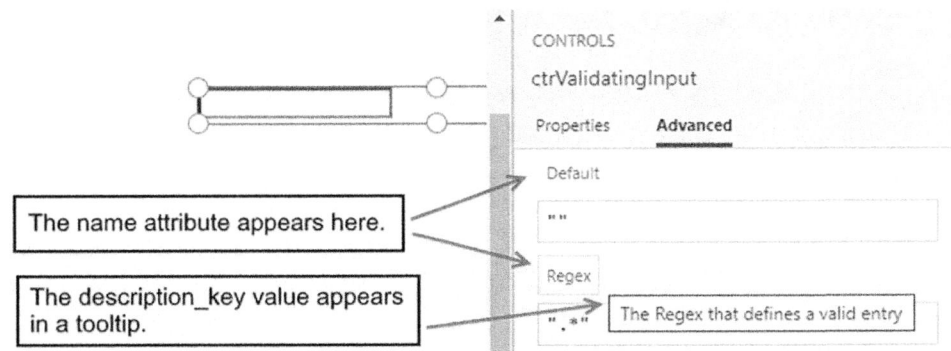

Binding, input, and output are all acceptable choices for the use attribute. An input and output property, a bound property can connect to a data field. In contrast, read-only data are entered into our control via an input property.

Finally, we may specify the type-group property to establish a list of suitable data types instead of defining the IsValid attribute. This would allow us to specify the data types that are compliant with the control for a bound property inside a model-driven application. The metadata file's built-in note explains how to use this syntax.

Writing the code

Then you are going to need to modify the TypeScript file. This is where the functionality of the control is defined and they include the HTML markups and the logic that runs with it.

Style the component with CSS

Making a CSS file and specifying the CSS classes we wish to use in our control are the last two tasks. We defined a link to the CSS file css/ValidatingInput.css in our manifest file.

It is vital to generate this file because it doesn't already exist. We start by making a blank file in Visual Studio Code (or another text editor), we can then add the following class to a file.

.notValid{background-color:red}

The notValid class that we use in the inputChanged method is defined by this. The red background color specified by this CSS class denotes the occurrence of an error.

The file must be saved as the last step. Any path that you specify in the manifest file is relative to the Typescript. Based on our example here is where we will save the file. C:\PCF\ValidatingControl\ValidatingInput\css\ValidatingInput.css

Building a control

The PCF control phase is now over. The creation and testing of our control is the following phase. We can verify that our control operates as intended during this process.

We employ the npm command to create our control. We launch a command prompt and go to the project's root directory. This is the following directory in our example:

C:\PCF\ValidatingControl\

The next command we execute is as follows:

Run **build npm**

Our initiative will grow as a result. The build process will fail if there are any mistakes, which will let us know what's wrong. For instance, the build output will specify the specific error and the file name, and the line number where the mistake occurs if our Typescript has syntax issues.

Testing a control

We launch a command prompt, go to the root directory, and type the following command to launch the test bed:

"npm start run"

When we run this command for the first time, Windows Defender will show a firewall notice. The option to let test environment Internet connectivity can be enabled. If everything goes as planned, we'll see the page depicted in the image below

We can modify the input properties of our control's values using the properties pane on this page. We may interact with our control through the main portion of this page and make sure it functions as intended.

We can use the keystrokes Ctrl+K and Ctrl+C to end the npm process at the command prompt.

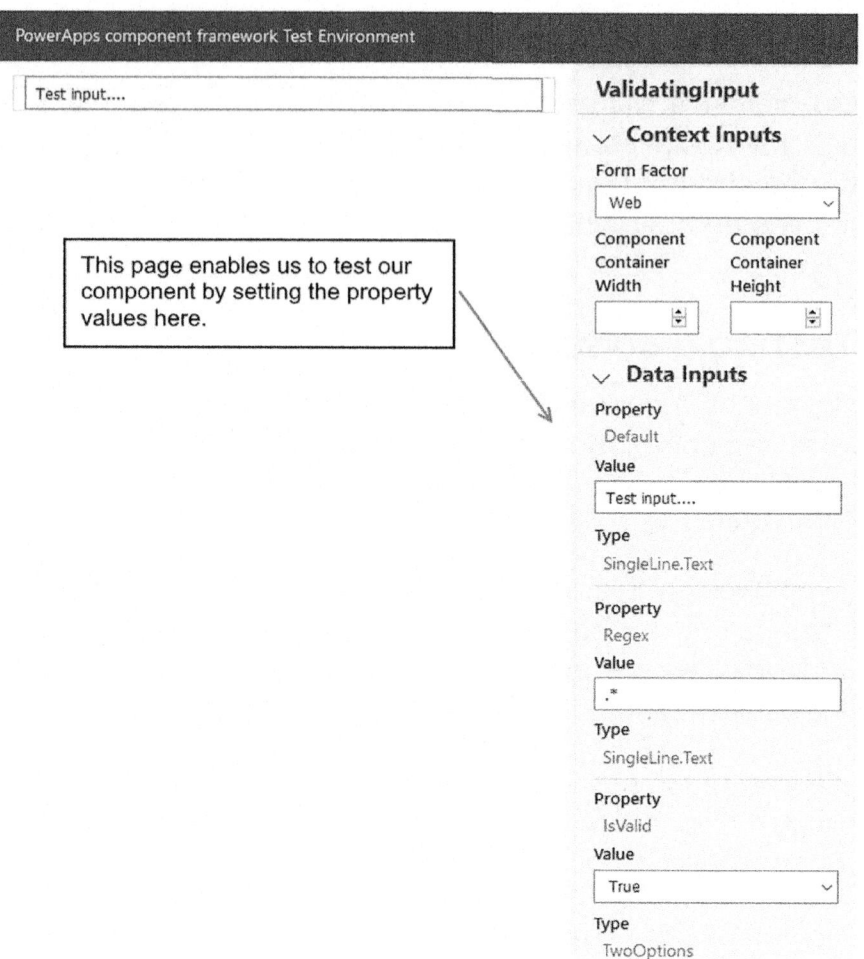

Deploying a control

We can proceed to package and deploy the control in the specific environment assuming that it performs as anticipated.

Using Power Apps, we can move objects across environments or deploy adjustments. Therefore, there are two stages to complete to deploy our custom control to a target environment. We start by developing a solution project. We next construct and package our answer into a zip file, which we may utilize to install our controls into the environment of our target.

Creating a solution

The first step in creating a solution is making a folder to house it. We'll build the following folder for this illustration:

C:\PCF\ValidatingControl\Solution

The following action is to launch a command prompt. We next proceed to our solution and execute the command

A solution is created using this command. Both a publication name and a publisher prefix are needed. A lengthy description that specifies the control's publisher may be used as the publisher name. The prefix that Dataverse adds to the solution's pieces is determined by the publisher prefix. As an illustration, we've seen how Dataverse uses a prefix to create logical table names (such as cr8a9 property).]

Then you need to enter a reference to the control project

Building a solution project

Now that our solution project is finished, we must construct our project. MSBuild is the name of the program used to create projects from the command line. We open the developer PowerShell session by typing "Developer PowerShell for VS2019" into the Windows Taskbar to begin building our project.

To recover all solution project dependencies, we visit the folder containing our solution (C: PCFValidatingControl) from the developer PowerShell window and enter the following command:

/t:restore MSbuild

Then the build is going to generate the output file. The output location is connected to the solution project. Here we can get the output if we go to the folder.

Installing a control

We can import the solution file into our target environment now that it has been built. Enter the Maker Portal and select the Solutions menu item to get started. From this point, we may select Import and upload our Solution.zip file. Then you are going to see the following:

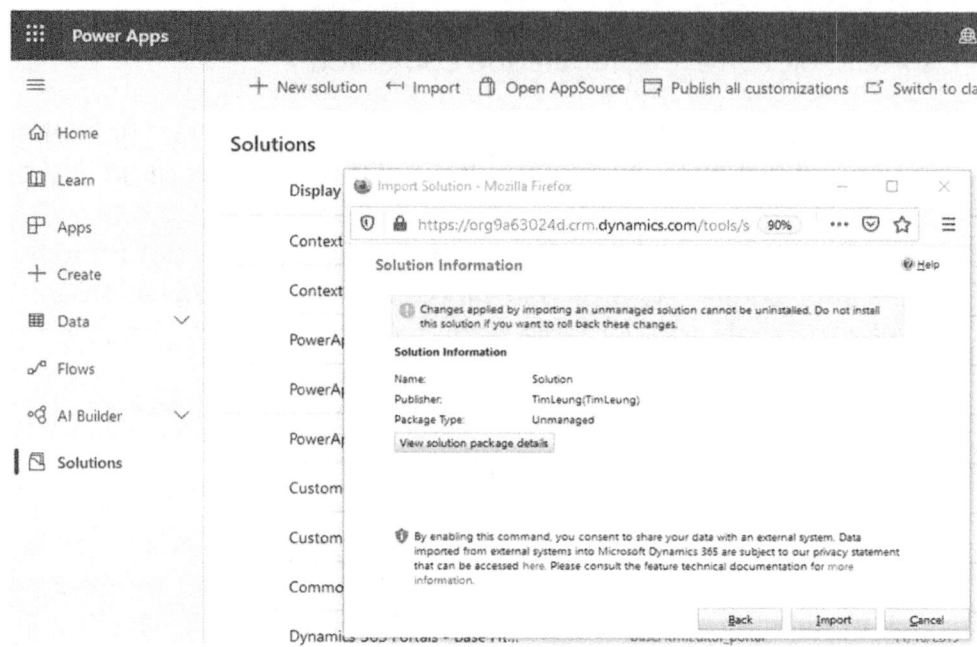

This prompts us to know that we install a managed solution that cannot be uninstalled. We are going to have to accept the warning and select the import button to finish the installation.

USING THE CONTROL

Then you can use the controls in the canvas app and the model-driven app.

Canvas app

There is a preliminary security step that we must complete to use a PCF control in a canvas program. Open the target environment settings from the Power Platform admin center, then go to the Product Features section. The "Power Apps component framework for canvas apps" option needs to be enabled .from here.

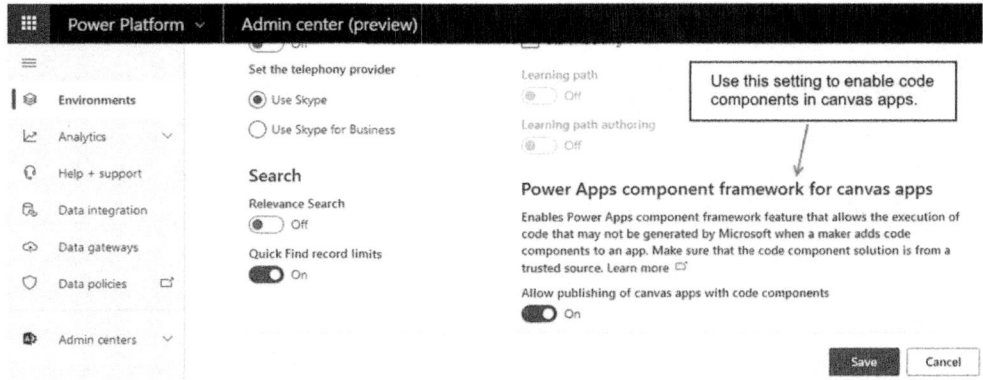

Then you need to edit the app or create a new one. Go to **Custom** and select **Import component.** Then choose the code tab to then import the control.

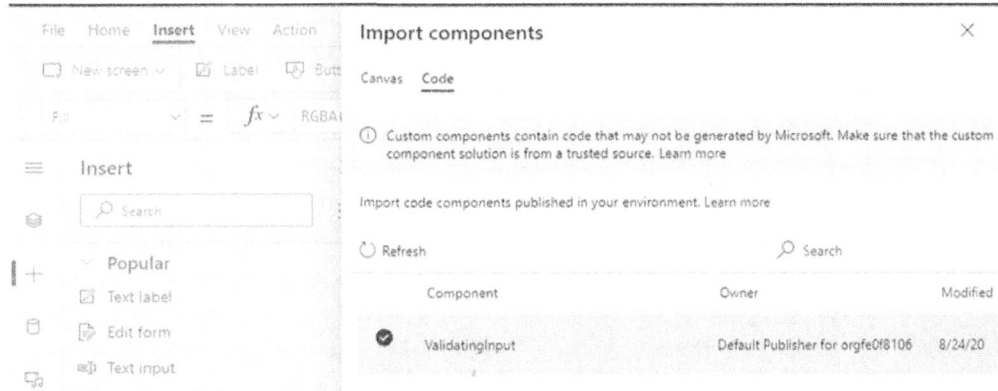

Model driven app

To then set the model-driven app for use with the PCF control, you need to associate the control with a field

Activity/ Review Question

- How do you build reusable code?
- Build a control using reusable code components.
- How do you create a project?
- Define a control manifest.
- How do you install controls into the data environment?

Summary

Using the Power Apps Component Framework, we discovered how to create controls in this chapter (PCF). With the help of this framework, we can easily create specialized controls that interact with canvas and model-driven applications.

PART SEVEN: OFFLINE AND INTEGRATION

CHAPTER TWENTY THREE

WORKING OFFLINE

Power Apps are made to run smoothly on mobile devices, however, occasionally, connections to the Internet are lost. It can be quite helpful for users to be able to keep functioning throughout these moments. Field service personnel, users who frequently work outside, and users who travel frequently should be aware of this in particular.

Power Apps provides the option to cache information just on local devices to account for these eventualities. We can create apps that function offline using this functionality. Offline model-driven programs can be supported well by Power Apps. However, creating a canvas app that only runs offline is a manual process that presents a highly challenging obstacle.

What happens offline?

Let's first look at what takes place on the smartphone player whenever a device loses Internet access. An automatically produced canvas app that goes offline in the middle of a session will still be largely usable. The search and sort options on the browse page will still function and display the data that was present before the app went offline. Even if we can access records on the edit screen to view the data, individual records would still open on the display screen.

Users can only run applications that have already been installed on the device when they launch Power Apps while they are not connected to the Internet. An app cannot access the data source's initial set of data when it loads while offline, hence it cannot display any data.

How do model-driven apps act when they are not connected to the internet? Model-driven apps previously only offered a few common Dynamics 365 entities with limited offline functionality. Model-driven apps can now access custom table's offline. Unlike canvas programs, it is a built-in capability, so we can offer offline support without having to create any intricate, unique algorithms.

Canvas formulas that enable offline working

Two formulas will make the canvas app be built offline.

1. Connection.Connected—this will return true if the device has been connected to a network.
2. Connection.Metered—this returns true if the device is connected to a metered network

This signal is capable of identifying metered connections in active connections. On smartphones, the mobile connection is typically set up as a metered connection. The app can be trained to conserve data, because of the ability to detect a metered connection. For instance, in this circumstance, we can create a formula to conceal photos.

Saving and retrieving local data

One of the most important parts of building offline apps is that you can save them locally. Here is the function to save and retrieve local data. SaveData and LoadData.

There are two parameters with the **SaveData** function. And that is the collection of the data to save and the name of the file. This is a simple example of storing data from a collection that is called **colproperties** inside a file called. Offlinepropertiesfile:

SaveData(colproperties, "offlinePropertiesFile')

The SaveData function isolates the data's storage and encryption from other customers and other programs. SaveData will replace an existing file with the same name if one already exists. We can call the LoadData method as follows to obtain the file data:

LoadData (colProperties, "OfflinePropertiesFile", true)

The destination collection for the data is specified by the first argument, and the file name from which it will obtain the data is specified by the second parameter. If the file doesn't exist, the third option instructs the LoadData method to proceed without error.

Only the data that we stored with SaveData within the same app may be retrieved by using LoadData. You cannot import data from other apps.

It should be noted that SaveData and LoadData capabilities are unavailable in the designer and do not operate on apps that run in browsers. As a result, when we use these functions, the designer displays errors inside the formula bar; however, we may disregard these mistakes.

Making a canvas app available offline

We'll now go through how to make an automatically produced app function offline. Although the Dataverse data source will be the foundation of our program, we may modify the methods to make it work with other data sources. Users will be able to browse, change, and add records when offline thanks to the adjustment we'll make.

We are going to be using the example that we have below in the image.

Application Start The app copies data from the Dataverse *Property* table into a local collection called *colProperties* .	Connection Status: ONLINE	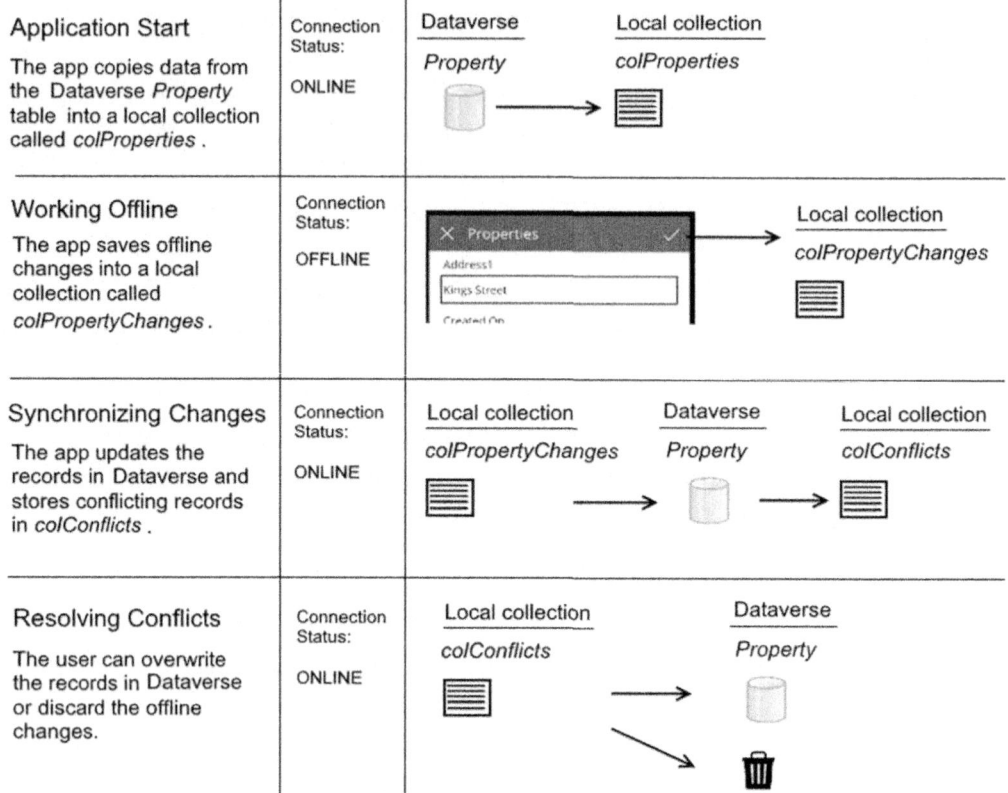
Working Offline The app saves offline changes into a local collection called *colPropertyChanges* .	Connection Status: OFFLINE	
Synchronizing Changes The app updates the records in Dataverse and stores conflicting records in *colConflicts* .	Connection Status: ONLINE	
Resolving Conflicts The user can overwrite the records in Dataverse or discard the offline changes.	Connection Status: ONLINE	

Data from Dataverse is loaded together into the local collection when the program first launches. All of the app's panels will be modified so that they interact with this local collection instead of the property table directly. If the device is connected to the internet, the app will store any modifications made by the user while adding or editing a record. The application stores the modifications to a holding collection if the device is offline (colProperties, in our example).

The app will use the SaveData function to access a local device cache during any data refresh or update activity. The app will try to load the information from a local file rather than from Dataverse if the device is offline when it first launches.

Then the app gives you a screen showing the records with the collection. Once the device is online, then the user can then make use of the screen in other to syn the changes to the Dataverse.

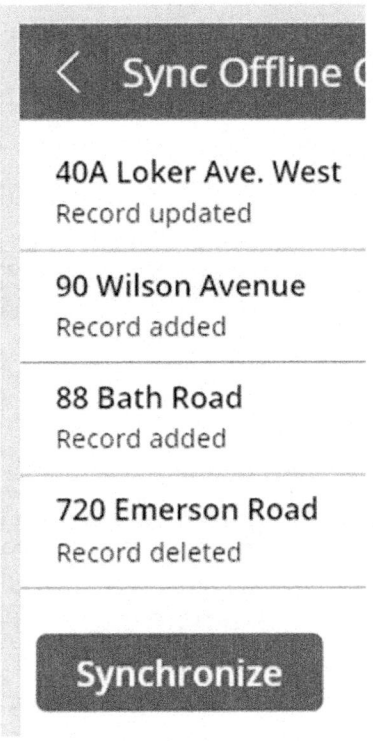

When the user cannot access the network for a long period, the other user can modify the record. If you do not want the other users to overwrite the changes that they make, the app runs a search to determine that there are no changes then it will synchronize the data. And when there are data discrepancies, then the user can discard the offline changes with the screen below.

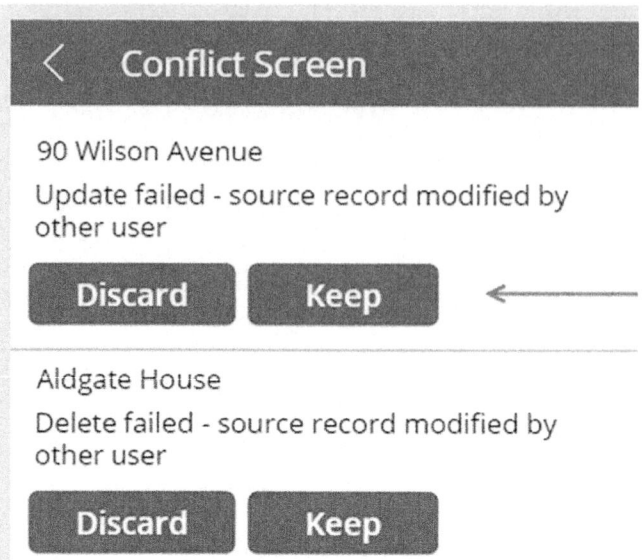

What you need for this example is first to build an auto-generated app based on a property table. There are two important fields that the app is going to be relying on inside the Property ID and the **modified** fields

Each entry in the database is identified only by its value in the PropertyID field, a custom autonumber field. The date and time of the most recent alteration are automatically entered into the usual "Modified On" column by Dataverse.

A built-in ID column of data type "unique identifier" is present in every Dataverse table (otherwise known as GUID). Therefore, instead of developing a bespoke autonumber field, why not use the built-in GUID field? The problem is that we are unable to seek records using GUID fields in a delegable manner. When synchronizing an offline modification, we are unable to reliably access the source record since we rely on a primary key field of the data type GUID. Especially when the Dataverse table exceeds 2000 rows

Last but not least, it's critical to recognize that creating an offline app is a very specialized procedure. The major goals of this example are to shed light on the difficulties that we face and to present a general framework that we can use to create offline applications.

Setting the Data source to a Local Collection

Once the app loads then what it does first loads the data source from the Dataverse table inside a local collection and also some other tasks.

This listing displays the code that is added inside the data ONstart property of the app. //1 Initialize collections that we use in the app

```
ClearCollect(colPropertyChanges,Blank());

//2 Main startup logic

If(Connection.Connected,

  ClearCollect(colProperties, Properties),

  LoadData(colProperties, "OfflinePropertiesFile", true)

);

UpdateIf(colProperties, IsBlank(Address1), {Address1:""});

UpdateIf(colProperties, IsBlank(Address2), {Address2:""});

UpdateIf(colProperties, IsBlank(City), {City:""});

UpdateIf(colProperties, IsBlank(Postcode), {Postcode:""});

UpdateIf(colProperties, IsBlank(Telephone), {Telephone:""});

SaveData(colProperties, "OfflinePropertiesFile");

LoadData(colPropertyChanges, "OfflinePropertyChangesFile", true)
```

Here is a breakdown of this formula:

The collections that we utilize in our app might optionally be initialized in the first section of this formula. The colPropertyChanges collection is initialized and given a value of zero in the first line of this formula. This is done to prepare the designer for it to identify the collection and won't flag it as having a red error if we later use the LoadData method to refer to it.

This formula's key component determines whether the gadget is online. If yes, colProperties receives a copy of the data from the Properties table in the Dataverse. When the device is offline, it accesses the file on the device to get the saved data and transfers it to the local collection.

The UpdateIf method is used in the following line of code to replace any instances of null in the fields we wish to utilize in our app with empty strings. This is done to address a problem with edit forms that connect to local collections that contain null data. If the initial value of a field in a local collection is null, a card on a form will not change the value of the field. Our solution is to first replace all null values with empty strings to get past this issue.

The SaveData function is called in the formula's subsequent part, which stores the data in a local file. If a user eventually launches the app while offline, this gives it data. The LoadData function is then used by the formula to load any unsynchronized data changes that may have occurred during an earlier offline session.

Then the next thing to do is to reset all of the screens inside the app so that we can then use the colproperties collection. This is based on the fact that the source Dataverse table is also called we need to rename all of the references of the properties that are called the data source to colproperties. Here are the three places to modify the app

- BrowseScreen1>BrowseGallery1>Items

- DetailsScreen1>DetailForm1>DataSource

- EditScreen1>EditForm1>DataSource

Then you need to adjust the refresh icon inside the browse screen for it to save the data inside and offline file once you make a refresh. Here is the formula.

If(Connection.Connected,

   Refresh(Properties);

   UpdateIf(colProperties, IsBlank(Address1), {Address1:""});

   UpdateIf(colProperties, IsBlank(Address2), {Address2:""});

UpdateIf(colProperties, IsBlank(City), {City:""});

UpdateIf(colProperties, IsBlank(Postcode), {Postcode:""});

UpdateIf(colProperties, IsBlank(Telephone), {Telephone:""});

SaveData(colProperties, "OfflinePropertiesFile")

Handling Offline Deletions

For apps to function fully offline, they should be able to handle the offline deletion of the data. The display screen will then have the delete icon. Here is a way to configure the formula in the icon so that it can support offline deletion.

```
RemoveIf(colProperties, BrowseGallery1.Selected.PropertyID = PropertyID);

If(Connection.Connected,

  RemoveIf(Properties,

      BrowseGallery1.Selected.PropertyID = PropertyID

  ),

   Collect(colPropertyChanges, {Record:BrowseGallery1.Selected, Status:"D",
OfflineID:BrowseGallery1.Selected.PropertyID});

   SaveData(colPropertyChanges, "OfflinePropertyChangesFile")

);

Back()
```

Deleting records from local collections

The most dependable approach to explain the syntax for removing an item from a collection is to use the RemoveIf function to delete the item using a unique identifier. It's natural to assume that the Remove function can carry out this operation when the following formula is used:

Remove (locProperties, BrowseGallery1.Selected)

It's vital to note that this syntax only functions with linked data sources, even though the delete icon first utilizes it to remove the chosen record from Dataverse.

The record we supply to the Delete method with a local collection must exactly match the record we wish to remove. Controls and values inside the item template of the gallery are likewise exposed through the chosen property of a gallery.

Handling Offline record updates

There are a few changes to make so that we can provide edits and make entries offline.

The edit form must be modified to prevent using the SubmitForm method to save the entry to the colProperties collection. This is a crucial change. The purpose is so that while the device is offline, we may create a temporary PropertyID value. When a device is offline, Dataverse does not create this value as it normally would. To be able to update or remove entries that were generated offline, we must allot a temporary PropertyID value. Our algorithm will produce negative PropertyID values to prevent the possibility of producing duplicate PropertyID values.

Building the Synchronization Screen

Then you are going to have to build the synchronization screen. The first thing to do to build the feature is to add a new screen then add a gallery control and configure **Items** property inside the **colproperties** collection. To show a field from the offline record, here is the syntax Thisitem.Record.<fieldname>

Then go to a label inside the gallery template, and provide a user-friendly description of the changing status with these syntaxes. Switch(ThisItem.Status,

"A","Record added",

"U","Record updated",

"D","Record deleted"

)

Under gallery control, then you can add buttons that sync the data. Set the **OnSelect** property of the button inside the formula. The formula has three logical parts and they consist of codes to sync the updated record, then code to sync the record that was deleted.

```
                    //1. Save the records that were added
                    ForAll(Filter(colPropertyChanges, Status="A"),
                        Patch(Properties,
                            Defaults(Properties),
                            {
                                Address1: Record.Address1,
                                Address2: Record.Address2,
                                City: Record.City,
                                Country: Record.Country,
                                Postcode: Record.Postcode,
                                Telephone: Record.Telephone
                            }
                        ,
);
RemoveIf(colPropertyChanges, Status="A");
Clear(colChangeReview);
Clear(colConflicts);
//2. Refresh the Dataverse data source. For records updated offline, retrieve
//  the corresponding current record.
Refresh(Properties);
ForAll(Filter(colPropertyChanges, Status="U"),
    Collect(colChangeReview,
        {OfflineRecord:Record,
         CurrentRecord:LookUp(Properties, PropertyID = OfflineID)
        }
    )
);
//3. If the source record is not found, add the record to the
//  conflict collection.
If(CountRows(Filter(colChangeReview,IsEmpty(CurrentRecord))) > 0,
  Collect(colConflicts,
        AddColumns(Filter(colChangeReview,IsEmpty(CurrentRecord)),
            "Status",
            "Update failed - source record deleted"
        )
  )
);
RemoveIf(colChangeReview, IsEmpty(CurrentRecord));
//4. Process the records that have not been modified on the server
ForAll(Filter(colChangeReview,
        CurrentRecord.'Modified On'=
            OfflineRecord.'Modified On'),
  Patch(Properties,
    CurrentRecord,
    {
        Address1: OfflineRecord.Address1,
        Address2: OfflineRecord.Address2,
        City: OfflineRecord.City,
        Country: OfflineRecord.Country,
        Postcode: OfflineRecord.Postcode,
        Telephone: OfflineRecord.Telephone
```

```
        }
      )
    );
    RemoveIf(
      colChangeReview,
      CurrentRecord.'Modified  On'=OfflineRecord.'Modified  On'
    );
```

```
    //5. The remaining  rows in colChangeReview  are conflicting records
    If(CountRows(colChangeReview)  > 0,
      Collect(colConflicts,
          AddColumns(colChangeReview,
                "Status",
                "Update  failed - source  record  modified  by other  user"
          )
      )
    );
    //6. Collect the records that were deleted offline into colChangeReview
    ForAll(Filter(colPropertyChanges, Status="D"),
        Collect(colChangeReview,
            {OfflineRecord:Record,
             CurrentRecord:LookUp(Properties,  PropertyID = OfflineID)
            }
        )
    );
    //7. Remove records that have also been deleted on the server
    RemoveIf(colChangeReview, IsEmpty(CurrentRecord));
    //8. Process the records  that were deleted offline
    ForAll(Filter(colChangeReview,
            CurrentRecord.'Modified On'=
                OfflineRecord.'Modified On'),
        Remove(Properties, CurrentRecord)
    );
    RemoveIf(colChangeReview,
          CurrentRecord.'Modified On'=
          OfflineRecord.'Modified On'
    );
    //9. The remaining rows in colChangeReview are conflicting records
    If(CountRows(colChangeReview) > 0,
```

```
Collect(colConflicts,
    AddColumns(colChangeReview,
        "Status",
        "Delete failed - source record modified by another user"
    )
)
);
Clear(colPropertyChanges);
//9. Update the offline file
SaveData(colPropertyChanges, "OfflinePropertyChangesFile");
//10. Build a message that we can show to the user
If(CountRows(colConflicts) > 0,
    UpdateContext(
        {ConflictMessage:
            Text(CountRows(colConflicts)) & " conflicting record(s)"}
    ),
    UpdateContext(
        {ConflictMessage: ""}
    )
);
```

The colPropertyChanges collection contains offline data alterations that are processed by this formula. This collection will be empty after processing all of the data.

colChangeReview

Here's a preview of the first 5 items in this collection
Learn about working with collections

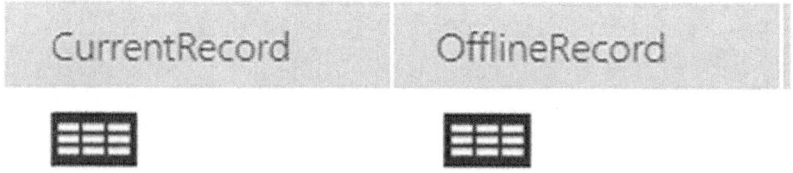

CurrentRecord	OfflineRecord

The source record was destroyed if the procedure is unable to find an updated record. The source record was altered by another user if the updated record displays a distinct last modified date and time. The formula keeps the conflicting data in a collection named colConflicts in both of these instances.

Building the Conflict Resolution Screen

We can provide consumers with a method for resolving these data conflicts if the synchronization procedure returns conflicting data. Users will then have the option to either keep the offline modification or go back to the record's most current server version. Create a screen, including a gallery control, and change the **Items** attribute to **colConflicts** to develop this functionality. Using the syntax **OfflineRecord.<Fieldname>**, we can tell the gallery control to display the fields that we want.

Then you need to add buttons to click to retain or remove any offline changes. Removing the offline copy of a record is all that is necessary to keep the server version of the record. To remove the offline change, we apply the following formula to the button's OnSelect property:

Remove (colConflicts, ThisItem)

Finally, when you want the users to open a conflict resolution screen, you can also add that button inside the synchronization screen.

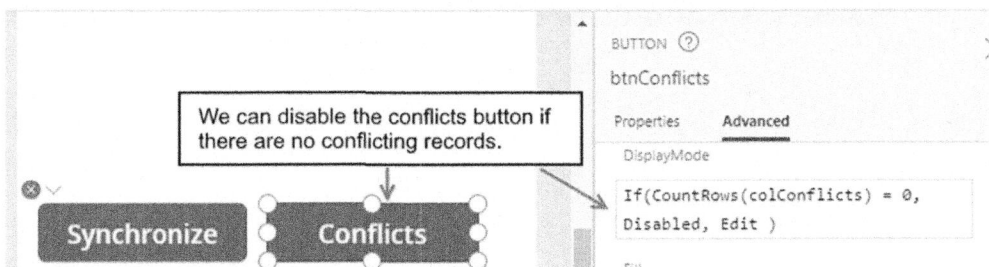

Making model drove App Offline

In this section, we are going to be using the process of how to make a model-driven app based on the Dataverse property table.

You have to first set up a mobile profile

The most important step in enabling offline working is to make a mobile offline profile. The tables and records that are accessible offline are specified in a mobile offline profile, which applies to a group of users. These profiles are defined at the level of the environment.

Power Apps establishes a local data cache on the mobile device when a user launches an offline-capable app. It updates this cache by syncing the data according to a timetable that we may set at the table level. The program keeps working with the cached data even if the device loses Internet access. Power Apps syncs any modifications that the user made while offline once the network connection is restored.

We must first activate all the tables that we wish to make available offline before configuring an app for offline access. We open the settings for every table from Maker Portal to do this. The next step is to allow offline access by checking the "Enable for mobile offline" button.

We can now develop a mobile offline profile. To begin, we access the target environment's settings via the Power Platform admin center. Choose the Mobile Settings menu item from the "Users + permissions" group. We select the option to establish a new offline profile from this page. We'll make an offline profile called "Property App Profile" for our example.

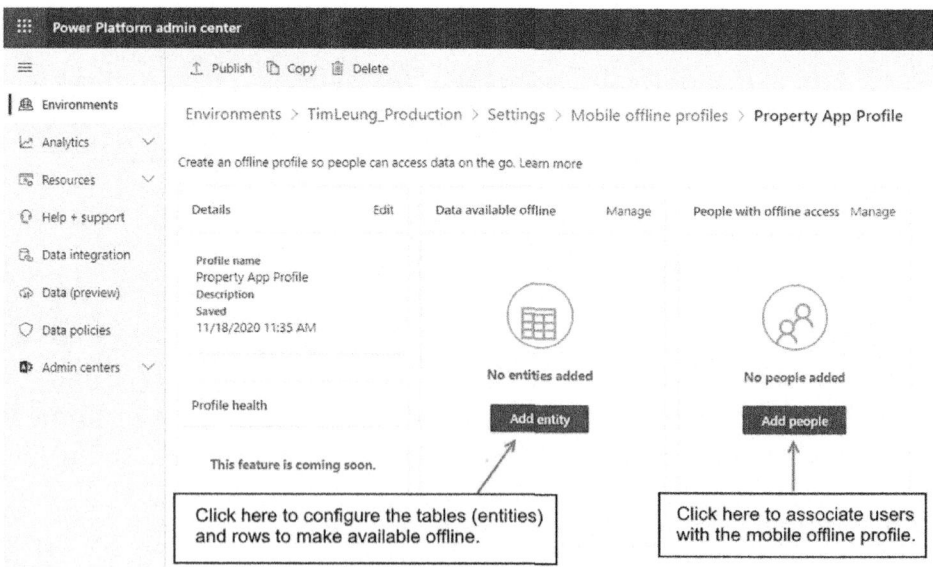

We choose the tables and data that we wish to make available offline from the "Data available offline" area. A list of all tables that are set up for offline access is shown when you click the "Add Entity" button. After choosing a table, we can choose the records we wish to create.

We have the option of making all records accessible offline. Smaller tables with fewer rows tend to work better for this. It's preferable to just make a portion of the records accessible offline for optimal performance.

Three checkboxes appear when the "Organization records" radio option is selected. These can be used to make offline records that belong to the user, the user's team, or the user's business unit available accessible offline.

The most potent method of configuring the records that are accessible offline is using the custom radio button. With this choice, a designer is provided that lets us create a filter based on the table's columns. As an illustration, we might develop a filter that only makes records that were produced recently available offline.

The setup of our program to function offline is the last stage. To do this, we visit our app's properties pane, select the mobile offline accounts to link to the app, and tick the "Enable for mobile offline" checkbox.

Configuring conflict settings

By default, any modifications performed by other users while the device was offline will be overwritten when it reconnects.

Activity

- Use the formulas in this chapter to create an app that works offline.
- What are the canvas formulas that can enable you to work offline
- How does one set a local source to a local collection

Summary

In this chapter, we looked at what occurs when an app goes offline and went through how to create an offline canvas app.

The explore screen of an automatically produced canvas app keeps displaying the data from before the app went offline. The refresh and save features won't operate, as expected. Users may launch previously run programs even when they are not connected to the Internet. A created app that launches offline, however, won't display any information. To prepare for future offline sessions, Power Apps does not immediately save app data.

CHAPTER TWENTY FOUR

CREATING CUSTOM DATA CONNECTORS

Through both free and paid data connectors, we can use canvas apps to connect to a variety of data sources. However, is it feasible to retrieve data sources that aren't natively supported? Yes, it is the solution. We can connect to any database server that is available through a web service by creating a custom data connection. Furthermore, we may get around this by creating our web service if the necessary data source lacks a web service interface.

Overview of web services and custom connectors

We can call it one of the countless online services available. All current social networking platforms provide online services for accessing functionality. These websites include many more, such as Twitter, YouTube, and Facebook.

Practical uses for business might include getting stock prices, currency exchange rates, translating IP addresses to locations, or monitoring brand reaction on social media. The list is essentially unlimited. If we have a general notion of what we want to do, we can generally use a search engine to locate a service that meets our needs. If there isn't a web service that meets our needs, we may create one ourselves or hire a developer to do it for us.

Making use of the Azure Functions feature of Microsoft Azure is a potent approach to take advantage of this capability. We may use a variety of languages to create code with Azure Functions to do tasks. These include non-Microsoft languages like Node.js, Python, PHP, and Java, as well as the.NET framework (C# and F#). We solely host the code functions that we develop in Microsoft Azure; no other infrastructure- or server-related duties are required. This type of cloud computing is referred to as "serverless computing" since end users do not need to worry about infrastructure-related duties.

Utilizing an Azure function has the extra advantage of allowing the designer to create an Open API specification for our function.

Overview of steps

As with the other built-in connections, like SharePoint, Excel, and SQL Server, after we create a custom connection, we can add that to our app and utilize it to access our data source. To call web service functions and get data, we can create a formula.

Here are the steps

- First, you have to identify or create a web service you want to connect to
- Then put down the web service then create a contract
- Then define the custom connector with the marker portal
- Inside the app, there is a data source that is based on the custom connector
- Write the formula to then call on the web service.

Understanding how the web works

Some of the languages might be perplexing to people who are not developers. REST, JSON, and other abbreviations are mentioned in the documentation. "RESTful API" is a different phrase we usually hear. What do all of these phrases signify, though?

Representational State Transfer, or REST, is a term that characterizes a typical feature of a contemporary online service. With REST, each call to a web service must include all the information required for the service to process a request. We can send this information by including arguments in the site address, the request body, or the headers.

One goal of REST is to prevent the need to limit interaction between clients and services to a single web server by doing away with the necessity to store session data on a particular server. As a result, infrastructure personnel may add more servers and simply load, balance, replace, or scale up a service. Each request's complete state information makes it feasible to cache results on any device acting as an intermediate between the client and the server, which can improve performance.

The acronym API, which means application programming interface, has been used in earlier chapters. One system can use code to access functionality or data from some other system using an API.

Making HTTP web requests

Through HTTP, web devices and web servers may communicate (Hypertext Transfer Protocol). With this protocol, separate requests and replies are used to communicate between such a client device and a server. A client sends a request to a web server whenever it needs data from the server. The communication is over when the server responds with a response. A succession of individual requests and answers make up a web session between such a device and a server.

A verb is a component of each HTTP request. This identifies the kind of request the client submits; there are four possible types: GET, POST, PUT, and DELETE.

A client always sends an HTTP request using the GET verb when it wants to get the information from the server. The customer may offer justifications along the way. The URL in this instance specifies an ID of 1729:

http://myserver.com/properties/item/1729

Through the use of query string parameters, HTTP requests may additionally specify arguments. The structure of a URL with a query string argument is shown below. The parameter values are name/value pairs that are separated by the = symbol and are found in the address following the? symbol:

http://myserver.com/properties.aspx?id=1729

A client commonly sends an HTTP request using the POST verb when it uses a web service to add or enter the data. The client's data will be included as an attachment to the request body.

Understanding HTTP responses

A status code is included in a web server's answers to HTTP requests. The 404 status code is presumably the one that most people are familiar with. When a user requests a site that doesn't exist, a web server responds with this status code. When a server finds a problem that the caller is unable to fix, it will return the error code 500 as another status code.

The desired response code when contacting a web service is 200. This status code denotes accomplishment. Another successful response code is 201, which denotes a valid POST or PUT request.

Documenting a web service

Let's step through the process of creating a custom connector that connects to the postal code lookup online service now that we are aware of the pertinent web protocols.

Finding a web service that offers this capability is what you are going to have to do first. The quickest approach to discovering a service is to type "zip code API" into a search engine. Numerous online services are returned by this sort of search that we might employ. Although we utilize Zippopotam.us in this example, we could just as well use any other online service.

Creating a web service description

Then you have to build a contract describing the web service. It is important to do this because it gives the power app the ability to understand methods, return values, and the parameters of the services.

Using postman

Postman is another desktop software you can run on Windows and Mac. If you want to use Postman, then you have to download, then install the application.

Creating an environment specifically for our purpose is the best method for Postman. We can declare variables in a container provided by an environment. We can rapidly alter parameter values for HTTP requests using the UI thanks to variables.

The designer may then be used to contact a web method, view the server's response, and build a new "request" object. In this instance, the GET request's value was set to the following:

http://api.zippopotam.us/us/{{zipcode}}

{{Zipcode}} serves as a placeholder for the variable zip code in this sentence. We may specify and assign a value to this variable using the environment settings.

Using swagger

Create an account, log in, and choose "Start a new API project" to utilize Swagger. The possibility to build a project using a template is offered by Swagger. The PetStore API template is a useful one. This template shows a lot of helpful syntaxes and was created for educational reasons.

Here is the listing that shows what the JSON exports. It is an Open APO document and the structure of it seems very similar to what the source YAML.

```json
{
    "swagger": "2.0",
    "info": {
      "version": "1",
      "title": "PostCode API",
      "description": "Call Zippopotam Lookup"
    },
    "schemes": [ "https", "http" ],
    "produces": [ "application/json" ],
    "paths": {
      "/us/{zipcode}": {
        "get": {
          "summary": "Get Postcode",
          "description": "Enter the postcode to search",
          "responses": { "200": { "description": "JSON postcode result" } },
          "parameters": [
            {
              "name": "zipcode",
              "in": "path",
              "description": "US Zipcode",
              "required": true,
              "type": "string"
            }
          ]
        }
      },
    "host": "api.zippopotam.us",
    "basePath": "/"
```

Creating a custom connector

The following step is to construct a custom connector, which may be done using the Maker Portal's Data Custom Connectors section. The "New custom connection" button here gives users the option to import the Open API file or Postman collection, build a blank custom connector, or construct a connector from an Azure service. We decide to import the Open API file in this illustration. This brings up the dialog box seen in the illustration. Here, we can give our connection a name and press the import Open API button.

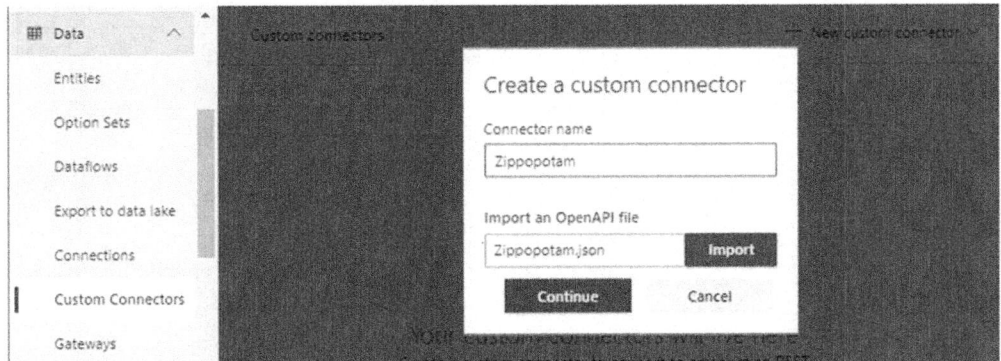

The image here is displayed when you click **Continue**. There are four steps involved in creating a custom connection, and we can see them by using the cookie trail option that shows at the top of the page. The General, Security, Definition, and Test phases make up these four phases.

We may upload an icon and enter a description on the General screen. Verifying that host and base URL settings correspond to the right base web address of the destination web service is the most crucial step.

The capability to connect to a web service through an on-premises gateway is a useful feature. To then connect to web services housed on internal networks, we can pick this option.

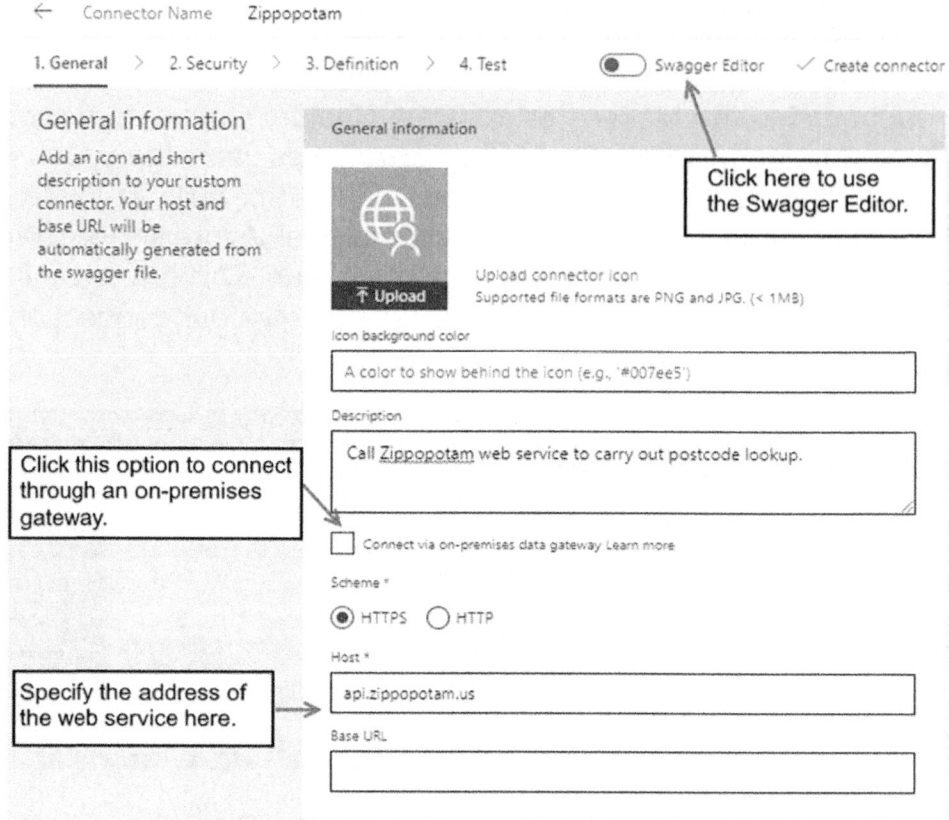

In the following screen, you can configure the web service security.

While many other online services need authentication, the Zippopotam web server does not. We utilize the options that are displayed to connect to a web service that needs authentication.

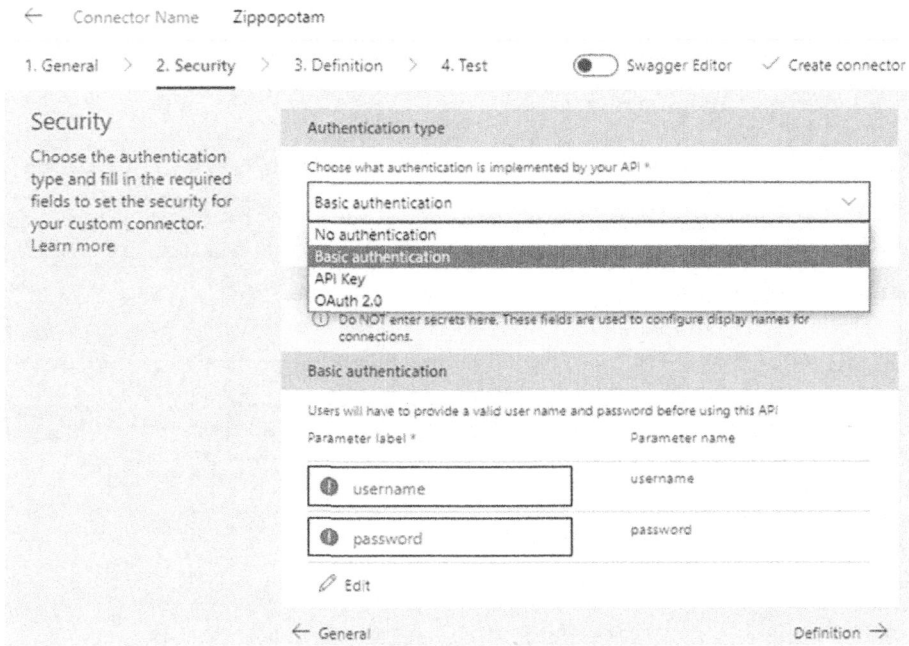

On the next page, you can define the web services or the actions of the custom connector.

Then you need to define the expected JSON result you want the web service to return. This way the power app is going to understand the structure of the data and also provide suitable intelligence inside the formula bar. Choose **200** response entries you see at the bottom of the page when you are in the response section.

On the next page, you can text the connector

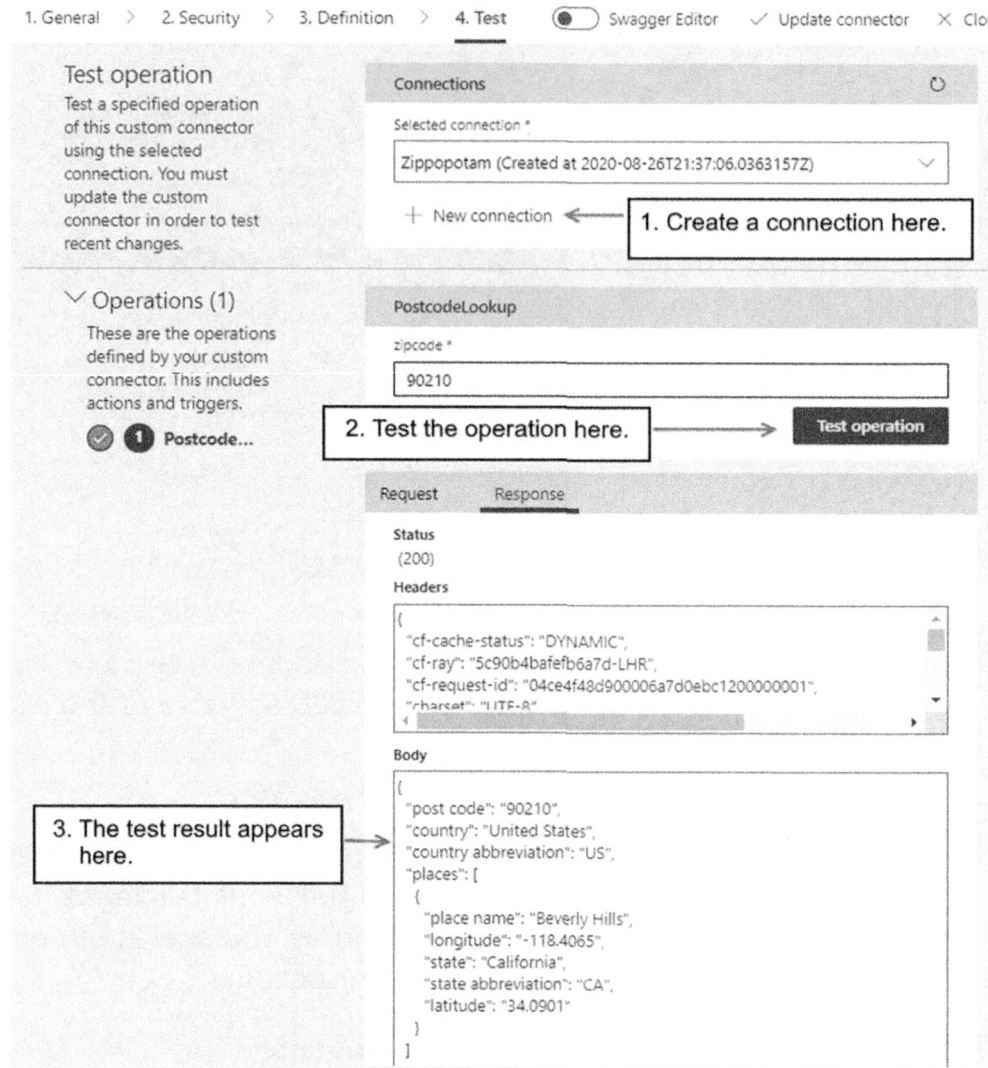

To achieve this, as seen in the figure we have here, we use the data panel to search for our custom connection by name (Zippopotam in this case). When you choose to add a connection, the Open API file's title setting will be used to determine the connection's default name. The Open API file for this example includes the title "Postcode API," therefore Power Apps establishes a connection with the name PostcodeAPI. We may use the term PostcodeAPI to designate this relationship in a calculation.

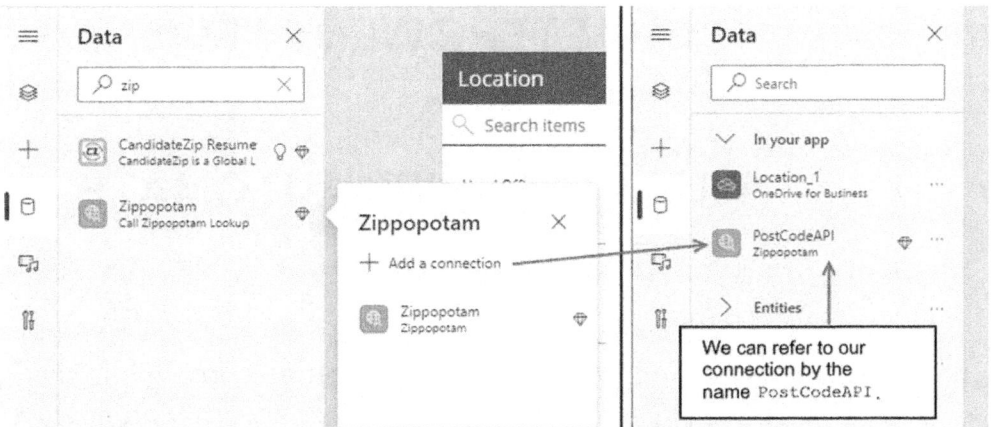

Here's how to modify the edit screen from an automatically created app to demonstrate how to fill data controls on a screen with information from our web service. We'll include a textbox where users may input their zip code and a button that calls up the Zippopotam service to acquire the relevant information.

Activity/ Review Question

- Create a custom connector with the online services.
- Create an HTTP web request.
- Create a custom connector

Summary

In this chapter, we discussed how to use a custom connector to connect to online services. Since it greatly expands the systems and data sources that we can connect to, the ability to invoke web service methods offers a significant advantage. Connecting to social networking websites, getting stock prices, or changing currency values are a few examples of the things we can do.

CHAPTER TWENTY FIVE

WHAT IS POWER AUTOMATE

Power Automate makes it easier to automate processes using flows. We can link to data and a variety of systems by creating flows. Looping logic and workflows with approval procedures are things we can build. Flows may be scheduled to run frequently and automatically.

Power Automate helps us get around the restrictions and gaps inside the functionality of Power Apps, which is one of the reasons why it is so helpful. It offers a glue that helps us to construct more comprehensive and well-rounded solutions.

Power Automate is a non-developer-focused alternative to Power Apps that enables the creation of automated business processes without the need for coding knowledge. We may create processes with Power Automate using a straightforward graphical web designer. There is no need to install any specialized software because the designer is web-based.

What can we do with Power Automate?

Here are some of the things that the power automate can do

- They can be used to create, copy and also carry out some file operations from one drive, etc.
- They can help you to perform SQL tasks.
- They can help you to use flows connect with AI builder.
- You can use it to access web resources.
- They are used for looping. Since there are no looping constructs in the power apps.
- They can help you to make some scheduling.

Managing and creating flows

You can use the flow section to create, manage and edit flows by using the flow section inside the portal maker.

The Maker Portal's Flows section divides things into four categories: Desktop flows, Cloud flows, Shared with me and Business process flows.

Cloud flow" shows the things that we can trigger using the power apps, the schedule, or when there is also a change inside the data source. Alternatively, "Desktop flows" enable the use of a screen recorder to record and replay actions. Through outdated systems without API access, they can assist in automating data entry and simplifying repetitive operations.

The "New" button provides a drop-down menu with a variety of choices to construct a new flow. A flow can be created from a template, scheduled, automated, and in other ways.

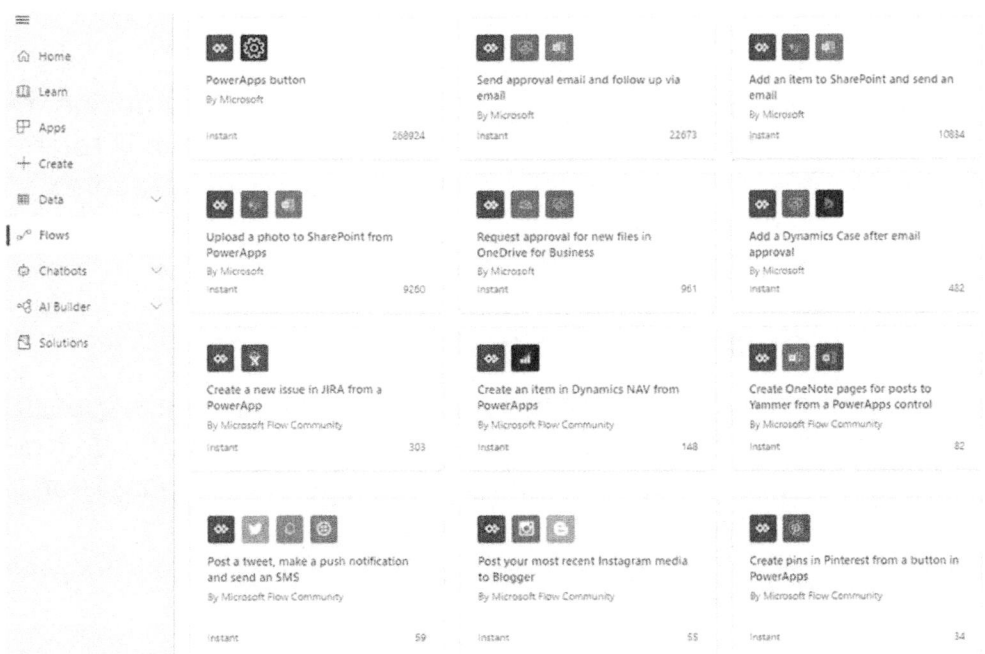

Defining triggers

A trigger initiates a flow's execution. Automated triggers and immediate triggers are the two basic types of triggers. Inserting a record into a database or a SharePoint list are examples of actions that can set off an automatic trigger. Additional types of automated triggers include the receipt of an email, the establishment of an event on the calendar, or the creation of a file in OneDrive.

An occurrence that is brought about by human involvement is known as an immediate trigger. The buttons we add to Power Apps or the buttons we put to the mobile app are two examples of immediate triggers. Last but not least, we may program flows to run at certain times or to recur at regular intervals.

Adding Actions

Once you open the designer, you are going to see the trigger. Then under the trigger, you can then add an action that also includes the data retrieval actions, the switch cases, the loops, and some other things.

After adding an action, then you can make use of the designer in other to attach some other actions. The most notable action is referred to as the condition. This way, you can define a condition if/else. You can also add some other branching actions like the switch and "do until" loops

Accepting Input Values

One typical necessity when connecting a flow to Power Apps is to send values from Power Apps into the flow. To do this, we first choose a field or property that will receive input from Power Apps. Then, we may choose the "Ask in Power Apps" option.

Calling Flows

Once you build the flow then you can run it in the canvas app or the model-driven apps.

From Canvas Apps

Here is how in the canvas app:

- Trigger the flow, then choose **An action** then choose **Power to automate.** This then opens the data panel. Then you can use the data panel to select the preferred flow.

From Model-Driven Apps

Inside the model-driven app, you do not have the option to add custom triggers. However, there are three methods:

Building an automatic procedure that activates whenever a Dataverse record is added, changed, or removed is the First method. We may execute a flow each time a user modifies a record by utilizing this trigger.

The second approach entails developing a flow that takes advantage of the "When a flow step is executed" trigger. Because of this, a Power Automate flow may be started from a particular phase in a business process flow. We may retrieve the fields from the stage in the business process flow using this kind of trigger.

Then in the third approach, you can build the flow using the **when a record is selected** trigger. This way, the user can navigate through the list and also use the built-in flow button in the top menu to start the flow.

Unattended: from a schedule

The first thing to do is build a flow based on the recurrence trigger.

Reviewing Call Histories

You can go to the **Run history** menu on the **Marker Portal** then it opens a list with the date and the time of all of the execution, the run status, and duration.

The data inputs and duration for each step are displayed in this view. Additionally, we can see how each stage responded. For instance, if one of the actions in our flow was to make an HTTP request to a web server, we could observe the server's response and any relevant error codes.

Working with Data

Through Power Apps, we have access to all the well-known standard and premium connections. Actions that handle data operations are exposed through data connectors. In addition, you may change an existing record and add new records, as well as retrieve rows and a single record.

Connecting to Data

The first thing to do is to start the data operation from the SharePoint data source. Then add an action and search for SharePoint. Then you are going to see a view like this.

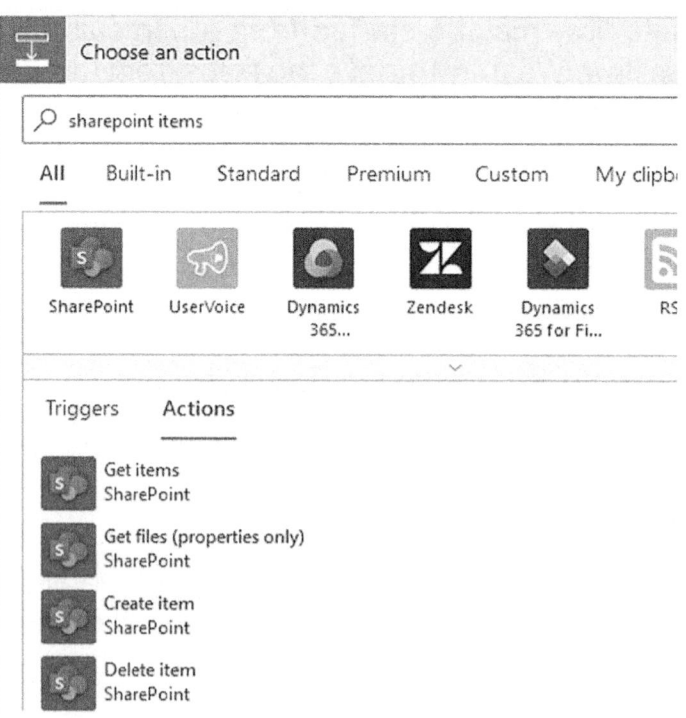

Filtering Data

- First, add a new action then choose the **SharePoint-get items** action.
- Then to filter the data, you are going to need an **OData** filter expression.
- Start by creating an expression in the Filter Query textbox to apply an OData expression that filters records by values the user enters using Power Apps. We choose the position where the date value should be, click the "Add dynamic content" button, and choose the "Ask in Power Apps" option rather than manually inputting hard-coded UTC date values.
- Then you can save and test the flow.

Working with Variables

Power Automate features a variety of looping constructions and supports variables. Here's how we can analyze our data from SharePoint and compute the sum of the "rent amount" column to demonstrate these functionalities. To get this total, we start a variable, iterate through the SharePoint rows, and then add the "rent amount" value for each row to the variable.

Then you need to add **Apply to each.** If you want to define the input, choose the **SharePoint value** object inside the **select an output from the previous text dialog box.** There the row is going to be defined

Constructing HTML Tables

After adding a step and looking for the data operation, you will find seven operations. The action you see there can then be used to create a CSV and the HTML tables, Parse JSON, and also to manipulate the values of the array

The create HTML tables collects input and also builds HTML tables that are based on the input.

We would create an action as seen in the image. To create an HTML table that contains the tenancy ID, start date, and rent amount. We supply the input from our SharePoint "Get items" action in this example. It is possible to explicitly set the fields and column titles or have the "Create HTML table" action automatically incorporate all columns from the input data.

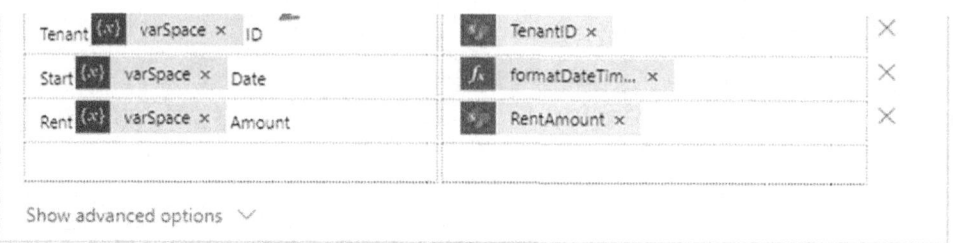

Then you can insert the output of the **created HTML table** in the message body.

Introducing Workflow Definition Language

These are the following ways that you can use this Workflow Definition Language

- For string manipulation;
- For date handling;
- For math;
- For the control of programs.

Applying Workflow Definition Language

You can use the workflow Definition Language in **data operations-compose** actions. You can use this action to calculate the output values for the user in some other parts of the flow.

Review Question

- What is Power Automate?
- What are the things that you can do with Power Automate?
- How does one filter data?

Summary

Power Automate is a tool that automates tasks using flows, which was the subject of this chapter. It can accomplish actions that are not feasible with Power Apps. For instance, we may use AI Builder to analyze data, run stored procedures to improve SQL Server performance and establish approval processes. By combining flows with the on-site gateway, file operations on internal networks are feasible. Even repeated tasks can be scheduled to run. Flows are particularly helpful for model-driven programs since they offer a method to conduct operations on data sources other than Dataverse.

INDEX

E

G

H

I

J

L

195, 196, 200, 203, 209, 210,
211, 212, 214, 215, 224, 229,
238, 248, 249, 253, 254, 255,
258, 259, 276, 296, 299, 300,
301, 316, 318, 329, 331, 333,
334, 335, 336, 338

power automate, 3, 210, 247,
331

Power BI service, 53

Power Fx, 255

Power Platform, 32, 192, 247,
249, 298, 316

Power Virtual Agents, 156

PowerApps, 7, 102, 125, 126,
142, 168, 216, 218, 226, 232,
233, 234, 239

Power App, 2, 3, 6, 12, 13, 14,
15, 18, 19, 27, 34, 39, 46, 49,
57, 61, 64, 66, 69, 70, 85, 87,
88, 99, 109, 125, 126, 132,
146, 163, 173, 177, 205, 211,
212, 215, 218, 226, 238, 246

Power Automate, 3, 156, 211,
215, 247, 248, 249, 253, 254,
331, 334, 336, 338

Power BI, 156, 157, 171

PowerApp, 18, 125, 126, 218,
236

Python, 320

subgrid, 189, 190

Printed in Great Britain
by Amazon

20141762R10208